THE EUROPEAN UNION AND DEMOCRACY PROMOTION: THE CASE OF NORTH AFRICA

BOOKS OF RELATED INTEREST

The Resilience of Democracy: Persistent Practice, Durable Idea
edited by Peter Burnell and Peter Calvert

Democracy Assistance: International Co-operation for Democratization
edited by Peter Burnell

Civil Society: Democratic Perspectives
edited by Robert Fine and Shirin Rai

The Internet, Democracy and Democratization
edited by Peter Ferdinand

Democratization and the Media
edited by Vicky Randall

Opposition and Democracy in South Africa
edited by Roger Southall

THE EUROPEAN UNION AND DEMOCRACY PROMOTION:

THE CASE OF NORTH AFRICA

edited by

RICHARD GILLESPIE
University of Liverpool

and

RICHARD YOUNGS
Norwegian Institute for International Relations

FRANK CASS
LONDON • PORTLAND, OR

First Published in 2002 in Great Britain by
FRANK CASS PUBLISHERS
Crown House, 47 Chase Side
London, N14 5BP

and in the United States of America by
FRANK CASS PUBLISHERS
c/o ISBS, 5824 N.E. Hassalo Street
Portland, Oregon, 97213-3644

Website: www.frankcass.com

British Library Cataloguing in Publication Data

The European Union and democracy promotion : the case of
North Africa. – (Democratization studies)
1. European Union 2. Democratization – Africa, North
3. Africa, North – Politics and government
I. Gillespie, Richard, 1952– II. Youngs, Richard, 1968–
321.8′0961

ISBN 0-7146-5292-X
[ISSN 1465-4601]

Library of Congress Cataloging-in-Publication Data

The European Union and democracy promotion : the case of North Africa /
edited by Richard Gillespie and Richard Youngs.
p. cm. – (Democratization studies, ISSN 1465-4601)
Includes bibliographical references and index.
ISBN 0-7146-5292-X
1. Democracy – Africa, North. 2. Democracy – Africa. 3.
Structural adjustment (Economic policy) – Political aspects – Africa, North.
4. European Union countries – Foreign relations – Africa. 5. Africa –
Foreign relations – European Union countries. I. Gillespie, Richard, 1952–
II. Youngs, Richard, 1968– III. Series.
JQ3198.A58 E97 2002
320.961 – dc21 2002001761

This group of studies first appeared in a Special Issue on 'The European Union and Democracy Promotion: The Case of North Africa' of *Democratization* (ISSN 1351-0347) 9/1 (Spring 2002) published by Frank Cass.

Printed in Great Britain by Antony Rowe Ltd., Chippenham, Wiltshire

Contents

Acknowledgements vii

Themes in European Democracy Promotion **Richard Gillespie and Richard Youngs** 1

The Challenge of Democracy in North Africa **Bechir Chourou** 17

The European Union and Democracy Promotion in the Mediterranean: A New or Disingenuous Strategy? **Richard Youngs** 40

International Markets and Partial Economic Reforms in North Africa: What Impact on Democratization? **Bradford Dillman** 63

From the Bottom to the Top: Civil Society and Transnational Non-Governmental Organizations in the Euro-Mediterranean Partnership **Annette Jünemann** 87

Dancing in the Dark: The European Union and the Algerian Drama **Hugh Roberts** 106

France, Democratization and North Africa **Jean-François Daguzan** 135

Two Cheers for Whom? The European Union and Democratization in Morocco **Said Haddadi** 149

Spain and North Africa: Towards a 'Dynamic Stability' **Bernabé López García and Miguel Hernando de Larramendi** 170

European Democracy Promotion in North Africa: Limits and Prospects **Richard Gillespie and Laurence Whitehead** 192

Abstracts 207

List of Contributors 211

Index 213

Acknowledgements

This volume is the first joint publication to emerge from the research project on 'The EU and the Promotion of Democracy: The Case of North Africa', directed by Richard Gillespie and co-ordinated by Richard Youngs. We wish to thank our principal funding body, the European Commission, for supporting the project, initially as part of the MEDA-Democracy programme (ref. 98MAG44B7050). We are also indebted to the Centre for European Studies Research (CESR) at the University of Portsmouth and the Europe in the World Centre (EWC) at the University of Liverpool for providing some of the infrastructural support that made possible the first two workshops held during phase I of the project, upon which this publication is based. The first of these took place at Langrish House, Petersfield, on 8 September 2000 and the second at the Foresight Centre, Liverpool, on 20–22 April 2001

In addition to the participation of contributors to this volume, the workshop discussions benefited hugely from the input of members of our advisory team (Imco Brouwer, Marc Schade-Poulsen and Saad Djebbar), other researchers (Laura Feliu, Tom Najem, Spyros Sofos and Graciela Malgesini) and Michael Docherty of the Commission. Outlines and drafts presented at the workshops were subsequently revised in response to critical discussion. Like all good research projects, this one has generated more questions than answers, at least early on. We have tried to examine the broader, more strategic questions here, leaving more practical, micro-level issues of democracy promotion to phase II of the project.

RICHARD GILLESPIE
Professor of Politics
Europe in the World Centre
University of Liverpool

RICHARD YOUNGS
Senior Research Fellow, Norwegian
Institute for International Relations
(NUPI) and University of Portsmouth

Themes in European Democracy Promotion

RICHARD GILLESPIE and RICHARD YOUNGS

The aims of this collection are situated within a distinct evolution of work on democratization processes. As is well documented, most analysis of political change prior to the 1990s was domestically-oriented. In the 1960s and 1970s, the pre-eminent focus was on the manner in which economic modernization, along with associated restructuring of social and class alliances, presaged particular changes in political structures. This gave way, in the 1980s, to approaches stressing the autonomous agency of domestic political actors in elaborating successful tactical strategies of transition. Both these frameworks relegated external factors to a relatively marginal role. The key role attributed to transnational civil society networks in bringing down communist regimes in eastern Europe at the end of the 1980s then brought international dimensions to political change centre-stage. There appeared to be some danger, however, of unwarranted determinism in the way in which international influences were assessed. The internationalization of communications technology, information flows, consumer preferences and civil society links was often portrayed as almost guaranteeing an unstoppable spread of democratic norms to those parts of the developing world that had still not undergone transition. Conversely, some analysts, witnessing the increasing strains and imbalances of globalization, became equally convinced that the structural evolution of the international economic system militated strongly against the development of sustainable, substantive democracy. Against this background, it was widely suggested that the complexities of the international dimensions to political change had been inadequately factored into studies of democratization. As western governments and international organizations committed themselves more systematically to encouraging democracy in the developing world, there were calls for works aimed at a better understanding of how external actors' purposive policies became intertwined with domestic and overarching structural features to condition political change.[1]

Responding to this challenge, the present collection provides a detailed study of the democracy promotion policies of one international actor, the European Union (EU), in one specific area, North Africa.[2] It is structured so as to provide a comprehensive analysis of the various factors and considerations pertinent to the external dimensions of democratization. The introduction expands on the range of themes judged to be relevant to the study of EU democracy promotion policies in North Africa, offering a contextual background for the issues that guide the collection's subsequent contributions. A number of these then go on to assess the nature of European policies and the motives behind the approaches to democracy promotion adopted by the EU member states. Related to this, a key theme is the assessment of how effectively the EU has deployed its resources as a unified actor and of the dynamics of convergence and divergence between the policies of different European governments, notably France and Spain. Other contributions seek to shed light on North African perspectives on the EU's democracy promotion commitment and to explore the political implications of the impact that European policy has had on social, economic and political conditions in North Africa. The collection also includes analysis of the dynamics that have unfolded at the level of civil society, taking the Euro-Mediterranean Human Rights Network as a case study. Finally, the conclusion seeks to draw together the different strands in order to assess whether there is a significant role that the EU can play in promoting political change in North Africa, either in the immediate future, with the prospects of democratization appearing remote, or at some future juncture, when democratic forces within the region have become more assertive.

In the original design of the project upon which this collection is based, we saw three dimensions to the study of the subject area: the activity of the EU to promote democracy in general and in North Africa in particular; the *problématique* of democratization in North Africa, viewed both as a discrete region and as embracing a degree of national diversity; and North–South mechanisms through which influences upon the democracy agenda were mediated, notably the Euro-Mediterranean Partnership (EMP) as the key multilateral framework of relevance to the topic. As the project developed, the sub-divisions proved difficult to adhere to rigidly: the EU has a substantial presence *within* North Africa, the inhabitants of the region are migrating to Europe in growing numbers and virtually every issue that we address is influenced by North–South dynamics and transnational networks.[3] For these reasons, in the end we have decided not to sectionalize the collection on this basis, for this would be to introduce more rigid divisions than the reality and the contents of the contributions actually merit.

Politics in North Africa – Plus ça change?

> in various states of the region respect for human rights, the democratic state and the rule of law have not shown significant improvement and … in some countries, the situation has even worsened.[4]

Much academic analysis has focused on the question of whether North Africa constitutes an exception to the established academic theories of democratization and to current democracy promotion efforts. The region was completely omitted from the purview of a major study of *Democracy in Developing Countries* just over a decade ago,[5] dismissed as having little democratic experience to learn from and very weak prospects of transition to democracy in the foreseeable future. Events may have vindicated the rather summary exclusion of North Africa from that comparative study, but have none the less generated a degree more optimism since that time, at least in certain quarters. During the late 1980s and 1990s, there was a notable increase in popular agitation for democracy in a number of Arab countries, and even developments that have encouraged some writers to deploy the vocabulary of 'democratization'.

The 'optimists' have tended to present almost any broadening of political participation as a first step in the process of 'democratization', opening up new vistas for political change in the future, particularly given what they see as positive developments within civil society.[6] Saad Eddin Ibrahim, for example, has outlined a scenario in which peaceful and relatively stable transitions to democracy might come about as a result of a regime's interest in sharing power with secular democratic opponents, when faced with a more radical challenge emanating from Islamic activists.[7] Alternatively, or additionally, it is the palpable growth in associational life that provides the substance for scenarios in which civil society emerges as the foundation of a more democratic future.[8] The 'pessimists' meanwhile embrace quite diverse perspectives and range from those inspired by essentialist and culturalist models, divorced from specific contextualization, to those who focus more on state and societal realities such as neo-patrimonialism. The reasons adduced for the persistence of authoritarian Arab regimes differ and are often contested. They include the existence of 'rentier states', largely immune from indigenous pressures for democratization; support for regimes from western countries, primarily concerned with access to energy resources; the undemocratic strands within Islamic cultures, and so on.[9]

Where the debate has progressed has been in relation to Islam, shown by a succession of studies to entertain diverse attitudes to democracy and human rights.[10] This has generated discussion of whether successful democratization requires an advance of secularism in North Africa, or might realistically be grafted upon certain Islamic concepts, including those of consensus and consultation.[11] The argument is also germane to the definition of civil society in this region. Does the notion of civil society automatically exclude religious-inspired associations,[12] or should it be elastic enough to embrace those sectors of the Islamist movements that accept pluralism, the rule of law and participation in electoral processes? The logic of excluding Islamic activists in general, together with the many secular associations that do not manage to survive as entirely autonomous bodies *vis-à-vis* the state, could be to dismiss the notion of civil society in North Africa altogether, not least as a foundation of future democratization. If, on the other hand, the logic of Islamic differentiation is pursued, this clearly suggests some potential for new political configurations and alignments to form, and perhaps to modify the existing balance of power.

This indicates the importance of political initiatives emanating from North Africa itself, to which the EU must be attentive. A significant diversity of national circumstances needs to be addressed by EU policy. The region is marked by diverse political regimes, economic structures and societies, albeit within recognizable North African parameters. In terms of government-led political reform of the kind that the EU wishes to encourage, there remains a total lack of movement in Libya and various symptoms of retreat in Egypt, Algeria and Tunisia. Even in Morocco, where the succession of Mohamed VI in 1999 prompted fresh hopes of political liberalization, developments in the second year of the new king's reign proved less encouraging than those during the first. Beyond government, the differential roles played by Islamist forces in the various countries of North Africa also demand country-specific democracy promotion measures within the common regional framework of the EMP. One of the questions being considered by the contributors to this collection is whether the existing policies – whether of the EU collectively or of key European actors such as France and Spain – are adequately fine-tuned to maximize their effectiveness in each country in question, or whether broad brush generalizations are being allowed to prevent this from occurring.

The European Union as Democracy Promoter

While situating itself within the general focus on international dimensions to political change, the collection also seeks to address a range of issues relating to the specific nature of the EU as a promoter of democracy. The various contributions offered here in different ways analyse the impact on democracy promotion strategies of the EU's *sui generis* nature as an international actor and the complex relationship between European states' national policies and common EU action. Although the United States began focusing more systematically on democratization slightly earlier than the EU, the latter has, since the early 1990s, explicitly sought to develop policy initiatives capable of challenging what many see as Washington's pre-eminence in this field. Analysis of the EU's role in promoting democratic change has focused to an overwhelming degree on its unique role in southern and, later, central and eastern Europe accorded by these regions' states' desire and eligibility to accede to the European Union. A key aim has been to extend European influence beyond Europe and to establish a more global presence, including in relation to democracy and human rights. The extension of the EU's democracy focus to the southern Mediterranean has, by virtue of the specific strategic and cultural challenges it involves, been seen as one of the most significant developments in European foreign policy. An assessment of the EU's activity in the area of democracy promotion – exploring both its strengths and weaknesses – must proceed from a careful appreciation of the complex nature of EU instruments and procedures, as well as of the evolving dynamics of co-operation between member states. It is hoped that a specific and detailed case study of democracy promotion efforts can in turn shed light on debates over these same complexities of European foreign policy co-ordination.

It is undoubtedly the case that, since the 1991 Development Council resolution first committed the EU to placing the promotion of democracy and human rights more systematically at the heart of its foreign policy, the EU has moved in significant ways to equip itself for implementing this declared objective. Resources allocated by the EU for democracy and human rights projects more than tripled during the 1990s.[13] To improve visibility and coherence, European Commission projects from different regions were grouped together within a European Initiative for Democracy and Human Rights. The formal remit for democratization work was expanded to incorporate a comprehensive range of democracy's institutional building blocks: civil society, parliaments, judiciaries, decentralized administration, unions, cultural organizations, conflict resolution, minority and vulnerable groups, education and democratic awareness-building were all identified as areas requiring attention. Provisions were also included in aid protocols for official development assistance (ODA) to be redirected to those states demonstrating progress in establishing democratic procedures. This mandate for positive assistance was accompanied by a new democracy clause agreed in 1995, providing for the suspension of aid and trade provisions in response to democratic reverses or shortfalls. Significantly, this clause was to be 'standardized' across regions and henceforth included in all new third country agreements.

A number of new instruments – Common Positions, Common Strategies, the High Representative for the Common Foreign and Security Policy (CFSP), the use of Special Envoys – were introduced to help increase the European Union's unity and diplomatic weight on the international stage, with the perceived need more effectively to convey support for democratic norms being a prime consideration in this regard.

Notwithstanding these developments, many analysts continued to lament the EU's limited capacities as an international actor. These were held to derive from both the paucity of co-ordination between member states and the EU's lack of competence over a number of relevant policy instruments. Critics argued that, in the absence of a firm obligation to agree a common line on foreign policy issues and with diplomatic co-ordination subject to the unanimity requirement, CFSP unavoidably gravitated to ineffectual 'lowest common denominator' positions. Despite the institutional changes introduced by the Treaty on European Union (1993), foreign policy co-operation had not become notably more effective or systematic, and for many still showed little sign of developing the kind of informal norms of co-operation that characterized even relatively loosely structured international regimes. Compounding the lack of substantive convergence within decision-making processes, member states' unwillingness to centralize key policy instruments was seen by many experts seriously to weaken the EU's external leverage. In particular, the absence of any significant common European security and defence competence was widely held to undermine the EU's general diplomatic weight: even if non-military instruments were far more relevant to the nature of contemporary challenges, it was the possibility of the US *in extremis* backing up its aims with effective force projection that still accounted for it being a far more potent influence in world affairs than the EU.

The range of new initiatives introduced at the European level suggested that the democracy promotion commitment had itself injected notable momentum into the development of the EU's internal procedures. However, significant weaknesses remained in the nature of those policy instruments specifically pertinent to influencing political change in third countries. Effective co-ordination of democracy assistance projects was conspicuously absent and evaluation mechanisms were slow to emerge. A Democracy and Human Rights Unit was created within the Commission only in 1999. This constituted a notable effort to inject greater coherence and efficiency into policy-making, but the lack of mechanisms for marrying national initiatives in particular developing regions to overall common guidelines on democracy still presented a serious challenge to effective concerted European action. Procedures for operationalizing the EU's democracy clause were not agreed until 1998 and even then the conditions that would trigger the use of political conditionality remained vague. Beyond this, a number of instruments pertinent to the democracy agenda continued to fall outside EU competence. This applied, in particular, to debt relief, investment promotion, export credit controls and most forms of sanctions. A new Code of Conduct introduced a very tentative degree of co-ordination over arms sales, but did not incorporate any direct democratic conditionality. The plans for the new EU Rapid Reaction Force revealed an intention to deploy military instruments more effectively to mitigate serious humanitarian crises, but it remained unclear whether this new military dimension would impact in any notable way upon the democracy promotion agenda. In all these domains there was a stated aim to improve co-ordination, but clear obstacles remained to the use of a wide range of important financial, commercial, diplomatic and security instruments in pursuit of the democracy promotion agenda.

Many analysts, however, became less dismissive of the EU's preparedness for effective international action. They insisted that the dynamics of EU policy-making evolved significantly during the 1990s and that an increasing degree of reciprocal compromise between member states could be detected. The incrementally ratcheted-up commitments to foreign policy co-operation had 'delegitimized exit': increasingly entrapped by their own rhetoric stressing the need for more effective external action, governments could no longer convincingly resort to a purely national policy rather than make the compromises necessary to preserve a common European strategy. Each time that commitments and instruments had been upgraded, however modestly, this had further raised expectations and modified governments' perspectives on the nature of their respective national interests. This had generated a self-perpetuating accumulation of co-operative norms and a steadily more regular pattern of co-ordination on external policy issues. Such informal dynamics rendered unsatisfactory minimalists' focus on the absence of majority voting and the EU's lack of a full range of policy instruments: the *de facto* norms of co-operation increasingly overrode the importance of such formal limitations. The EU was widely held to have carved out an increasingly influential international role despite not possessing the same degree of material force or diplomatic clarity as a unitary nation-state. Indeed, the EU's international 'presence' was seen to be based on the development of an extensive network of socio-economic links and stable contractual partnerships with developing countries and was in this sense, it was suggested, rather well suited to the dissemination of norms and political values.[14] In sum, contrasting perspectives on the EU's international 'actorness' have been advanced, with important implications for democracy promotion policy. This debate informs the accounts included in this collection.

Explaining Democracy Promotion Policies

A central concern of the collection is to apply to EU policies in North Africa competing explanations of the West's new focus on democracy promotion. Such an aim is judged to be of interest against the backdrop of keen disagreement over the relationship between western interests and democratization in developing states. Compared with the strategic certainties of the cold war, the existence of sharply contrasting perspectives on governments' new security and commercial challenges was a notable feature of debate during the 1990s. The ideological conflict of the bipolar era had, of course, largely subordinated preferences for particular political forms to the imperatives of competitive alliance-building throughout the developing world. This did not always militate against the encouragement of political liberalization, but it did ensure that the latter was judged apposite not in its own right but only when it was likely to reinforce rather than weaken a country's pro-western leaning. The fall of the Berlin Wall engendered a reassessment of these assumptions and, as western governments assumed their commitment to promote democracy, a variety of views emerged on the dynamics both propelling and likely to dilute the realization of this new policy agenda.

One perspective suggested that the elaboration of democracy promotion strategies should be seen as driven by calculations of strategic self-interest. Primarily in the United States, an assumption emerged in the immediate aftermath of the cold war that the focus on encouraging democratization neatly reconciled ethical and pragmatic concerns. If the cold war had invariably required support to be given to anti-communist, non-democratic regimes, within the new security paradigm the promotion of democracy was itself seen as the best guarantee of western security and commercial interests. This thinking owed much to the influential 'democratic peace' hypothesis, whose proposition that conflict was unlikely between democracies established itself as an apparently axiomatic tenet of US foreign policy. The implication of the reasoning was, of course, that the spread of democracy would reduce the array and degree of threats to the West. Starting from the observation that no two democracies had ever gone to war with each other, a number of grounds could be advanced for expecting the proliferation of democracy to lead to a more generally harmonious international system. In balancing contending views, political pluralism tended towards moderation. Governments held accountable to their own populace would be encouraged to devote resources to social and economic betterment rather than external aggression. Transparent systems of governance would make the evolution of policies more predictable, while procedural checks and balances and the rule of law would reduce the scope for arbitrary acts, undertaken with an autocrat's personal prestige in mind. Democracies would also be more inclined to international co-operation, as this represented an extension of internal bargaining procedures. Democratically-elected elites were less likely to have to revert to aggressive nationalism as a means of injecting legitimacy into the system of government. Based on such reasoning, democracy promotion strategies were widely advocated as a geo-strategic priority.

These propositions were, however, as vigorously rejected as they were propagated. Critics pointed out that, with there having been so few democracies throughout history, the correlation between democracy and peace was not a statistically convincing demonstration of causality. Moreover, the transition from authoritarian to democratic regime was most commonly an extremely destabilizing period, during which elites were often encouraged to offset internal strains by pursuing more, not less, aggressive external policies. Nationalism was commonly a child of the disorientating collapse of established orders. Where grave social and economic costs of adjustment were suffered, the perception that liberalism's supposed panaceas had failed could provoke a generalized hostility towards the West.[15] Indeed, some saw the attempted imposition of democratic values as one of the gravest threats to the West's own security interests, to the extent that it could be expected to provoke a backlash against western governments.[16] In a more direct sense, political liberalization would often give formal voice to organized political forces hostile to the West and more protecting of local markets.[17] Others continued to doubt that a country's internal political characteristics were likely to be in any way an indication of its external behaviour. It was pointed out that international instability had almost always arisen as a result of conflict over economic and social resources, rather than as an externalization of regimes' inherent political characteristics. The nature of the economic interaction between states was, from this perspective, the main determinant of how conflictive the security environment was likely to be. Globalization, in this sense, bound states together in mutually dependent economic relations, but was also responsible for an aggravation of social tensions – the precise way in which it was managed would determine the balance between these positive and negative dynamics.[18] Some cautioned that democracy would often actually unleash local ethnic conflict, seen by many as the most acute threat to international stability after the cold war.[19] For many analysts, these factors combined with particular resonance in relation to political Islam, making democratization in the Arab world – either for reasons of inherent religious doctrine or contingent socio-economic imbalances – a prospect more preoccupying than comforting to the West.

Parallel to these differences over approaches to security, the relationship between democratization trends and western economic interests was also the subject of debate. The traditionally widespread presumption that the nature of political structures in themselves mattered little to international investors was increasingly questioned. From a critical perspective, it was argued that western governments' new commitment to democracy promotion reflected the pressure of transnational capital for 'low intensity' democracy. From this perspective, multinationals' interests were assumed to have played a prominent role in the perpetration of the democracy promotion agenda, but had also ensured that only a very limited, formal concept of democracy was to be encouraged in the developing world. International investors pushed for democratization insofar as this conferred greater legitimacy on governments' economic policies and was consequently a more effective means of retaining stability and disciplining labour. To this end, a form of democracy with inbuilt limits on the influence of unions and other possibly anti-market forces would be preferred.[20] Others saw the private sector's role in more positive terms as a force for benign change in the developing world, built on the kind of high quality, socially harmonious, well-educated and prosperous democracy that would best further investors' own interests.[21] A key consideration, in this sense, was the relationship between the good governance and democracy agendas. While some held these to be essentially separate agendas, others – including even the World Bank – began to question whether the sorts of governance issues of concern to international business (corruption, transparency, judicial security) were themselves related to broader political structures.[22]

Against these explanations, one of the most prominent strands of analysis expressly turned the focus away from western governments' actions to the growing influence of transnational civil society networks. A staple of much theorizing during the 1990s was the concern to highlight the increasing sway of non-governmental organizations (NGOs) over governmental decision-making. Building on the role of cross-border advocacy networks in Latin America and eastern Europe, many theorists argued for recognition of the role played by an increasingly extensive cosmopolitan civil society in shaping political choices in both western and developing countries. Governments' incorporation of new 'ethical' goals relating to human rights and environmental protection was, they held, primarily a testament to this influence. Crucially, civil society agency was secured not simply through pressure and campaigning, but also through the way in which cross-border networks were able to structure a new discourse on normative values. Developing influential ideas advanced by new constructivist approaches, analysts argued that such discourse could bring about an adherence to certain normative values as governments' perceptions of their own identities evolved.[23] Rebutting the notion of an impersonal, automatic transmission of political values across borders, it was widely stressed that governmental agency was still crucial in giving manifestation to these normative values. However, this role could not, it was argued, be reduced to rationalized calculations of material self-interest. Rather, a different type of logic was afoot. A different type of international discourse had permeated international relations, mediated through the interaction between NGO networks, governments and international institutions. Governments were seen as having to react defensively to this, but also as having their own outlook gradually converge around these values in an incrementally more positive and cognitively rooted fashion. A study of democracy promotion policies must clearly investigate the force of such an explanatory framework. Indeed, given that such approaches were applied overwhelmingly to human rights policies, it would seem to be of particular interest to assess whether or not they can convincingly be extended to the broader question of democracy promotion policies.[24]

Crafting Democratic Change in the Context of the Euro-Mediterranean Partnership

A further set of questions relates to the way in which an international actor can most effectively help construct high quality and balanced democratic institutions. Western governments' democracy promotion commitment provoked lively debate between the proponents of top-down, coercive policies, on the one hand, and the advocates of bottom-up, positive approaches, on the other hand. Most analysts expressed strong reservations over the wisdom of punitive strategies, arguing that these often risk being counterproductive in the construction of positive 'consent' around democratic norms. Experience suggests that, while conditionality probably has a role to play, this may have the desired effect only in rather specific circumstances: for instance, at a time of crisis when economic sanctions might hasten the departure of an already debilitated authoritarian regime; in response to a sudden regression towards authoritarianism following political liberalization; or when internal reformers are appealing for international pressure. Much more attention has been given to the positive assistance of modest liberalization measures in the realms of civil society and economic governance, and the grounds for expecting that these will eventually spill over into pressure for democratization. Experts on the more specific phenomenon of democracy-related aid projects have highlighted the unfulfilled potential of such initiatives. They have also cautioned, however, that democracy assistance can fail to make a significant impact owing to the difficulty of obtaining an appropriate and effective sequencing of the various initiatives adopted *vis-à-vis* civil society, the economy and the political sphere, respectively, and because bottom-up approaches often lack a suitable counterpart at the intergovernmental level, designed to encourage top-down democratization efforts. Bottom-up approaches have, that is, themselves come in for criticism, particularly the hopes that have been pinned upon economic liberalization acting as a catalyst for political liberalization.[25]

The main orientations that democracy promotion in the South has inherited from similar activity focused on the East include three types of activity aimed at generating or reinforcing a bottom-up dynamic in the countries concerned: support for civil society, in the belief that this will apply internal pressure for democratization; an extension of economic liberalization, on the assumption that this will spill over into political liberalization; and sponsorship of the 'good governance' agenda long associated with the International Monetary Fund (IMF) and World Bank, and seen by the EU as possessing broad democratizing potential. The EMP was faced with many of the same dilemmas of democracy promotion that were encountered in relation to central and eastern Europe, but with two crucial differences: first, that most of the Mediterranean partners do not have in prospect the possibility of future EU membership; and second, that the EMP is also very much an exercise in region-building,[26] embracing a much more diverse set of regimes and societies than the EU has been addressing in central and eastern Europe. Libya aside, the EU made great efforts to develop an inclusive approach through the EMP, not least as a means of supporting conflict resolution efforts in the eastern Mediterranean. This collection focuses on assessing the crucial relationship between the EMP's security dimension and the specific strategies adopted towards promoting political change. The inclusive approach would appear to make it exceptionally difficult for the European Union to apply the principle of conditionality in its dealings with the Mediterranean partners, for fear of disfiguring the multilateral partnership. Critical voices have demanded more 'conditioned' European policies – for instance, in certain Nordic countries at the end of phase one of the EMP – but may be criticized themselves for the deceptively easy solutions they advocate.

In the context of the EMP, placing the emphasis more on positive forms of conditionality (that is, rewarding progress) than on negative forms (sanctions) has clearly been preferred by the EU in order to facilitate partnership-building with southern governmental authorities. The intergovernmental domain may not be the only level at which the partnership is being built, but it is an essential component of the EU outlook on the Barcelona Declaration (1995), given that increased co-operation by southern authorities is sought over a whole range of issues, including priority matters such as illegal northward migration – subjects that EU governments can hardly ignore in the interests of pursuing more coherent long-range policies designed to facilitate democratization. Since the EMP extends to so many policy areas in which enhanced North–South co-operation is sought, it becomes very difficult to develop a democracy promotion strategy that does not conflict with efforts that require consent and collaboration in other areas. The temptation then is to rely primarily on bottom-up approaches insofar as the democracy agenda is concerned. This raises questions – central to many of the contributions to this collection – over whether the possible shortcomings of the bottom-up logic raised by many analysts have been adequately factored into EU policy. This issue is particularly pertinent to critics' insistence that the economic liberalization promoted through the EMP is in fact more likely to 'destabilize' the southern countries and actually reinforce existing anti-democratic forms of 'neo-patrimonialism'.[27]

Even support measures for civil society must confront huge difficulties, given that legality in the Arab world is rarely conferred enthusiastically upon genuinely autonomous organizations, and that some very significant non-governmental organizations are religiously inspired and intolerant in their attitudes to other sectors of society. The EMP emphasis on NGO support raises questions over the extent to which this is a viable alternative to state-oriented democracy promotion efforts and the EU's preparedness to fund projects opposed by officialdom within the respective Mediterranean partner states. At times, EU officials seem to hide behind the pretence (or, more charitably, the aspiration) of partnership in order to avoid taking steps that will create political tension with southern counterparts and thus get in the way of immediate trade and security objectives

EU policy towards the Mediterranean, while setting ambitiously short-term targets for trade liberalization efforts, has an infinite temporal horizon when it comes to democracy promotion. The partnership approach arguably constrains the EU more than it does its partners. It implies an attempt over many years to socialize both the political class and civil society in the South into a greater acceptance of European-compatible democratic political ways. Thus it would appear that content, rather than form, is being privileged by EU policy-makers, who have seen all too many 'empty shell' democracies established in the past largely to satisfy the conditions set by aid donors. In North Africa in particular, elections have not proved to be 'harbingers of democracy', except perhaps, paradoxically, in Algeria.[28] Yet this socialization strategy of the EU, even if sincerely pursued, risks making the EMP appear to North Africans as itself 'an empty shell devoid of any political substance'. And the failure of the EU to address the lack of legitimacy of many of its southern interlocutors may be fuelling Arab suspicions that Europe is not really committed to democracy in the South, for fear of what the result might be.[29]

Given these dilemmas, the early years of the EMP left many policy-makers somewhat sceptical about the merits of its democracy component. Although during 2000 a number of EU member states called for political conditionality to be implemented, they were defeated by a majority of more cautious countries that saw such proposals as potentially damaging to the evolution of the partnership, already hit by the breakdown of the Middle East peace process. Officials even suggested *sotto voce* that the Barcelona Declaration's democracy agenda had been a mistake, and that 'good governance' alone would have achieved just as much at the political level, while presenting fewer problems for North–South intergovernmental relations. Implicitly, the sceptics were echoing the sentiments of many observers of the North African scene, who long before the Barcelona Conference had regarded the region as a 'special case', resilient to the 'waves' of democratization that swept through other parts of the world during the final decades of the twentieth century. Against this background, the EMP's structure and broad range of concerns provide both opportunities and constraints as regards the type of democracy promotion strategy adopted by the EU: assessing the balance between these enabling and constraining dynamics is central to this collection's aims.

NOTES

1. This proposition most notably underlays: L. Whitehead (ed.), *The International Dimensions of Democratization: Europe and the Americas* (Oxford: Oxford University Press, 1996); G. Pridham (ed.), *Encouraging Democracy: The International Context of Regime Change in Southern Europe* (Leicester: Leicester University Press, 1991); and G. Pridham, E. Herring and G. Stanford (eds.), *Building Democracy: The International Dimension of Democratization in Eastern Europe* (Leicester: Leicester University Press, 1994).
2. For a broader perspective, see R. Youngs, *The European Union and the Promotion of Democracy: Europe's Mediterranean and Asian Policies* (Oxford: Oxford University Press, 2001).
3. It must also be acknowledged that, owing to resource limitations, we were not able to investigate some themes as extensively as we would have liked. Our search for evidence of North–South demonstration effects led us to commission a study of Moroccan migration to Spain, the results of which were presented in a paper by Graciela Malgesini entitled 'Migration, Communications, the Media and Demonstration Effects'. Malgesini's limited study, conducted mainly in Madrid, found little evidence of democratization issues featuring in the motives of Moroccans migrating to the Spanish capital, and for this reason it is not being included as part of this collection.
4. European Parliament, Resolution of March 1997, PE 257.133/45.
5. L. Diamond, J.J. Linz and S.M. Lipset, *Politics in Developing Countries: Comparing Experiences with Democracy* (Boulder, CO: Lynne Rienner, 1990).

6. H. Deagan, *The Middle East and the Problems of Democracy* (Buckingham: Open University Press, 1993).
7. S. Eddin Ibrahim, 'Crises, Elites and Democratization in the Arab World', *Middle East Journal*, Vol.47, No.2 (1993), p.303. It is sad to reflect that voices such as his have been silenced and at present are unable to intervene in academic debates on political change in North Africa. Ibrahim's imprisonment in Egypt underlines real limitations to external democracy promotion activity. Saad Eddin Ibrahim is not only a US citizen, but also was imprisoned precisely for offences connected with the receipt of EU democracy promotion funding.
8. A.R. Norton (ed.), *Civil Society in the Middle East*, 2 vols. (Leiden: E J Brill, 1994 and 1996).
9. O. Schlumberger, 'The Arab Middle East and the Question of Democratization: Some Critical Remarks', *Democratization*, Vol.7, No.4 (2000), pp.104–32.
10. J.L. Esposito and J.O. Voll, *Islam and Democracy* (New York: Oxford University Press, 1996); F. Halliday, *Islam and the Myth of Confrontation: Religion and Politics in the Middle East* (London: I.B. Tauris, 1996), ch.5; and A.S. Moussalli, 'Discourses on Human Rights and Pluralistic Democracy', in A. Jerichow and J. Baek Simonsen (eds.), *Islam in a Changing World: Europe and the Middle East* (Richmond: Curzon, 1997).
11. Esposito and Voll, op. cit., pp.21–32.
12. L. Diamond, *Civil Society and the Development of Democracy* (Instituto Juan March de Estudios e Investigaciones, Madrid, Estudio/Working Paper 101, June 1997), offers a relatively restricted definition of civil society in this regard. After commenting that 'One of the most misleading and even trivializing conceptualizations of civil society is to treat it as simply "organizations that are independent of the state"', he insists that civil society organizations, in addition to being 'voluntary, self-generating, autonomous, and rule-abiding', must be concerned with public rather than private ends, not seek to control or participate in the state, and encompass pluralism and diversity. Associations based on religious orientation would be excluded for not being 'voluntary' and some for competing in elections. A.R. Norton, 'The Future of Civil Society in the Middle East', *Middle East Journal*, Vol.47, No.2 (1993), pp.205–16, does include Islamists as part of civil society and defends the utility of the concept in relation to the Middle East. S. Eddin Ibrahim, 'The Troubled Triangle: Populism, Islam and Civil Society in the Arab World', in Jerichow and Baek Simonsen, op. cit., p.27, defends the treatment of religious-based parties as part of civil society so long as they accept the principle of pluralism and 'observe a modicum of civility in behaviour toward the different "Other"'. He sees potential for Islamist parties to develop into something comparable with European Christian Democratic parties or religious parties in Israel.
13. For a breakdown of figures and an analysis of EU democracy assistance, see R. Youngs, *Assessing Democracy Promotion: The Case of European Union Strategy*, CEPS Working Paper, No.167 (Brussels: CEPS, 2001).
14. Edited collections analysing recent developments in CFSP invariably contain contributions from proponents of both the pessimistic and more optimistic perspectives. See J. Petersen and H. Sjursen (eds.), *A Common Foreign Policy for Europe: Competing Visions of the CFSP* (London: Routledge, 1998); K. Eliassen (ed.), *Foreign and Security Policy in the European Union* (London: Sage, 1998); J. Zielonka (ed.), *Paradoxes of European Foreign Policy* (The Hague: Kluwer Law International, 1998); and E. Regelsberger, P. de Schoutheete and W. Wessels, *Foreign Policy of the European Union: From EPC to CFSP and Beyond* (Boulder, CO: Lynne Reinner, 1997).
15. For an example of the debate over democratic peace theory, see 'Give Democratic Peace a Chance?', special edition of *International Security*, Vol.19, No.2 (1994).
16. K. Waltz, 'America as a Model for the World? A Foreign Policy Perspective', *PS: Political Science and Politics*, Vol.24, No.4 (1991), pp.667–70; and S. Huntington *The Clash of Civilizations and the Remaking of World Order* (New York: Simon and Schuster, 1996).
17. G. Segal, 'International Relations and Democratic Transition', in Pridham, *Encouraging Democracy*, p.40.
18. J. Gray, 'Global Utopias and Clashing Civilizations: Misunderstanding the Present',

International Affairs, Vol.74, No.1 (1998), pp.149–64; and T. Barkawi and M. Laffey, 'The Imperial Peace: Democracy, Force and Globalization', *European Journal of International Relations*, Vol.5, No.4 (1999), pp.403–34.

19. S. Hoffman, 'A New World and Its Troubles', *Foreign Affairs*, Vol.69, No.4 (1990), pp.115–23.
20. B. Gills, J. Rocamora and R. Wilson (eds.), *Low Intensity Democracy* (London: Pluto Press, 1993); W. Robinson, *Promoting Polyarchy* (Cambridge: Cambridge University Press, 1997); and H. Smith, 'Why is there no International Democratic Theory?', in H. Smith (ed.), *Democracy and International Relations: Critical Theories/Problematic Practices* (Basingstoke: Macmillan, 2000).
21. A. Bernstein and P. Berger (eds.), *Business and Democracy: Cohabitation or Contradiction?* (London: Pinter, 1998).
22. World Bank, *Anti-Corruption in Transition: A Contribution to the Policy Debate* (Washington: World Bank, 2000).
23. A. Wendt, 'Anarchy is What States Make of It: The Social Construction of Power Politics', *International Organization*, Vol.88, No.2 (1992), pp.384–96.
24. The most sophisticated and pertinent recent application of the civil society framework to the human rights agenda, which also suggests the approach is likely to be relevant to broader democratization dynamics, is T. Risse, S. Ropp and K. Sikkink (eds.), *The Power of Human Rights: International Norms and Domestic Change* (Cambridge: Cambridge University Press, 1999).
25. On democracy assistance, see T. Carothers, *Aiding Democracy Abroad: The Learning Curve* (Washington: Carnegie Endowment of International Peace, 1999); and P. Burnell (ed.), *Democracy Assistance: International Co-operation for Democratization* (London: Frank Cass, 2000).
26. The question of which 'region' is being built remains an area of fundamental ambiguity within the EMP. While the idea of recreating or reinforcing a Mediterranean region is possibly supported by the emphasis on 'horizontal' co-operation and South–South economic integration, it remains problematic owing to the EU/Mediterranean Partner division among the riparian countries. The simultaneous emphasis upon building a Euro-Mediterranean entity is reflected in the EMP's institutional structures and in the plans to build a free trade area, yet any notion of region-building at this level is undermined once again by the EU/Mediterranean Partner divide, by the one-sided EU provision of direction, funding and administrative support for the project, and by the one-sidedness of the original free trade area design (omitting agriculture, under protest from southern countries).
27. E. Kienle, 'Destabilization through Partnership? Euro-Mediterranean Relations after the Barcelona Declaration', *Mediterranean Politics*, Vol.3, No.2 (1998), pp.1–20; O. Schlumberger, 'Arab Political Economy and the European Union's Mediterranean Policy: What Prospects for Development?', *New Political Economy*, Vol.5, No.2 (2000), p.258; and Schlumberger, 'The Arab Middle East', pp.118–22.
28. B. Dillman, 'Parliamentary Elections in North Africa', *Government and Opposition*, Vol.35, No.2 (2000), p.211.
29. Bechir Chourou, 'Security Partnership and Democratization: Perception of the Activities of Northern Security Institutions in the South', in Hans-Günter Brauch, Antonio Marquina and Abdelwahab Biad (eds.), *Euro-Mediterranean Partnership for the 21st Century* (Basingstoke: Macmillan, 2000), p.188.

The Challenge of Democracy in North Africa

BECHIR CHOUROU

Following the fall of the Berlin Wall and the end of the cold war, authoritarian regimes in eastern Europe and other parts of the world have been overthrown and replaced, more or less successfully and durably, by democratic forms of government. However, this 'wave of democracy' has missed the Middle East and North Africa (MENA) region. Thus in 2000–01, Freedom House, an organization that monitors the status of freedom and the existence of political rights and civil liberties around the world, found Algeria and Tunisia were not free and Morocco was only partly free; it gave them, respectively, scores of 6, 5 and 5 on political rights and 5, 5 and 4 on civil liberties (1 being the best score and 7 the worst).[1] It is interesting to note that for the period 1972–2001, Algeria's scores on political rights and civil liberties were consistently 6 or 7 and the country was always deemed to be not free, except in 1990–92 when both scores improved to 4 and the country was considered as partly free. Tunisia, on the other hand, has gone through three different phases. During the period 1972–79 Freedom House considered it as not free and gave it a score of 6 on political rights and a score of 5 on civil liberties. For the period 1980–93 the first score was either 5 or 6, but the second improved to 4 in 1988 and to 3 in 1989, and the overall political system was deemed to be partly free. Then from 1994 onward Tunisia reverted to the situation that had prevailed in the 1970s. As for Morocco, it was found to be partly free throughout the 1972–2001 period, and its scores on political rights and civil liberties were never above 5 and were even 3 or 4 in 1977–80 (except in 1992 when the score for political rights was 6); these were scores that neither Algeria nor Tunisia had ever obtained.[2]

Despite pressure exerted by national and international actors in favour of political liberalization, North African governments have been reluctant to adopt substantive reforms. In fact, North Africa – like most of the Arab region – appears intent on maintaining authoritarian rule for the foreseeable future; whatever reforms that may have been adopted remain mostly formal. In reality, as a European senior official noted concerning government attitudes towards democracy, Tunisia is going backwards, Algeria is going round in circles, and Morocco is undecided about which direction to take.[3]

What follows is an evaluation of the prospects for democratization in Algeria, Morocco and Tunisia. It is divided into four sections. The first deals with the immediate post-independence period. It is argued that at that time, conditions in the three countries were favourable for the adoption of a democratic system of government, but that independence leaders and movements failed to take advantage of the opportunity. The second section deals with the 1980s, a period during which North Africa faced major economic difficulties and social unrest that threatened to undermine the social fabric and political systems of the region. Reforms were adopted in an attempt to deal with the crisis, but they proved to be inappropriate and insufficient. As a result, the crisis widened and deepened, and the region was threatened by social, economic and political disintegration. The process is most visible in Algeria but, it is argued in the third section, is also at a dangerously advanced stage in the neighbouring countries, albeit in a less visible manner. The consequence is that democracy in the region has never been as remote a prospect as it is today. Nevertheless, it is suggested in the last section that despite major obstacles, future prospects for democracy are not totally dim, provided that urgent steps are taken to allow its emergence. In particular, attitudes towards Islamism have to change fundamentally: Islamist movements may well be a threat to democracy, but the solution is not to give preference to current regimes, as they are also a clear and present obstacle to democracy. Therefore, the appropriate policy should not be to maintain the regimes as the preferred or only way of avoiding the potential threat from the fundamentalists at the present time, but to ensure that (1) all forms of authoritarian rule are effectively blocked, and (2) that no party or movement has a monopoly over the political field or overwhelming arguments to prevail over other contenders for political leadership. It will be argued that the European Union (EU) played a role in the emergence and continuation of the current regimes and that it should play an equally decisive role in bringing about the demise of authoritarianism.

The Early Independence Period: Missed Opportunities

The nationalist movements that fought against French colonial rule in North Africa used the same basic argument to demand independence: the right to self-determination and self-rule. They claimed that democratic principles and practices recognized and respected in France applied equally well to North Africa. However, as soon as independence was achieved, those ideas were set aside. The new argument was that there were more urgent and vital tasks to be undertaken: building the state, achieving economic development, supplying social services to the population and so on. The nation had to devote all its energies to those sacred goals. Issues such as tenure of public office, methods for choosing leaders and representatives, and accountability of public servants were declared irrelevant and unworthy of debate.

In the general euphoria that prevailed after independence, the general public had no difficulties accepting such ideas. In Morocco and Tunisia, the leaders of the independence movements became the heads of the new states. The majority of the population in each country saw this as a natural transition, and clearly would have approved of Mohamed V and Habib Bourguiba regardless of the method of consultation. In Algeria Ahmed Ben Bella's popularity was perhaps less extensive. However, in no country did the leaders enjoy the same widespread support within their respective nationalist movements. Obviously, the struggle for independence was not carried out by a single person or group, yet in the end recognition was not given to all participants, awards were not obtained by all who expected them and the jackpot – supreme power – did not necessarily go to the candidate that other leaders would have chosen. Nationalist groups or factions agreed on the final objective – independence – but they did not have a common vision concerning the nature, institutions, policies or leadership of the future state. At some point a dominant view and figure did emerge, and minorities either gave their support to the majority, went into active opposition, stood aside biding their time, or left the game altogether, whether by choice or under duress.

In any event, this would have been an ideal opportunity for the winners to lay the foundations of a democratic state. Once in power, the new heads of states had political capital that could have lasted for years. Their auras and the popular support they enjoyed at the time were sufficient to guarantee success in any political contest. Had they organized such a contest, they could have used its inevitable outcome to consolidate their legitimacy and, perhaps, discredit their opponents. However, it quickly became apparent that the prime concern of the liberators went much further than mere politics. They found that it was only natural that they be awarded the highest office in the land as a sign of gratitude for their struggle and sacrifices. But they considered that their mission did not end with the ousting of the colonial power. Rather, it extended to the eradication of poverty, ignorance and underdevelopment in general. They had achieved independence and that made them the most qualified to carry out the new task – a task so ambitious that it could not be bound by any time limit and so vital that it could not be submitted to crass political bickering.

In Morocco, Mohamed V, the 'Revolutionary King', emerged as the most prominent figure of the nationalist movement. Political parties, including the largest one, Istiqlal, lacked a mass following, and their leaders drew support mostly from the elite. There was a high degree of political freedom, but the parties used it mostly for waging attacks against each other. In 1959 Istiqlal ended up splitting into two parties. This may have led the king to conclude that it would be futile, perhaps dangerous, to involve such ineffective forces in government. In 1960 he decided to become his own prime minister, thereby directly involving the monarchy in partisan politics. The king was no longer content to reign, he wanted to rule. Although the decision was the result of the inability of political parties to govern rather than a gambit by the palace to institute an absolutist monarchy, it did open the way to an increased involvement of the monarch in day-to-day politics.

When Hassan II came to power in 1961, he maintained this course. Members of his first government were chosen more on the basis of loyalty than political affiliation or ability. His first task was to draft a constitution (approved by referendum in 1962) which set up a 'constitutional, social, democratic' monarchy, but which in effect concentrated most powers and prerogatives in the hands of the king. Thus Morocco settled into the familiar pattern of authoritarian rule. Political freedoms, modest as they were, gave way to the repression of any form of opposition or protest. Social and economic problems were left unattended, leading to sporadic riots, attempts on the king's life and generalized instability.

In Tunisia the nationalist leader Habib Bourguiba, who gave himself the title of '*al-mujahid al-akbar*' (Supreme Combatant), had a much simpler situation to deal with. His party, the Néo-destour, was the only organized political movement in the country and enjoyed broad popular support. Shortly before independence, Salah Ben Youssef, secretary general of the party, briefly challenged Bourguiba's leadership, but his attempt failed and he was forced to flee the country.[4] As a result, when the French left in 1956 neither Bourguiba nor his party had to contend with any competition. The mostly ineffective Bey (king) was quickly and easily deposed and the monarchy abolished. Bourguiba was designated acting president of the new republic while a constitution was drafted. When the constitution was promulgated in 1959, presidential and legislative elections were held. Bourguiba and his party ran unopposed. For nearly three decades they then held a tight grip on power. None of his policies, domestic or foreign, could be discussed or criticized, no matter how erratic or ineffective they may have been.

Until the mid-1970s there were few fundamental or widespread causes of discontent. Despite uncertainties created by the government's hesitation between liberalism and socialism, the economy appeared to be moving ahead. Public enterprises and the administration were recruiting most job-seekers; housing, education and health services were readily available and poverty was declining. With time, Bourguiba became convinced – and expected everyone to recognize – that every success was attributable to his genius and that no further progress would be possible without his enlightened guidance. Even within his party, which had been renamed the Socialist Constitutional Party (Parti socialiste destourien, PSD), the freedom of expression in internal debates which the leadership enjoyed for a time gave way to an insipid enumeration of Bourguiba's achievements and exceptional qualities, creating disenchantment among a growing number of the party's leaders. Every major event related to the president's life – his birthday, his deportation by the French, his return from exile, his ascent to power – became public holidays and occasions for lengthy festivities during which he would listen with visible enjoyment to people glorifying him in songs and poems.

Throughout this period Bourguiba had ample opportunities to set Tunisia on a course towards democracy. He could have allowed freedom of expression, the separation of powers, an independent judiciary, freedom of association and the separation of state and party – all this without seriously jeopardizing his own position or powers. The only drawback was that he would have had to recognize that he was not indispensable and to set a schedule for his departure, opening the way for others to take over. Unable or unwilling to do so, he preferred instead to saddle the country with a president for life and thus deprived it of learning under his guidance and moderating influence how to transfer power in an orderly and peaceful manner. Worse still, as Bourguiba grew older, succession moved higher up the political agenda and, while the scramble for power intensified, the country was left to drift.

When the president's health started to deteriorate, those with grudges against him or his regime came forth. Seeing plots and counterplots everywhere, insiders and outsiders used every available means to consolidate their positions and eliminate opponents. Demonstrations degenerating into riots became commonplace, especially on university campuses, forcing the government at one point to close the universities for an entire year. By 1980 the crisis was so deep that no one could foresee how or when it would be resolved.

Algeria's situation was quite different from that of its two neighbours. For one thing, independence was achieved by soldiers rather than by diplomats. When the war was over, there were few politicians (and their standing was lower than that of military men). There were only two political institutions that could effectively run the country: the Front de Libération Nationale (FLN) and the Provisional Government of the Algerian Republic (Gouvernement provisoire de la République algérienne, GPRA). The FLN and the GPRA, both formed in 1958, were made up of members of the National Liberation Army (Armée de libération nationale, ALN), which in effect was the only national structure sufficiently well-organized to be able to fill the vacuum left by the precipitous departure of the French at independence. Furthermore, no one in the ALN emerged as an intellectual leader or a theoretician of the revolution; hence no vision or blueprint was prepared for the post-independence period.

When negotiations with France were concluded and a date for independence was formally set, the Algerian high command met in Libya to form a government. Immediately divisions appeared among the factions of the ALN as well as between these and the GPRA. There was actual fighting among army factions when everyone returned to Algiers to take office. Ahmed Ben Bella prevailed, due to the decisive support of chief of staff Houari Boumédiène. The FLN then proceeded to choose a slate of candidates for a future parliament. Elections were held in September 1962 and the new Assembly chose Ben Bella as head of government. Within a year Ben Bella managed to become head of the FLN, have a constitution adopted setting up a presidential regime and get himself elected president of the republic.

The ruling elite, particularly the army (by then called the National Popular Army, Armée nationale populaire, ANP, instead of ALN), interpreted these moves as attempts by Ben Bella to increase his powers at the expense of his allies. This led to a confrontation between the president and Boumédiène, his defence minister and erstwhile supporter. Ultimately Boumédiène won and Ben Bella was overthrown in June 1965. The two-year-old constitution was suspended and all powers were vested in a 21-member Council of the Revolution.

During the subsequent 12 years, politics in Algeria came to a standstill. Political institutions, including the FLN, became perfunctory. It was decreed that all energies were to be devoted to economic development. Almost immediately a strategy of heavy industrialization was launched, financed by state capital. That decision and others adopted in the late 1960s and in the 1970s were to have long-lasting effects on the country. Even without the benefit of hindsight, one could argue – and in fact many did at the time – that all these decisions were ill-advised and should at least have been submitted to public debate before becoming national policies.

Despite a major rise in the country's GDP following the 1973 oil price increase, Algeria continued to experience high unemployment, housing shortages and many other social and economic problems. In 1976 public participation in political life made a comeback when the population was asked to approve a National Charter and a new constitution. A large and quite open debate took place, followed by overwhelming approval of both documents, although neither of them called for democratic principles or practices. In fact, by virtue of the new constitution, Boumédiène ran unopposed for president and so did all FLN candidates to the National Popular Assembly.

In sum, neither the Moroccan monarchy, nor the Tunisian secular modernizing regime, nor the Algerian revolutionary junta, showed much interest in creating democratic systems of government in their newly independent states. In all three cases conditions were conducive to such a development, or at least were not totally opposed to it, and the leadership had enough power, prestige and influence to ensure the success of such an endeavour. This was most clearly the case in Tunisia. When the country achieved independence, it had standing political institutions and a functioning administration in which most positions were held by nationals, except at senior levels. During the protectorate period, France had not pursued a policy of heavy-handed assimilation or systematic discrimination towards the indigenous population, as it did in Algeria. Thus, the number of settlers and other French nationals was not large. Schools for Tunisian children were available and the curriculum included French language and culture as well as subjects related to Arab and Islamic culture taught by Tunisians in Arabic. Secondary schools existed even before the protectorate and one of them, the famous Collège Sadiki, supplied the country with its elite. They continued to function during the protectorate, and their graduates could either work for local institutions and public enterprises (such as administration, the post office, transport companies and the mining industry) or enrol at universities in France. As a result, a sizeable minority of the population was able to acquire a modern education without being cut off from its national culture, and in time this class was to supply the leadership of the nationalist movement as well as the managers of the future independent state.

In Morocco, France pursued a similar policy of non-interference in local culture and traditions, and made no efforts to impose western values and practices on the population. But neither did it adopt any particular steps to promote social welfare in the country. The net result of this policy of 'benign neglect' was to maintain Moroccan society in a state of underdevelopment, with such signs as illiteracy, poor health conditions, poverty and an absence of industry.

In Algeria, however, France pursued a radically different policy. Whereas in Tunisia and Morocco it was content to rule through existing political institutions and structures, in Algeria it opted for the systematic elimination of all forms of self-government. Furthermore, it launched a large-scale programme of settlement that drew a constant flow of migrants, attracted by the prospect of acquiring confiscated land at symbolic prices. Those French nationals who migrated to Algeria quickly became the dominant economic and political group in the country, and over the years forced the French government to adopt a series of measures which, by the end of the nineteenth century, had created a virtual system of apartheid, imposed by some 364,000 Frenchmen on nearly 4 million Algerians.[5]

At the time of independence, the three countries were at different stages of development. However, they were not completely without resources. Clearly, most skills needed for social and economic development were scarce. Furthermore, traditional beliefs and practices were dominant. Nevertheless, people were politically aware and capable of understanding such ideas as freedom, self-determination and human rights. If this were not the case, it would have been difficult to mobilize them politically and militarily to achieve independence. So when the French departed, more or less hastily, the countries may have lacked teachers, technicians and engineers, but not political discernment. In fact, up until a few years after independence, active involvement in *assiyassa* (politics) was considered both a right and a duty. It should be borne in mind that, without the active support of their populations, the nationalist leaders would not have been able to carry out the struggle for independence, nor would they have been entrusted with power as leaders of the new states. But in the end those early leaders allowed their ambitions and personal interests to prevail over their civic duty. As a result, they may come to be remembered more as failed nation-builders than as successful national liberators.

The 1980s: A Time of Procrastination

By 1980 an entire new generation was coming of age in North Africa. Large numbers of this generation were literate, informed, politically sophisticated and articulate. They had never lived under colonial rule, and to them the national liberation movement was just another chapter in their history books to be memorized for exams. Bourguiba was viewed as an ailing and somewhat senile dictator, Ben Bella a dissident in exile, Boumédiène the protector of a predatory class and Hassan II a king to be respected as 'Commander of the Faithful' (the title that Moroccan kings traditionally claim to legitimize their rule) but feared as commander of the secret police. In each country the population considered that it had a tacit contract with the rulers whereby the latter would be left to rule unhampered so long as the people could be guaranteed a minimum standard of living. A vivid illustration of this passivity towards politics is the Tunisian popular notion of *khubzist*, or follower of the 'bread party'. By and large, politics and politicians were scorned, ridiculed, envied, courted or, most often, feared and avoided. However, passivity gave way to activism when the contract was broken.

During that period, the world was grappling with a serious recession. The economies of the industrialized countries stagnated. Sluggish demand for raw materials, energy products and manufactured goods in Europe, the United States and Japan had a direct impact on the economies of Arab states in general and North Africa in particular. More than 75 per cent of North Africa's trade was with Europe. Most of Algeria's revenue was generated by oil and gas exports. Consequently, any contraction in European markets or oil prices would have severe repercussions on North Africa.

Other major developments of the period were the demise of the Soviet Union and the end of the cold war, followed by uprisings in eastern Europe that led to: the overthrow of authoritarian regimes which had been in power for decades; the discrediting of socialism as a form of social and economic organization; and the growing notoriety of Islamic fundamentalism, perceived in the West as a source of violence and instability.

The convergence of these factors created havoc in North Africa. High rates of demographic growth cancelled or even outstripped those of economic growth, except in Tunisia, which had introduced a vigorous and effective family planning programme years earlier. Previous policies that could not be easily reversed, such as export-led growth, import substitution activities and heavy industrialization, started to have their full impact. As a result of declining public revenues, subsidies for staple products and expenditure on social services had to be curtailed.

By the mid-1980s both Tunisia and Morocco had to call on the International Monetary Fund (IMF) for help. Structural adjustment programmes (SAPs) were put into place, with the standard injunctions to cut budget deficits and public spending, liberalize trade, prices and wages, and so on. The social effects of those measures, although predictable, were ignored.

Popular reaction to the widening and deepening crisis was inevitable, and because it lacked channels for orderly expression it took violent forms. This forced governments to modify or even abandon some decisions, but overall it was mainly a question of violent means being employed to repress the articulation of grievances and demands for a re-evaluation of economic policy. The Algerian uprising of 1988 was the most dramatic illustration of this trend. In Tunisia riots broke out in 1984 and instability continued until 1987. Also in 1984 violent demonstrations took place in 48 towns and villages in southern Morocco, and the intervention of the army and the police left 25 people dead and 114 wounded, according to official figures.[6]

However, hopeful signs began to appear here and there. In Tunisia Bourguiba was deposed in 1987 in a bloodless 'medical' coup carried out by his prime minister, Zine el Abidine Ben Ali. The new president promised not only to resolve economic problems but also to achieve national reconciliation and establish a democratic government. In Algeria a new constitution, adopted in February 1989, and a law on political associations promulgated a few months later, instituted a free press and led to the formation of some 20 political parties. Only Morocco seemed to lag behind. A few days after the 1984 riots were crushed, Hassan II went on television to announce that the violence had been fomented by traitors supported by communist, Zionist and Khomeinist organizations. He further warned that minors caught demonstrating would be punished as adults and that their parents would be held responsible for their acts. Finally, he advised Moroccans in other parts of the country who might be tempted to join the protest movement to remember what he did as crown prince when people took to the streets in 1958–59.

By the end of the decade, rulers and ruled appeared to have reached a tenuous truce, if not a tentative peace agreement. Although none of the fundamental problems had been resolved, a new discourse was being established, particularly in Tunisia and Algeria, and most people were willing to wait in the hope that positive developments would take place. That hope was shattered at the beginning of the 1990s.

The 1990s: Racing Towards Disintegration

Events taking place in North Africa at the onset of the decade appeared ominous: riots followed by repression; police harassment, illegal detention and the disappearance of dissidents; cancelled or rigged elections and similar events – all multiplied. It was evident that the second-generation rulers of North Africa were no more interested in, or committed to, democracy than were their predecessors.

It was at this juncture that 'political Islam' became a hotly discussed issue. In Algeria, following the adoption of a new constitution in 1989, the country's main Islamist party, the Islamic Salvation Front (Front islamique du salut, FIS) was legalized. It took part in the 1991 legislative elections, and it was clear from the first round that the FIS was going to repeat its performance in the 1990 local and regional elections and score a major victory. Without waiting for the second round, in early 1992 the army cancelled the elections and took power on the grounds that an FIS victory would have jeopardized national security.

Do Islamic (or Islamist or fundamentalist) groups represent a threat? If so, who is threatened? What is the nature of the threat? Is the presumed threat a sufficient reason for preventing those groups from participating in politics? Such questions were scarcely raised when those groups became active in North Africa in the 1960s and 1970s. In fact, many of them had been created with the encouragement – if not at the behest – of governments as a counterweight to liberal or radical movements that sought to form opposition parties. But when the political arena was wiped clean of any organized opposition or dissidence, and as social and economic conditions worsened, the fundamentalists stepped in to identify and denounce those responsible for the people's hardships and to provide immediate and concrete help to alleviate those hardships. Their success on both accounts was easy – and logical, for the ruling regimes had few qualities that endeared them to the citizens. Day-to-day living standards were worsening and no relief was in sight. Avenues for expressing needs or grievances, and particularly for influencing events, were lacking. In addition, the fundamentalists spoke of values that a Muslim understood and upheld – justice, honesty, solidarity, morality – in a language that the common man understood. Most importantly, the Islamists dealt with concrete problems such as hunger, poverty and illness and they provided food, medical care and money – not just words. It is not surprising that the fundamentalists had a large and growing appeal or that at some point they should decide to use it in order to seek political power.

This is what the FIS did in Algeria; but when it became clear that its (predictable and predicted) victory was going to materialize, the game was cancelled at half-time and the army confiscated the ball. This intervention in the electoral process has precipitated Algeria into a crisis from which it still does not appear ready to emerge. But it was welcomed with relief in Europe as well as by Algeria's two immediate neighbours. Hassan II and Ben Ali, who had been neither consulted nor informed beforehand about Algerian president Chadli Benjedid's decision to legalize the FIS, were concerned that an FIS victory would lead to a resurgence of Islamist movements in Morocco and Tunisia. Consequently, not only did they consider the Algerian army's move appropriate, but they also took precautions to prevent their own fundamentalists from following in the FIS's footsteps.

It is clear that the crisis has brought great pain and anguish to the Algerian people. What is less clear is whether there are any lessons to be learned from it, especially by other North African countries and by Europe. In particular, one has to ask whether North Africa – and the rest of the Arab world – is condemned to choose between institutionalized democracy and radical fundamentalism; whether the choice could be made without precipitating social disintegration; whether both alternatives are bound to result in such a disintegration; and lastly whether the EU can or should provide any help to find answers to these questions.

The Challenge of Democracy in North Africa

Democracy has not existed in North Africa in the past, although it could have done; nor does is exist now, notwithstanding all claims to the contrary; nor is there any inherent reason for it not to exist in the future. Without going into a lengthy dissertation on the nature of democracy, it will suffice here to consider as democratic any polity in which citizens delegate authority to individuals who are freely and fairly chosen on a periodic and regular basis, and who are held responsible for their actions and decisions while in office. Democracy does not guarantee good or efficient government, nor does it always yield desirable results. The main merit of democracy is that it leaves the way open to different choices or corrective actions the next time around.

Democracy requires adherence to some values, such as belief in the virtues of dialogue, tolerance of different opinions, acceptance of criticism and abiding by majority decisions, however adverse they may be. Such values may have to be acquired through practice, but the learning process has to start sometime and it is postulated that everyone is capable of undertaking it. In this regard, several scholars have attempted to determine whether or not the emergence and persistence of democracy do in fact require certain social and economic conditions such as minimum levels of per capita income, literacy and industrialization. As part of this continuing debate the author has argued elsewhere that there is no compelling evidence to support the proposition that democracy can be instituted only when certain conditions are met.[7] Consequently, claims that certain societies are not sufficiently ready or 'mature' for democracy are most likely casuistic justifications for the continued existence of authoritarian regimes.

This is not to say that the adoption of democracy will not create problems. However, it can be argued that the nature and severity of these problems are more likely to be determined by the length and degree of ruthlessness of dictatorial rule than by some characteristics of the society in which democratization takes place: the longer the period of dictatorship, the greater the likelihood of a disorderly transition to democracy. This is because authoritarianism prevents the development of a tradition of dialogue and compromise, and creates deep-seated mistrust of authority in general and of those previously associated with it in particular. In the absence of effective structures capable of aggregating and articulating interests, any political opening is likely to lead to the formation of a multitude of narrowly-based groups whose members are eager to secure and protect interests that have been repressed or ignored. These groups may be formed along racial, ethnic, religious, regional or professional lines. Once constituted, and being fully aware that their interests may be opposed by others, they become convinced that their objectives can be achieved only through the exercise or the direct control of power. To put it differently, interest articulation may become politically dysfunctional in the absence of efficient structures for interest aggregation.

This is in fact what occurred in Algeria and in many parts of sub-Saharan Africa where democratic experiments have taken place. In Algeria, political reforms adopted in the wake of the 1988 revolt led to the creation of a multitude of political parties and other forms of associations whose membership rarely overlapped. There was also a proliferation of newspapers whose editorial lines or political orientations were quite similar, but which represented or were aimed at a particular section of society.

The same trend is likely to be observed in other North African or Arab countries that might adopt democratic reforms, including those that appear to have rather cohesive societies. Tunisia is a case in point. This is a country where there are practically no racial, ethnic, religious or linguistic minorities. Social services such as education and health have been more equally distributed than in many other countries. Women have been granted more rights than elsewhere in the Arab world. Stark poverty is not as highly visible as it is elsewhere. Nevertheless, such achievements have not prevented, or in fact have resulted in the emergence and growth of, a desire for political freedom. If citizens were to be left free to express and organize themselves, they would be likely to exercise all the rights that have been previously denied or repressed, including the right to participate in the exercise of power. The process is certain to be disorderly, as groups and parties find difficulties in trusting each other and show a tendency to be mutually suspicious of their motives for existence.

Such a development would only be natural: whenever goods which had been scarce reappear on the market, people tend to consume them without moderation and to hoard them. However, the transitional disorder may be prolonged in time and/or degenerate into violence under a number of circumstances: some players are not admitted to the game; the rules of the game are not strictly observed; the regime in power deliberately manipulates groups to prevent the emergence of coalitions that threaten its hold on power. One cannot expect democracy to emerge quickly or easily in North Africa, but the process may be greatly facilitated if the following obstacles are downsized or eliminated.

The first and perhaps most formidable obstacle is represented by each of the regimes currently in power in North Africa. In Morocco, the monarch wants both to rule and to reign, and considers himself untouchable in both capacities. The country has some of the features of a democratic system, such as a parliament and a number of political parties, but ultimate power is in the hands of the king. Most acts depend on his initiative and goodwill, including those that are defining characteristics of a democracy, such as respect of laws and human rights. The regime in Morocco (and elsewhere) commits various abuses, but rejects any condemnation for such acts. However, when the government decides to suspend such practices, it presents this as an act of magnanimity and goodness to be admired and applauded. Similarly, regimes have now and then proposed 'national charters' or 'pacts of good behaviour' designed to regulate relations between rulers and civil society. These stipulate, *inter alia*, that the signatories shall abide by the law and that lawbreakers shall be punished – as if such matters should be subject to a negotiated agreement.

In Algeria the army continues to be the main political player and to hold ultimate power. During the early months of 2001, there was speculation that it was preparing to depose President Abdelaziz Bouteflika after earlier having engineered his election to office. Interestingly, Algeria has been the country with the least pretence of democratic government and has been considered by many the least likely to democratize. Yet it became the first – and so far the only – country in the region to carry out a genuinely democratic experiment. But the experiment came to an abrupt end because its first outcome was deemed unacceptable. The ensuing crisis is not likely to be resolved unless that outcome is validated or the experiment is repeated in its original format, that is, with the participation of the FIS. But this can happen only if the army withdraws from politics.

In Tunisia, Ben Ali successfully deposed Bourguiba in 1987 and declared that Tunisia was sufficiently mature for democracy. He called for a broadly-based dialogue to determine the future of the country, and initiated a number of reforms aimed at resolving the crisis that had nearly precipitated the country into a civil war. However, the initiative was short-lived. Barely two years after coming to power, the regime reverted to the old pattern of authoritarian rule that it was supposed to have put to rest. Having been in power ever since then, and confronted with a constitutional amendment (adopted upon his own initiative) that bars him from seeking an additional term once his current one expires in 2004, Ben Ali is reportedly seeking a plausible scenario that would keep himself in power for one or more additional terms. It would be helpful if the scenario could be made to fit democratic principles, but this is probably not a major requirement.

Clearly, democracy cannot be instituted in North Africa as long as current power structures remain unchanged. If ruling regimes were to open the way to democratic rule, this would mean in practice that they would prepare for their own demise. This has happened in some sub-Saharan African countries, but there is no reason at present to believe that it will happen in North Africa. Of course, current conditions may make it difficult for authoritarian rule to persist indefinitely. In particular, northern governments and international institutions can no longer be counted on to refrain from interfering in the internal affairs of sovereign states. However, North African regimes know that no practical measures can be taken to force them to give up their power. Nevertheless, they have shrewdly chosen to pre-empt or prevent international criticism. Thus, they adopt measures designed to improve their image and standing on the international scene: freeing prominent political prisoners, authorizing carefully screened parties to play the role of opposition, and promulgating laws setting up all the mechanical procedures of democracy. Outside observers may view such a policy as a pragmatic approach leading towards a gradual and orderly transition to democracy, or as an indicator of the adaptability and resilience of regimes to change. However, North African societies consider that most measures adopted by their governments constitute a façade behind which rule continues to be exercised by force.

This leads to the second major obstacle to democratization, namely, the attitude of citizens towards politics. At present citizens are barred from any meaningful participation in the political process and are afraid to petition for the right to such participation. As a result, most people have withdrawn from active citizenship to become passive subjects of whoever happens to rule. Anomie, considered to be a threat to the survival of democracy, must also be considered a threat to its emergence. However, misery, despair and pent-up resentment may at any time take people out of their apathy and onto the streets to 'kick the rascals out' and replace them with whomever seems most likely to bring about effective change.

To prevent such a dangerous development, people have to be offered alternative ways of achieving the desired end. At present most opposition parties in North Africa are unable to offer alternatives because their very existence depends upon the goodwill of the regimes, and as a result they have little credibility and would attract little support in future free elections. Some opposition leaders who refused co-optation have been forced to go into exile to escape arrest. But they are aware that they cannot undertake any serious political action from afar. That is why they demand guarantees that would allow them to return home and to operate legally. In this respect, fundamentalist groups have skilfully exploited their illegality to acquire credibility and legitimacy, and those who support them do so as a way of defying the regimes and anyone directly or indirectly connected to the regimes. One can even argue that the fundamentalists do not need to destroy democracy once they have used it to come to power: if they can just manage to prevent further deterioration of the economic and social situation, they can realistically expect to be elected again and again, because voters will be inclined not only to give them time to undo the consequences of decades of mismanagement, but especially to block the return of faces and groups associated with the bad old days. Resentment does not fade easily and some wounds heal very slowly; even if people do not turn vindictiveness into vendettas, and if they can resist the desire to make the oppressor taste his own medicine, they will still do everything to prevent a return to a hated past.

A factor that may become the third obstacle to democratization in North Africa is the EU's inability to devise an effective, coherent and consistent policy toward the region. At present popular attitudes towards the West (the EU being perceived as a mere underling within the group) are negative and are not improving. The reasons for this are too numerous and too well known to warrant their discussion here, but some, which are particularly prominent in North Africa and apply specifically to the EU, need to be mentioned.

The EU has come to view the Mediterranean as an important region that deserves a specific and long-term policy. Therefore, it launched an initiative that eventually led to the adoption in 1995 of the Barcelona Declaration, which set a number of objectives to be achieved in common by the EU and 12 partners from the southern and eastern Mediterranean. The overall aim of the Euro-Mediterranean Partnership (EMP) is to turn the Mediterranean into an area of peace, stability and shared prosperity, where some fundamental principles – such as non-interference in internal affairs, the rule of law, respect of human rights, democracy – prevail. The Barcelona Declaration also envisages the creation of a Euro-Mediterranean free trade area by virtue of partnership agreements concluded between the EU and each of the Mediterranean non-EU countries (MNCs).

So far, little progress has been made towards the objectives defined at Barcelona, and the process towards achieving them – the Barcelona process – is now being reviewed in the hope that it can be relaunched or reinvigorated. Ironically, but not surprisingly, the process has created – at least in Morocco and Tunisia – a consensus among governments and populations who are now questioning it, although for entirely different reasons.

Governments saw the EMP as something that might bring material and political benefits at little cost. Economic measures such as privatization, trade liberalization and other adjustments have been presented as being required by the EMP, but they have been implemented in such a way that most of their benefits have gone to a small elite while all of their costs have been borne by the rest of the population. At the same time, implementation brought rewards from the EU in the form of funds and political support, if nothing else. None of this was very objectionable, but when the EU started alluding to other EMP measures that had been neglected, such as democratic rule and respect of human rights, governments bristled. The public, on the other hand, had to endure the negative effects of the free trade agreements (unemployment, higher prices and so on), but saw no compensation coming in the form of progress towards the positive objectives of the EMP, particularly in the areas of democratization and human rights.

As a result, the EMP and its initiator the EU came under attack from both sides. On the one hand, governments have given a *fin de non recevoir* to EU suggestions that greater attention be paid to the political 'basket' of the Barcelona Declaration. The breakdown of the Middle East peace process in late 2000 provided a convenient reason for postponing further discussion of the issue. What will happen when or if the question comes up again? If the EU stands by its recently-adopted resolve, many MNCs will, in the author's estimation, threaten to renege on the Barcelona Declaration (which is not legally binding anyway) and, in the case of Morocco and Tunisia, even to rescind the association agreements.

On the other hand, societies – particularly segments that are not officially considered to be 'civil' – will grow restless as economic difficulties increase and political expectations remain unmet. It is already widely believed that the EMP is a thinly disguised form of imperialism designed to exploit and dominate the Arabs, and that the EU will do nothing to destabilize regimes needed to carry out its plan. Past behaviour and declarations by EU members and organs have done little to contradict such perceptions. The EU's recently proclaimed intention to take a more proactive approach in favour of democratization may thus be greeted with some degree of cynicism and seen as an effort to placate legitimate aspirations for genuine democracy.[8]

The EU finds itself in a quandary. If it leans too heavily on current regimes, it will alienate them without necessarily achieving the desired goal of democratization, and it may lose the EMP as a forum in which it can exert further pressure on them. On the other hand, if the EU opts for gradualism and patient persuasion, it will be accused by public opinion of temporizing in order to allow regimes to tighten their grip on their societies. It cannot even consider a policy of the 'iron fist in a velvet glove' because the regimes will focus on the fist and try to avoid it, while public opinion will see only the glove and denounce its softness. To complicate the situation further, the fundamentalists stand to profit most from any solution adopted to resolve this dilemma: if democracy is instituted and elections are held, they are likely to be voted into power; if not, they can put the blame on the regimes and their foreign patrons, and wait for the mobs to carry them to power.

Devising a suitable policy is most difficult, especially when time is short. Nevertheless, the situation may still be salvaged provided that the EU's resolve does not dissolve. What is needed is a series of measures that would bring quick, tangible and widespread results in the eyes of increasingly sceptical populations. Whatever the measures adopted, they should seek to compensate for the negative effects of liberalization, amend and complement clauses of the Partnership Agreements that have created social and economic difficulties, and create hope of a better life in the not-too-distant future. Furthermore, the EU should clearly indicate its firm intention to invite any interested groups and individuals to participate in the identification, implementation and follow-up of these measures and ask governments to refrain from any attempts to prevent, discourage, manipulate or sanction such participation.

If successful, such a strategy would yield several benefits. It would make people feel that they are no longer limited to a choice between forced obedience or violent protest. It would give them confidence in their ability to influence events relating to their own welfare. It would encourage them to take initiatives and make decisions, as well as reassure them that their actions would be judged strictly on the basis of merit. And they would see and experience first-hand the virtues – and the difficulties – of discussion, negotiation and compromise.

However, such a strategy is not likely to open the way to democratic rule unless it is accompanied by a qualitative change in the way the EU and its members deal with unco-operative and unresponsive governments. Until now the EU has been much too lenient toward regimes that are clearly authoritarian. Its failure to condemn the cancellation of the 1991 elections in Algeria has particularly damaged its image and may ultimately lead to the failure of its current efforts in favour of democracy. EU commitment to democracy is seen as opportunistic, insincere, inconsistent and wavering. European countries may intervene collectively or individually when a prominent opposition figure is persecuted in North Africa, but remain silent and inactive regarding less famous victims of detention, torture, harassment and other violations of human rights. Not only are such acts continuing unabated but their perpetrators are received in European capitals with honour and respect.

The EU will have to be more circumspect in its dealings with North African politicians. If it chooses not to reprehend them openly, it should at least not condone their crimes. In any case, it may no longer be sufficient to rely on discreet diplomacy. What goes on behind the scenes will have no impact on public opinion. The EU will be expected to speak its conscience louder and with greater conviction.

Conclusion

The following conclusions may be drawn from the preceding discussion.

First, the nationalist leaders and movements who put an end to colonial rule could have built the new independent states on democratic foundations. There were no social, economic or political obstacles to the implementation of such a choice. In earlier periods, other societies that were not more advanced than those of North Africa at that time had successfully established democratic governments. Furthermore, democracy would not have prevented North Africa's leaders from exercising power and would even have consolidated the legitimacy of their leadership.

Second, regimes in all three countries adopted commendable policies and achieved positive results. They claimed credit for successes, but were willing neither to adjust to the logical consequences of successful policies nor to assume responsibility for those that failed. Thus, they wanted recognition for having improved educational levels, health conditions and living standards, but they would not accept that citizens whose utilitarian needs have been satisfied are likely to want to participate in public life and demand the right to hold leaders accountable for their acts. Policies that presented potential negative consequences were not submitted to public debate and those that did prove harmful could not be criticized or denounced. Had the leaders invited or encouraged public participation in the political process, they would have spared their countries the consequences of ill-advised decisions, and would have established the ways and means for avoiding similar errors in the future through a peaceful and structured political dialogue.

Third, as problems grew in number and intensity, it became increasingly difficult to deny their existence. Paradoxically, this made the leaders more adamant in their claims that these were not problems but mere 'challenges' imposed by external factors (globalization being the current favourite culprit), more entrenched in their belief that only they could meet such challenges and protect the nation's welfare and integrity, and more intransigent towards critics and dissidents.

Fourth, having come to the conclusion that the regimes were neither interested in, nor capable of, resolving urgent problems, people endured their suffering in forced silence while remaining on the lookout for the slightest opportunity to express their discontent collectively. The fundamentalists were skilful in turning this situation to their advantage. Having legitimate venues (mosques), legitimate reasons for gathering crowds (praying, preaching) and legitimate issues to raise (religious values that happen to apply to politics), the *imams*-turned-politicians could denounce all wrongdoers and call on all God-fearing men to wage a *jihad* to establish God's kingdom on earth.

Fifth, such a message left no one indifferent, but the reactions of two groups are of particular interest here. The first is that of the governments in power. They accused the fundamentalists of mixing religion with politics and denied them any right to pose as the exclusive or most competent defenders of Islam and of Muslim values. They then declared them subversives and even heretics! This reaction is understandable and perhaps not too far-fetched. But then they went from there to argue that all critics by definition had fundamentalist tendencies, and defined all those who challenged power-holders or sought to exercise power as equally subversive – an attitude which is not understandable and is indeed quite far-fetched.

The second reaction is that of the West, including the EU. Initially, the reaction tended to be hysterical, although the large number of spectacular terrorist acts carried out by Arab and Islamist groups may have explained, if not justified, official and popular attitudes toward Islam at that time. It is quite clear, however, that not all Muslims were fundamentalists or potential terrorists, and that not all fundamentalists were bent on violence and confrontation, but this argument has had little effect on western perceptions. In particular, the EU continued to equate fundamentalism with terrorism, and to consider both as threats to its security. Moreover, it gave credence to North Africa's regimes, which played on this fear and claimed that any move in the direction of democracy was bound to result in an increase in fundamentalist power ('look at Algeria', they said) and to create instability in the region. This attitude, however, has been revised since.

All three North African countries missed early opportunities to establish democratic systems of government; had they grasped these opportunities, these countries would have become mature, stable democracies by now. Over the years, they have adopted institutions and processes usually associated with democracy, but they have failed to make them operational. If one were to evaluate the North African political systems on the basis of their current constitutions, one would find them quite acceptable and perhaps superior to those of some western countries. But few elements of those constitutions are actually applied or respected.

The challenge of democracy is in effect the challenge of a speedy and effective implementation of existing constitutions. North Africans must meet that challenge by themselves, but the odds against them have to be improved. In this respect the EU could play a useful role, not so much by assisting democratic forces as by helping to level the playing field and by ensuring that Europe does not unwittingly aid and abet anti-democratic forces.

In the short run, the prospects for democracy in North Africa are not encouraging. Indeed, Tunisia is moving backwards; in Morocco the new king initially seemed to be liberalizing the regime but he appears to have had second thoughts. In both countries the fundamentalists are keeping a low profile, but are by no means out of the picture. As for Algeria, it is caught between the army, which does not want to loosen its iron grip on power, and the Islamists, who want to reclaim what was taken away from them by force.

If fair elections were held now anywhere in North Africa, the Islamists would be likely to obtain good results, if not outright victories. But this should not become an argument for postponing the establishment of the democratic process or an excuse for nipping it in the bud. That would simply condemn the countries to greater repression at the hands of frightened regimes or uncompromising fundamentalists. A better approach would be to give people fewer reasons to opt for radical solutions, and convincing arguments that better alternatives are available and forthcoming.

NOTES

1. All scores are available on Freedom House's website at http://www.freedomhouse.org/research/freeworld/FHSCORES.xls.
2. The table below shows the scores for all three countries for the period 1972–2001:

TABLE 1
FREEDOM RATINGS IN NORTH AFRICA, 1972–73 TO 2000–01

Year	Algeria	Morocco	Tunisia
1972–73	6.6, NF	5.4, PF	6.5, NF
1973–74	6.6, NF	5.5, PF	6.5, NF
1974–75	6.6, NF	5.5, PF	6.5, NF
1975–76	7.6, NF	5.5, PF	6.5, NF
1976–77	6.6, NF	5.5, PF	6.5, NF
1977–78	6.6, NF	4.3, PF	6.5, NF
1978–79	6.6, NF	3.4, PF	6.5, NF
1979–80	6.6, NF	3.4, PF	6.5, PF
1980–81	6.6, NF	4.4, PF	6.5, PF
1981–82	6.6, NF	4.5, PF	5.5, PF
1982–83	6.6, NF	4.5, PF	5.5, PF
1983–84	6.6, NF	4.5, PF	5.5, PF
1984–85	6.6, NF	4.5, PF	5.5, PF
1985–86	6.6, NF	4.5, PF	5.5, PF
1986–87	6.6, NF	4.5, PF	6.5, PF
1987–88	6.6, NF	4.5, PF	5.6, PF
1988–89	5.6, NF	4.5, PF	6.4, PF
1989–90	6.4, PF	4.4, PF	5.3, PF
1990–91	4.4, PF	4.4, PF	5.4, PF
1991–92	4.4, PF	5.5, PF	5.5, PF
1992–93	7.6, NF	6.5, PF	6.5, PF
1993–94	7.6, NF	5.5, PF	6.5, NF
1994–95	7.7, NF	5.5, PF	6.5, NF
1995–96	6.6, NF	5.5, PF	6.5, NF
1996–97	6.6, NF	5.5, PF	6.5, NF
1997–98	6.6, NF	5.5, PF	6.5, NF
1998–99	6.5, NF	5.4, PF	6.5, NF
1999–00	6.5, NF	5.4, PF	6.5, NF
2000–01	6.5, NF	5.4, PF	6.5, NF

Source: Freedom House, 'Freedom in the World Country Ratings 1972–73 to 2000–01', ibid. The freedom status of a country is calculated on the basis of scores given for political rights and civil liberties, measured on a scale of one to seven, with one representing the highest degree of freedom and seven the lowest. 'PF' and 'NF' stand for 'partly free' and 'not free' respectively. Countries whose combined averages for political rights and civil liberties fall between 1.0 and 2.5 are designated 'free'; between 3.0 and 5.5 'partly free'; and between 5.5 and 7.0 'not free'.

3. This remark was attributed to French foreign minister Hubert Védrine, during a private meeting with the press following his brief visit to Algeria in February 2001. It was reported in *Nord-Sud Export*, No.415, 2 March 2001.
4. After independence he tried to organize an armed rebellion but this also failed and he was later assassinated in Germany, probably on Bourguiba's orders.
5. For a more detailed account of French colonization policies in each of the three North African countries, see Jamil M. Abun-Nasr, *A History of the Maghrib*, second edition (Cambridge: Cambridge University Press, 1975), especially ch.9.
6. These figures were reported by local newspapers as having been provided by the Ministry of the Interior. However, foreign reporters estimated that the number of dead and wounded was much higher. See François Della Sudda, 'Le Maroc du silence', *Le Monde Diplomatique*, December 1988, p.15.
7. Bechir Chourou, 'Security Partnership and Democratization: Perception of the Activities of Northern Security Institutions in the South', in Hans-Günter Brauch, Antonio Marquina and Abdelwahab Biad (eds.), *Euro-Mediterranean Partnership for the 21st Century* (London: Macmillan, 2000), especially pp.167–76.
8. Support for democracy and human rights is found in the Barcelona Declaration as well as in the association agreements that the EU signed with Morocco and Tunisia, which contain articles (art.2 of the Tunisian Agreement) stipulating that democracy is an 'essential element' of the agreement. Since then, repeated violations of human rights and lack of progress towards democracy have been denounced in the European media and by the European Parliament. However, official pronouncements by the Council or the Commission have been scarce and indirect until recently. Thus, the Presidency's Formal Conclusions issued at the end of the Fourth Euro-Mediterranean Conference of Foreign Ministers (Barcelona IV), held in Marseille on 15–16 November 2000, indicate that the participants 'took the view that there should no longer be any taboos where questions of common interests were concerned, and expressed a desire to extend the [political] dialogue to other topics [than security] such as regional trends as regards ... the process of consolidating the rule of law and respect of human rights and democratic principles' (para.12). More recently, the European Commissioner responsible for external relations, Chris Patten, declared in a speech delivered in the European Parliament on 31 January 2001 that greater efforts are needed 'to promote respect of human rights and democratic freedoms in the region' and that 'the EU should use *all* appropriate fora to press for progress on those issues; the MEDA Democracy programme should continue to be used to fund positive actions; and MEDA allocations themselves should be more dependent on adequate progress' [emphasis in the original text]. MEDA refers to the 'Mesures d'Accompagnement', that is the financial and technical measures, established by the EU to support structural reform in Mediterranean partner countries, as part of the Euro-Mediterranean Partnership. The speech may be found at: http://europa.eu.int/ comm.external_relations/ news/patten/speech_01_ 49.htm.

The European Union and Democracy Promotion in the Mediterranean: A New or Disingenuous Strategy?

RICHARD YOUNGS

As in other regions, prior to the 1990s European concern with democracy and human rights in the southern Mediterranean was subordinated to the strategic logic of the cold war. While a commitment to the promotion of democracy was enshrined within new European Union policy initiatives towards the Africa-Caribbean-Pacific (ACP) states, central and eastern Europe and Latin America during the late 1980s and early 1990s, it remained absent from the EU's Renovated Mediterranean Policy adopted in December 1990. This invited suggestions that the Mediterranean was perceived to be subject to unique considerations which militated against a prioritization of democracy promotion. Tensions after the second Gulf war against Iraq's invasion of Kuwait and the rise of political Islam, most dramatically demonstrated by the Islamic Salvation Front (FIS) victory in the subsequently revoked 1991 elections in Algeria, could, for some, be cited as justification for such exceptionalism. While the European Parliament's withholding of assent for new aid packages to Morocco and Syria in 1992 was widely seen as an important departure, this coercive action was strongly opposed by European governments and was explicitly directed at specific human rights issues rather than broader democratic shortfalls.

Against this background, it appeared highly significant that, from 1995, Mediterranean policy was brought into line with other areas of the EU's external relations. Those states negotiating new association agreements – initially Morocco and Tunisia – were obliged to sign up to a clause stipulating a commitment to democratic reform. The democracy promotion aim was then regionalized through the new Euro-Mediterranean Partnership (EMP), formally established in Barcelona in November 1995, within whose inaugurating declaration the 12 Mediterranean partners were required to sign up to principles of political pluralism. This commitment was still apparently subject to limitations: the EMP's political intentions were vague and tentative alongside the extensive and detailed timetables for economic liberalization; the substance of the democratic principles to be encouraged was not specified beyond a list of fundamental freedoms; and, sitting uneasily with the common commitment to political liberalization, the principles of non-intervention were affirmed, according each partner the right 'to choose and freely develop its own political, socio-cultural, economic and judicial system'. Notwithstanding this, the extension of the democracy promotion agenda to the Mediterranean basin appeared to represent a historic change in the EU's declared objectives in the region. The inception of this new approach to the Mediterranean invited a number of considerations, which form the subject of this account. What strategy did the EU adopt to implement the democracy promotion agenda after the Barcelona summit? Did the nature of that strategy suggest that the commitment to encourage political reform was genuine, or did it infer that it reflected a reluctant incorporation of a discourse guiding EU policy towards other areas but whose substantive materialization in the Mediterranean was to be decidedly circumspect? Did European policy succeed in linking together the various different strands of its Mediterranean policy in a way that enhanced rather than diminished the prospects for democratization? How effective was internal EU co-ordination in the Mediterranean, a region towards which member states have traditionally held strongly contrasting perspectives? In exploring these issues, the article highlights the significance of the EU's declared holistic approach to democracy promotion in the Mediterranean, but concludes that European policy failed fully to adhere to the logic of its own philosophy.

The Rationale: Mediterranean Democracy and European Interests

The tardy incorporation of the democracy promotion agenda into the EU's Mediterranean policy suggested that the influence of 'standardization' was considerable. The central concern of EU policy-makers during the early 1990s had been to reform instruments and procedures so as to standardize – and thus, it was hoped, depoliticize – provisions relating to democracy and human rights across different regions. In this sense, the EU appeared to be almost reluctantly obliged by the logic of its own stated approach to extend to North Africa and the Middle East an objective adopted in less sensitive circumstances elsewhere in the world. However, the architects of Mediterranean policy during the latter half of the 1990s insisted that the new commitment to democracy promotion also reflected a genuine reassessment of European interests.[1] Political liberalization was, they maintained, now seen as the best means of engendering both stability and moderation in the Mediterranean, and of helping to generate the economic growth that would eventually ease migratory pressures. The Barcelona process was predicated on the expectation that economic liberalization, political reform, cultural understanding and strategic stability would be mutually reinforcing. Political liberalization, combined with deeper economic interaction and social co-operation, would enhance well-being, stability and Europe's own security. Contrary to the presumptions most commonly attributed to western governments, it was argued that, in the post-cold war era, repressive government in the Mediterranean was doing little to advance or safeguard western European interests. A 'comprehensive' approach towards security would henceforth be pursued, consistent with and informed by new theorizing advocating a more proactive shaping of political structures judged most conducive to peaceable international relations. This appeared to position the EU firmly within the 'contingent' perspective on political Islam: if the latter had come to advance anti-democratic and anti-western views, this was less an inherent and unchangeable trait of Islamic tenets than a reflection of the deteriorating economic conditions suffered by Mediterranean populations under years of pro-western autocratic government.[2] European policy would seek to address the social and economic roots of radical Islam, such that political liberalization would be less likely to produce anti-western orientations and over time provide the means of more effectively securing a Euro-Mediterranean area of shared prosperity and stability.

Despite declaring this new approach, however, policy-makers acknowledged that in practice EU strategy also remained subject to more traditional caveats. European governments cautioned that their key concern would be to ensure that political change did not engender instability in the short term. No EU member state maintained that the democracy promotion agenda should, in the case of the Mediterranean, contain any aspiration to undermine incumbent regimes. While pluralism was seen as a means of reducing migratory pressure over the longer term, European governments continued to be concerned – without apparent clear supporting evidence, critics suggested – that in the shorter term it would benefit Islamists and actually encourage greater migration. It was feared that ongoing arms control negotiations could also be complicated by precipitate regime change. Most significantly, of course, several of the region's governments were crucial to the Middle East peace process. In countries such as Egypt and Jordan, the curtailment of political space had contained opposition to the peace process. In this sense, despite the insistence that the success of the EMP could help lay the foundations for a peace settlement, in practice EU policy-makers were resigned to the EMP's subjugation to the peace process. A more active democracy promotion strategy would need to await sustained progress in the peace process, rather than – as the 'democratic peace' hypothesis might proffer – itself being seen as a means of instilling moderation and making Arab–Israeli reconciliation more likely. While the EU had advanced a general approach to conflict resolution that explicitly and apparently unreservedly conceived of democracy as conducive to reconciliation, in the Mediterranean such logic collided with the more immediate imperatives of keeping the various tracks of the peace process alive. In the Palestinian Territories themselves, the EU's clear priority was to shore-up Yasir Arafat's position against those forces opposed to the peace process, this encouraging tolerance of the Palestine Liberation Organization (PLO) leader's centralization of power and his creation of a highly repressive police force.

Consequently, the EU expressly committed itself to playing the 'long game' in the Mediterranean. It was this that accounted for the stated aim of constructing a deeply embedded sense of partnership with the Mediterranean partners, informed by the notion of ongoing 'contractuality'. The aim would be to press discreetly for the development of the precursors to democratization, such that political change would be facilitated over the longer term within a context more conducive to tempering the negative effects – for Europe as well as for North African states themselves – of transition. To this end, the foci of strategy would be: to carve out a modest widening of the space available for civil society; to generate democratic 'awareness' or 'capacity'; and to facilitate the move away from 'rentier' economic activity towards the type of dispersed and varied commercial structure widely seen as going hand in hand with the diffusion of political authority. Alongside this, there would be engagement directed purposefully towards affecting a convergence of Islamist opinion around basic democratic norms. Most notably, this policy mix was portrayed as a means of correcting a passivity towards Algeria's worsening conflict, as even here – the case most frequently cited in demonstration of the EU's prioritization of immediate security issues over democratization – European governments professed a stronger desire to encourage democratic reform. While apparently tolerant of the serious imperfections in the post-1995 political reform process initiated by President Liamine Zeroual, the EU sought to construct a more meaningful low-level social and economic engagement with Algeria, through which influence could be brought to bear and, at the same time, the prospects for a stable democratic transition enhanced. In sum, European governments sought an improvement in basic economic and political rights rather than making relations in any substantive sense conditional upon the adoption of a set of 'western' liberal democratic structures. Significantly, many North African and Middle Eastern experts had come to advocate just such an approach, which was seen as an appropriate middle way between absolute relativism and heavy-handed imposition of western political forms.[3]

In the EU's case, this approach was not only seen as conceptually justified, but was also the result of internal 'bargains' between member states. While broadly shared by all member states, the caution characterizing EU policy was adhered to in particular at the behest of southern EU member states. The latter, confronted more directly with the challenges arising from potentially destabilizing change in North Africa, remained wedded to more traditional views on security than their northern European counterparts. Indeed, at Barcelona southern EU states reportedly expressed a willingness to exclude references to democracy and agreed to insist on such a commitment only after northern states sanctioned new aid funding for the region.[4] This well-documented north–south split was more marked in the Mediterranean region than most other regions and, significantly, was seen by many policy-makers as not having narrowed by the end of the 1990s. The nature of democracy promotion strategy consequently flowed from ongoing mutual compromise between member states. Northern EU states judged the EMP to have tied southern EU states into at least some critical focus on democracy, while southern states welcomed it as a means of constraining the idealistic fervour, as they perceived it, of the northern states. The deepening of internal European integration did to some extent 'Europeanize' southern member states' concerns: the Schengen Agreement (1985) on open borders and, later, the Amsterdam Treaty (1997) commitment to move towards a common immigration policy meant that Mediterranean immigration was increasingly seen as an issue of potential concern to all EU states. However, northern EU states still argued that there was more scope to pusher harder for political change without endangering stability in the short term. The Mediterranean Forum, in which five southern EU states participated with five southern Mediterranean states, and from which any critical pressure in relation to democracy was conspicuously absent, was seen by some states as undermining the EMP. The EU's north–south division was paralleled by differences between the regional Mediterranean and Common Foreign and Security Policy (CFSP) policy-making communities within the EU, the former urging flexibility, the latter concerned more with the overall consistency of European strategy.

The EU's Mediterranean policy was, in a comparative context, notable for the extent to which it was driven more strongly by strategic than by commercial considerations. For the first time in a decade, investors did insist that the nature of internal governance structures was of greater concern to them than basic security considerations. A commonly advanced presumption has been that multinationals have become increasingly exercised by rising levels of corruption and the absence of transparency in commercial proceedings, but not by the lack of formal, political democracy. In the Mediterranean, the investors' main focus was indeed on relatively narrowly defined good governance issues. Pressure from the private sector was influential in encouraging policy-makers to look beyond the traditional range of trade liberalization measures and incorporate into the EMP aims relating to the transparency of customs procedures, the functioning of dispute settlement mechanisms, public procurement liberalization, more open certification procedures and the establishment of a rules-based process of standards harmonization. The overwhelming majority of investors cited such shortcomings in good governance as one of the primary obstacles to further commercial engagement. Significantly, however, policy on these issues was conditioned by the input of the European private sector to a far lesser extent in the Mediterranean than in areas such as East Asia and Latin America. The limited presence of European companies outside the energy sector arguably indicated a greater degree of untapped potential than in other emerging markets, but in practice business pressure for upgraded policy initiatives in the Mediterranean was conspicuous by its relative absence. None the less, it was a significant development that a more acute concern with good governance issues could clearly be detected on the part of European companies interested in the Mediterranean, and this undoubtedly informed EU policy-making.

Beyond the issues of corruption and transparency, there was no direct private sector pressure for more active diplomacy aimed at political liberalization. Indeed, some companies expressed concern that the politicization of human rights and democracy could impede concrete progress on the good governance matters of most immediate relevance to investors.[5] However, the view that the nature of broader political structures was of little import to investors fails fully to capture the extent to which European companies' perspectives on the Mediterranean basin did evolve. Standard claims that narrow improvements in good governance sufficed to awaken the interest of many investors were guilty of looking primarily at the extractive companies already present in the region, and with contracts often directly sponsored by incumbent regimes, rather than the views of the far larger number of companies choosing *not* to invest in the Mediterranean. Most investors consciously moved towards a broader and longer-term perspective, within which they recognized good governance to be a political, and not entirely technical, issue. They listed a range of preoccupations that touched upon the political sphere. There was concern that technical capacity to take forward market reforms had not been generated throughout economic and political systems because governments had kept implementation responsibilities within a very small circle of reformers. The frequent non-implementation of pro-market ministerial decrees was seen as related to the fact that governments had little incentive to build up broad-based alliances behind reform efforts. Governments' reluctance to allow for the freer provision of information was undermining the quality of the kind of market and statistical information necessary for investment plans. Overvalued exchange rates were judged to flow from governments' protection of favoured importers. There were general concerns over arbitrary decision-making and the fact that the 'cult of the strong leader' had fomented rather than tempered radicalism. The absence of moderating political dynamics was also seen as having contributed to the lack of co-operation between the different Mediterranean economies, which investors insisted was the region's main disadvantage relative to other developing areas.

All this appeared to fit closely with the view of western governments – and, increasingly, even of the World Bank – that robust democratic processes could play an important role in underpinning investor-related good governance reforms. However, the notable fact was that companies did not always associate the failings with which they were increasingly concerned with the region's lack of democracy. While attesting to the kind of political concerns seen by most analysts as intrinsically related to an absence of democracy, European investors did not themselves see their resolution as entailing or rendering desirable full democratization. Some companies did express outright scepticism towards democratization, fearing this would, in the particular circumstances of the Mediterranean, be profoundly destabilizing. Some claimed to be positively keen on political liberalization as the best means of securing faster and more sustainable growth rates. Most companies, however, were deeply ambivalent. As one commercial officer noted, there was genuine 'confusion' among European companies over the sort of political evolution consistent with their own regulatory and good governance priorities. Companies were, for instance, far less ambiguous than officials in enumerating concerns over Islamists being given greater political space, but they also recognized that the region's increasingly irreversible integration into the European economic space had in practice reduced the likelihood of such groups adopting protectionist policies. In overall terms, there was no strong private sector pressure for democratization, but nor did investors seek actively to dissuade EU governments from their democracy promotion agenda.

Democracy Promotion Strategy

The nature of these aims was reflected in an approach to political reform that focused primarily on the need to establish a 'discourse' on democracy. European policy-makers claimed to see the Barcelona Process as most notable for introducing the discourse of democracy to EU–Mediterranean relations, for the first time explicitly identifying political pluralism as a norm that should govern relations between western Europe and the Arab world. The EMP framework would ensure the embedding, or institutionalization, of a dialogue predicated on a shared espousal of democratic norms. The key to fostering 'socialization' around democratic norms was to maximize the regime-like features of the EMP, 'nesting' the aim of promoting democratic reform within a comprehensive range of institutionalized co-operation. It was this 'holistic' approach that was promoted as the main change to the European approach. The EU offered to the Mediterranean partners most of the same forums of co-operation, at a similar level of commitment, that were being developed with the central and eastern European applicants. Indeed, policy-makers expressly sought the form, without the fact, of accession for the Mediterranean states. The aim was to build up an internal momentum or dynamic to the EMP and to avoid prioritizing particular concrete results over the retention of an ongoing process of co-operation. Democratic norms could only effectively be disseminated through an institutionalized process within which mutual trust had accumulated and genuine 'consent' to the normative value of political pluralism could be generated. In this sense, European policy corresponded closely to constructivists' arguments that the agency of values-based discourse was increasingly eclipsing that of purely material instruments.

In tune with this focus on socialization dynamics, substantive punitive conditionality was not imposed in relation to actual democratic shortfalls. There was no consideration of suspending MEDA funds on political grounds, this contrasting with the EU's willingness to withhold parcels of aid where economic reforms failed to materialize. Libya was ostracized owing to events related to the terrorist attack on the Pan-American airliner over Lockerbie, not its lack of democracy: after a deal was reached on staging the trial of Libyan suspects at the Hague in 2001, sanctions were removed and Libya was invited to sign up to the EMP without any concrete conditionality being applied to internal political conditions. Even the EU's rhetoric was cautious: the scarcity of CFSP statements with any degree of critical edge pertaining to political developments in the Mediterranean was conspicuous alongside the ubiquity of such criticism towards the Lomé Agreement with the ACP states and towards eastern Europe. Fraudulent elections failed to elicit the kind of expression of concern with which the EU frequently greeted similar irregularities in other regions, and the incremental tightening of political space in countries such as Egypt and Tunisia met with no substantive response. Algeria remained the most sensitive case for European governments, but was in fact the one country with which the EU completely broke off association agreement negotiations (in 1997). While this was presented as a means of pressing the Algerian government to construct more robust institutions capable of implementing commitments entered into under such an agreement, no direct democratic conditionality was imposed, and talks were renewed in 1999 with conditions seemingly more stable but with political pluralism little advanced. The new sovereigns in Morocco and Jordan were given almost unconditional support, with European governments judging it inappropriate to seek to press the monarchs to extend what in the early part of their respective reigns remained extremely tightly controlled processes of reform. Suggestions that the Common Strategy for the Mediterranean adopted in the autumn of 2000 might intimate a more coercive approach – this being possible 'at 15' in a way that was not possible 'at 27' within the EMP – was supported by only a minority of member states and not adopted. Far firmer pressure was exerted in relation to individual human rights cases than democracy: the EU did oblige Mediterranean states to justify and address individual cases of abuses, with some success in Morocco, Tunisia and Algeria. The willingness to develop a tougher approach to human rights served further to highlight the absence of a similar approach towards democracy promotion. It was significant that the non-governmental organization (NGO) community engaged in Mediterranean issues focused almost entirely on human rights, and far from pressing European governments to impose coercive instruments in relation to democracy many themselves expressed unease over any linkage of human rights to a western liberal democracy template.

There was a degree of more 'positive' or 'rewards based' conditionality, but this was linked to progress on democratization only to a relatively limited extent. Some political criteria were apparent, with Morocco and Jordan becoming high per capita recipients of official development assistance (ODA), while Syria continued to attract extremely limited flows of development aid. However, European aid to the region, for well-established strategic reasons, remained skewed disproportionately towards Egypt. The extent to which MEDA funds were conditional upon economic, not political reform, was demonstrated by Tunisia's success in securing a disproportionately high share of this aid package.[6] Several states increased aid to Morocco after 1999 and the country established itself as the third highest recipient of Commission aid anywhere in the world, but these efforts fell short of a comprehensive, common European package targeted specifically at assisting democratic change. In practice, a rather confused picture emerged, indicative of the split in aid competences between member states and the Commission. At the bilateral level only France advanced significant amounts of aid to North Africa. Other states' negligible ODA donations were justified mainly by the region's medium-level development indicators, but were also seen as not entirely unconnected to the paucity of democracy. However, the rises in Commission-managed aid to the Mediterranean caused overall EU aid increases to the region over the latter half of the 1990s to exceed those to Latin America, Asia and the ACP states, meaning that, in fact, the EMP represented the EU's most significant deviation from rewards-based conditionality. The Mediterranean states that had implemented the most far-reaching political liberalization increasingly expressed their frustration that they had not been rewarded for doing so.

Thus, the emphasis on the dynamics of socialization was of far greater significance than concrete, purposive policy measures, predicated on the use of democratic conditionality, the development of which remained conspicuously limited. Some would doubtless see the EU's approach as a legitimate, appropriately 'consensual' strategy, while critics of the 'constructivist turn' in international relations might contend that it reflected pure unwillingness to adopt any 'real' democracy promotion policies. It would seem unduly glib to dismiss the discursive approach as a purely disingenuous façade, insofar as its foundations were themselves predicated upon a degree of more traditional materially-based pressure. The EU's insistence that Mediterranean partners agree to democracy forming a legitimate part of the EMP was firm, as was its imposition of the new democracy clause. European governments also insisted on Mediterranean governments accepting a provision allowing the EU to fund democracy projects without recipient governments' consent. This degree of coercion – what might be termed *a priori* 'value' conditionality – helped establish the base from which the dynamics of socialization might function. Egypt signed its association agreement only in June 2001, Algeria and Lebanon months later, and by early 2002 Syria had still not concluded an agreement; the human rights and democracy clause was one of the points of difference in all these cases. This indicated that the declared approach to democracy promotion was not completely lacking in some degree of force and substantive content. Mediterranean governments certainly felt that a degree of pressure to modify their discourse had derived from the formal codification of the commitment to democracy within the EMP.

However, the EU's strategy could more convincingly and justifiably be criticized *on its own terms*, to the extent that the logic of the 'socialization dynamic' was in practice not fully followed through. Having expressly promoted the Barcelona process as a means of ensuring mutually-reinforcing progress in different areas of policy, the EU's leverage over democratic change was significantly diminished by its own reluctance to agree to Mediterranean states' demands on other issues – trade, migrants' rights, a reduction of EU pressure for southern states to readmit migrants, co-operation on terrorism, the presence in European countries of exiles accused of violent acts. Whatever the validity of these concerns, the EU's refusal to make concessions undoubtedly undermined its negotiating power on democracy. Most damagingly, the EU's insistence on a rather artificial separation between the peace process and the EMP was interpreted by the latter's Arab members as the most glaring demonstration that a 'comprehensive' partnership was, in practice, not sought by European governments. In this sense, the EU's refusal to use the economic provisions of the EMP to pressure Israel into concessions related to the peace process reduced its negotiating leverage over internal political developments in Arab countries – although in the summer of 2001 the Commission did for the first time intimate the possibility of invoking the human rights clause against Israel. All this undermined, in the eyes of Mediterranean states, the spirit of trust and mutual compromise upon which the EMP was supposedly predicated, and was the direct cause of a number of civil society initiatives being blocked.[7] It cooled the enthusiasm even of those Mediterranean NGOs most critical of their own governments and whose engagement EU policy-makers saw as crucial to the human rights and democracy agenda. While there was regular talk of moving to a sub-regional structure to help rectify the 'infection' of the peace process, this was supported neither by many EU member states nor by the Mediterranean partners, and hence a major determinant of democracy promotion policy towards North Africa was the extent to which this had been unwittingly linked to the deterioration of the Arab–Israeli conflict.

In addition, the pursuit of comprehensive dialogue and societal engagement was in practice relatively limited. In response to opposition from the Mediterranean partners, and to the increasing chagrin of European private sector representatives, EU policy-makers acknowledged that they had not insisted on any significant dialogue even on fairly technical good governance reforms, expressly limiting themselves to taking up particular corruption-related grievances suffered by individual companies. The Civil Forum, central to the civil society aspirations of the EMP, was kept marginal to decision-making structures. The various programmes of decentralized co-operation, aimed at facilitating direct civil society–civil society links, failed to get off the ground in any significant way. Several initiatives seen as being key to giving effect to the socialization approach – an Arab version of Euronews, a Euro-Islam Dialogue Forum – were either abandoned or diluted in response to Arab objections. EU governments in practice eschewed any direct support for initiatives that might be seen as aimed at 'norm dissemination'.[8] EU projects aimed at fostering inter-religious dialogue shied way from any notable inclusion of Islamist opposition forces, and were in fact gradually scaled down at the end of the decade. The much hoped for and widely advocated engagement with Islamists on common minimum standards of political pluralism conspicuously failed to emerge, with national governments preferring to pursue such an approach discreetly through bilateral channels and expressly without EU co-ordination. There was no systematic attempt to distinguish between moderate and less-moderate Islamist groups, and no sustained effort to engage with those whose commitment to democratic rules remained ambiguous. The EU was keen for local NGOs to undertake this task, but did not press them in any significant way to do so and declined to prioritize this as an area of funding. Islamist groups themselves were not attracted to more systematic dialogue, the EMP having failed to convince them that European governments were intent on a genuinely more conciliatory approach. Given that it was precisely in this domain where value-based socialization was integral to the essence of the EU's Mediterranean policy, such a shortcoming appeared to represent a serious lacuna. Only after the 11 September attacks did the commmission propose new co-operation initiatives involving Islamist groups, though still in a tentative fashion.

Hence, if the holistic framework was in line with the kind of approach experts had long been advocating, its practical realization was far from comprehensive. Substantive disconnection was compounded by the standard problems resulting from the EU's institutional fragmentation. In some senses, it would be easy to overstate this ubiquitously cited criticism of European policy-making. Expressly so as to facilitate the holistic approach, institutional coherence was improved through member states appointing EMP co-ordinators to link together the partnership's different volets.[9] However, problems remained. While improving institutional coherence became a stated priority for the EU, inter-issue linkages were still hindered more than they were facilitated by policy-making structures. Indeed, within the Commission decisions relating to democracy promotion strategy were taken out of the department dealing with Mediterranean policy, actually aggravating the 'disconnect' between regional and global considerations. In sum, notwithstanding the supposedly comprehensive and holistic approach, in reality the new democracy promotion agenda was deliberated on as a 'bolt-on' to existing policy, rather than the overall objective to which the whole range of instruments and commitments was to be harnessed. Assessment was made of how much scope for democracy promotion was left as a residual from other priorities, with the intricate causal connections between democracy strategy and other areas of policy not being addressed to any significant degree within day-to-day policy decisions.

Trade Liberalization and Political Reform: A Misconceived Link?

At the heart of the EU's gradualist approach was the overwhelmingly pre-eminent emphasis on economic reform. With the prospective free trade area constituting by far the most significant substantive element of the EMP, there was clearly considerable hope and expectation invested in a spillover from market reforms to political liberalization. The region's resistance to the third wave of democratization was seen as integrally related to its limited insertion into the world economy. It was, indeed, the introduction of economic reforms in the mid- to late 1980s that had initially encouraged North African elites to seek to 'distribute blame' for structural adjustment by dispersing a degree of political power. Helping to ensure that political reform was in fact followed through required a more concerted move way from the rentier state that had obviated the need for significant amounts of taxation and thus representation. The pursuit of free trade and structural reform within the institutionalized partnership of the EMP would facilitate both a more far-reaching process of economic liberalization and a more controlled process of change than that driven by the multilateral financial organizations.

Both prior to the Barcelona Conference and during the early years of the EMP's existence, it was the perception of the EU's heavy-handed imposition of unduly harsh economic liberalization on the Mediterranean partners that attracted most criticism from commentators. Even if most acknowledged the potentially positive impact of the region's deeper economic integration with western Europe, the EU was almost universally berated for its insistence on a process of trade liberalization strongly skewed to its own advantage. The friction that emerged in relation to the EU's lack of generosity in opening up its agricultural and textile markets is well documented. The magnitude of the MEDA fund, aimed specifically at assisting structural reform, was seen by most as negligible relative to the scale of transformation contemplated. Moreover, the EMP contained no initiative on debt relief, this most important of issues for the Mediterranean partners falling outside EU competences. The nature of the economic commitments was held to impact prejudicially upon the democracy promotion agenda in two ways. First, economic instability and tension was held to be inimical to generating sustainable democracy. Theorists' growing concern with the 'incivility' of civil society in many parts of the world seemed particularly apposite in North Africa: if Islamist groups' anti-western and anti-democratic discourse was indeed a product of the adverse effects of perceived western hegemony, it was reasonable to fear that the asymmetric economic impact of the Barcelona Process might simply aggravate such radicalism. Second, in a more direct sense, the rigorous requirements of the timetable towards the Free Trade Area (FTA) would encourage elites actually to gather additional power and discretion so as to be able more effectively to implement reforms. Many analysts saw this latter concern increasingly coming to fruition as governments sought to micro-manage preparations for the association agreements and the FTA, co-opting selected companies in a way that reinforced their own networks of patronage and quashed any spillover to the political domain. This was particularly notable in Tunisia, Egypt and Syria, while Morocco was a partial exception.[10]

The EU did show some signs of adapting policy in response to such concerns. European policy-makers continued to argue that in the longer term political elites would be obliged to cede control as economic reforms progressed – and in this sense the bunkering down of a number of the region's governments had been facilitated by the limits to, rather than the existence of, economic liberalization. They did, however, claim to be increasingly aware of the potential dangers of an unbalanced process of trade liberalization. Several southern European member states argued that policy should move away from such unquestioning faith in an automatic and mutually-reinforcing link between a deepening of free markets and political liberalization. MEDA aid was oriented more markedly towards offsetting the social costs of adjustment. Of particular note was the Commission's role as the largest contributor to Egypt's Social Development Fund: the fact that 100 times more funding was donated to this than to democracy projects in Egypt might be taken to qualify the frequently expressed criticism that the EU appeared intent on forcibly imposing democracy blind to the dangers of attempting this within a context of increasing social marginalization. An increased share of funding went to rural development, service provision networks and literacy projects, such basic issues recognized to be important as underpinnings of both economic and political reform. Indeed, a number of northern states expressed concern that MEDA had moved too far away from its supposed remit of private sector structural reform into a more traditional development budget. Extensions to a number of transition periods for liberalization were granted to Mediterranean partners. As a number of the agreements' review clauses became operational in 2000, agricultural and textile quotas were increased, and additional concessions were made to Egypt in order finally to conclude the latter's association agreement. While the €5.3bn MEDA II aid package agreed in November 2000 represented a small decrease in real terms in relation to MEDA I, a growing concern with the social costs of adjustment did elicit flexibility from those member states (and some parts of the Commission) that had expressed a desire to shift funds more markedly away from the Mediterranean towards Balkans reconstruction and more poverty-focused development work.

Notwithstanding these changes, however, concerns clearly remained. Despite stronger pressure from the Commission and some member states, there had still been no significant progress on agricultural access by 2002. Apart from any direct economic impact, the EU's stance on commercial issues deprived it of precisely the kind of institutionalized engagement it itself held to be requisite to gaining purchase over political reform. The differences on agriculture ensured either that association agreements were not concluded or that Mediterranean partners finally accepted market access arrangements well below their original bottom line positions. The EU's lack of flexibility was another factor making both European and southern Mediterranean NGOs reluctant to engage more fully and enthusiastically with the EMP as a potential force for securing political liberalization. While criticism of the EU's lack of generosity in its readiness to open markets and increase financial transfers to the Mediterranean became a standard element of analyses of the EMP, the shortcomings of EU strategy must be recognized as extending beyond the simple refusal to increase a number of tariff quotas or allocate more ODA. Rather, the EU's more critical deficiency was its adherence to an overly vague assumption that economic reform would eventually filter through to political change in the absence of any detailed engagement capable of analysing or effecting such spillover. There was little evidence of deliberation on the kind of complex issues relating to how shifting domestic coalitions and the reconstitution of patterns of control over economic resources mediate the path-dependent relationship between economic and political reform. Policy-makers with a remit over democracy promotion had little input into detailed commercial policy decisions. There was no engagement aimed at carving out alliances of support for political reform specifically on the basis of the nature of unfolding economic changes. Indeed, it seemed reasonable to suggest – as Bradford Dillman argues in this collection – that much European aid was going directly to reinforcing government-controlled networks of patronage.

The main vehicle for securing the link between economic and political liberalization was to be the increase in foreign investment that the comprehensive strategy of the EMP would engender. In practice, not only did European foreign direct investment (FDI) remain at low levels compared to other regions (the Mediterranean partners attracting under 2 per cent of EU FDI) and the private sector unenthusiastic about engaging in EMP forums, but there was little effort to work out a strategy to encourage a type and form of economic engagement conducive to prompting political change. Most of the European investment that did flow to the Mediterranean remained limited to precisely the kind of utilities infrastructure – energy, telecommunications – that provided state elites with direct 'rent'. With a broader range of investment – especially by smaller companies most in need of systemic-level good governance reforms – having been seen as crucial to facilitating the link between economic and political liberalization, its failure to materialize clearly undermined such spillover potential.

Democracy Assistance: A Viable Strategy in the Mediterranean?

The EMP was notable for providing the EU with a formal remit to fund democracy assistance projects in the Mediterranean, in particular through a separate Commission-managed programme, MEDA Democracy. Between 1996 and 1999, the Commission allocated Ecu 27m to democracy assistance in the Mediterranean partners.[11] While later to start than in other regions, democracy funding in the Mediterranean came to account for a significant 14 per cent of the Commission's overall democracy assistance budget in the second half of the 1990s. The approach pursued through the Commission's programme was avowedly and strongly 'bottom-up', focusing on support for NGOs, grass-roots advocacy networks, awareness-building and civic education, in particular for marginalized and vulnerable groups. In addition, increased amounts were allocated within economic reform programmes for judicial and administrative reform. Here, bilateral donors, and in particular France, advanced significant new packages to assist reform, often making important contributions to large-scale World Bank initiatives. This new EU work compared favourably with that undertaken by the US. The Maghreb was one of the few areas of the world where the EU assumed clear primacy over the US in democracy assistance, the United States Agency for International Development first initiating democracy promotion in the region in Morocco only in 1999, with a modest $1.3m to be spent over two years. The development of democracy assistance work was seen as a particularly notable aspect of the EU's relationship with Algeria: while other, more high politics aspects of this relationship remained problematic, Algeria emerged as the third largest recipient of MEDA Democracy funds.

While a significant development, the EU's democracy assistance efforts in the Mediterranean remained relatively cautious and subject to a number of limitations. The scale of democracy assistance funding was modest. Funds allocated for democracy assistance over the latter half of the 1990s amounted to less than 0.5 per cent of all aid to the region. Over 200 times more money was given under the main MEDA budget for assisting the process of economic restructuring. Significantly more funds were allocated for traditional developmental priorities than for democracy. Democracy assistance spending in the Mediterranean remained at a lower level than in the ACP countries (taking 21 per cent of the budget) and even Latin America (accounting for 17 per cent of spending). Spending on democracy assistance represented less than €1 per capita in all Mediterranean partners except the West Bank and Gaza Strip, and in most countries was below €10 cents per person. Moreover, there was a decrease in funding in 2001, and MEDA Democracy was disbanded as a separate programme and merged into horizontal democracy budgets, apparently increasing even further the disarticulation with Mediterranean-specific socio-economic deliberations. To an even greater extent than with overall spending, member states' democracy assistance efforts remained limited because of governments' preference for this area of funding to be led by and associated with the Commission. France, as North Africa's main donor, remained one of the states least convinced of the merits of increasing political aid work, and allocated only 0.3 per cent of its aid to the Maghreb to human rights and the rule of law (see Daguzan's contribution to this collection). Investing resources in democracy assistance in the Mediterranean was a priority neither for north European donors increasingly focused on poverty-reduction ODA nor for southern EU states traditionally oriented more towards commercial co-operation.

In addition, the range of work undertaken was relatively narrow. While policy-makers presented the bottom-up approach as a positive strength of European strategy, it also reflected a reluctance to engage in more politicized top-down democracy assistance. In practice the Commission shied away from using the provision enabling it to fund projects opposed by non-EU Mediterranean governments. While 290 NGO projects were undertaken, only 16 provided funds directly for the reform of state institutions. Up to 1999, only 22 projects were classified directly as aimed at building democracy, compared with the 77 going to civil society, 38 aimed at basic human rights, 54 for vulnerable groups, 45 for education and 30 for the rule of law. The Commission was not entitled directly to fund political parties, and bilateral donors refrained from engaging in this type of work – with the exception of a small number of projects financed by the German party foundations. Those projects that did cover more political issues – the role of armed forces, parliaments, institutional reform, media and trades unions – did so in an indirect fashion, through NGO-organized training, education, awareness-building campaigns, seminars and conferences. EU states themselves were concerned that such events usually failed to engender concrete follow-up co-operation or make any tangible impact. Most proposals for work on strengthening trades unions was either scaled down or dropped due to difficulties in identifying and/or gaining access to genuinely independent organizations. When Nordic states and the European Parliament suggested that conditionality be stipulated in relation to the full participation in EU projects of genuinely autonomous organizations, the idea was rejected by the majority of member states. This was despite an acknowledgement that Mediterranean regimes had complicated many areas of work by incorporating the externally-led values agenda through creating government-controlled human rights groups, with the aim of stemming a flow of funds to actually independent organizations.

Despite the undoubted value of the bottom-up approach for countries in which the legacy of authoritarian government rendered the constructing of basic grass-roots democratic capacity particularly urgent, the EU's political aid could more accurately be classified as aimed at specific human rights issues than at a comprehensive range of democracy assistance projects. The profile of democracy assistance work in the Mediterranean was significantly narrower than in Latin America, central and eastern Europe and the ACP countries. The EU provided no support for the range of groups widely identified as elements of a potential Arab form of democracy – professional associations, syndicates, mosques, teaching circles, neighbourhood organizations or craft groups. The proposed Confidence Building Measures, that were seen as an indirect means of instilling democratic norms into the region's armed forces and rebalancing civil–military relations, remained subject to political sensitivities. The allocation of funding was largely reactive, responding to those proposals received in an effort to encourage 'local ownership' of projects, rather than a proactive identification of the specific areas where further emphasis might be needed in each individual country. As Annette Jünemann points out in this collection, where selection was made European funding targeted less conflictual civil society organizations. Funding in Morocco, for example, went overwhelmingly to the three large, party-linked, officially-sanctioned human rights organizations. As elsewhere, no assessment of overall EU efforts in the Mediterranean was compiled. This absence of a complete picture of how bilateral and Commission projects related to each other militated against any fine tuning of the profile of democracy assistance funds to respond to areas of either neglect or duplication.

Unsurprisingly, the obstacles to political aid work were particularly acute in the region's most closed polities. Morocco, Jordan and Lebanon were relatively high per capita recipients of MEDA Democracy funds, while Syria and Tunisia received only 1 per cent each and Egypt only 4 per cent of the total funding. This reflected government hindrance not only of the implementation of projects but also of the submission of independent proposals to the European Commission. In precisely those states where, arguably, democracy assistance work appeared to be most urgent, the reactive approach to funding in this way militated against any significant EU engagement. The Syrian government blocked a number of apparently innocuous projects assisting grass-roots developmental organizations, fearful of incipient civil society momentum. In Egypt there were several high-profile cases of EU funding counterproductively unleashing tighter state restrictions: the head of the Egyptian Organization of Human Rights was arrested for accepting funds from the UK; another European-funded organization, the Group for Democratic Development, closed down in the face of official harassment; and in 2000 the EU-funded institute of one of Egypt's most prominent academics was closed and its head imprisoned.[12] The tensions engendered by these cases, combined with the fact that the number of independent proposals originating from Egyptian civil society actually dropped sharply after 1998, encouraged the Commission to favour an even narrower remit for funding under MEDA II, focusing more exclusively on children's and women's rights.

Perhaps as unsatisfactory to the EU, even the more reformist states remained sensitive to welcoming EU democracy assistance. In Morocco, even after the succession in 1999, projects were heavily focused on women's rights, with no more than a negligible amount of work undertaken to strengthen political society institutions. Indeed, precisely because of Mohamed VI's apparent commitment to increasing transparency, if not to full democratization, the Commission and, even more so, the principal bilateral donors such as France and Spain became more reluctant to engage in any area of work not directly solicited by the Moroccan government. The latter enthusiastically sought co-operation on some aspects of reform, such as increasing judicial and administrative transparency, while opposing EU intervention in the reform of political and state institutions. In Morocco, it was the US National Democratic Institute that was acknowledged to have taken a conspicuous lead in attempting to develop projects aimed at strengthening political parties and the parliament. With over 40 per cent of MEDA Democracy funds going to Israel and the Occupied Territories, the budget appeared in practice to be primarily aimed at underpinning the peace process. While undoubtedly making a major contribution to the setting up of Palestinian institutions, EU funding in the Occupied Territories was targeted mainly at building up a Palestinian police force capable of fulfilling its security commitments under the peace accords. Funds were actually shifted away from NGOs, many of whom harboured misgivings over the peace accords – although this trend was reversed slightly at the end of the 1990s.[13] In this case, the EU appeared more interested in executive, rather than broad ranging democracy, assistance. As the corruption and repression associated with Arafat's leadership deepened, so the EU's original confidence in equating democracy assistance with peace process support looked increasingly misplaced.

Good governance assistance proved to be slightly less controversial and an area in which the preparations for the FTA did give the EU significant influence. An increasing amount of good governance work was carried out as an integral part of the economic measures funded by the main MEDA budget, including the training of civil servants, judiciaries and market regulators, the harmonization of technical standards and the transparency of procurement procedures. Even the Tunisian government was open to some co-operation in relation to designing new regulatory frameworks in preparation for the FTA. In Lebanon, the Commission worked with local authorities to revise the country's fiscal system, necessary to replace revenues which would be lost through tariff removal, and played a direct role in putting in place more transparent structures. The Syrian government, still extremely sensitive to external pressure on good governance, blocked significant funding for such work until 2000, but did then agree to co-operate with the Commission on a project for regulatory reforms to public procurement rules and the tax system.[14] A range of good governance questions were addressed in the various sectoral forums of the Barcelona process, for example those covering energy and industrial co-operation developed projects related to issues of judicial security and transparency, expressly related to the needs of potential European investors in these sectors. The main focus of the Commission's work in Morocco was on strengthening administrative capacity and tax reform, areas where co-operation aimed to introduce more transparent institutional structures. While blocking a number of proposals in more controversial areas of judicial reform, Mediterranean states were generally keen to co-operate with and benefit from the technical expertise and resources of the EU in relation to good governance issues. This agenda did proceed more productively than the more overtly political democracy assistance work, and did appear to provide a more promising, indirect entry-point to encouraging institutional change in the Mediterranean. Many were concerned that funding for good governance was not being maximized because association agreements remained blocked due, in part, to the EU's democracy clause. Some policy-makers expressed concern that the new separation between the MEDA fund and the Democracy and Human Rights Unit inside the Commission would make it more difficult to feed democracy-building initiatives into technical, regulatory reforms specific to each Mediterranean partner state.

Conclusion

The EU's tentative incorporation of the democracy promotion agenda into its Mediterranean policy was predicated on a genuine uncertainty over the nature of its own strategic and commercial interests, combined with a more positive belief in a socialization- rather than coercion-based strategy. This appeared to reinforce the standard claim that the EU's particular strength as an international actor lay in the construction of broad, partnership-based patterns of socio-economic co-operation and political dialogue. If most of those viewing the creation of the EMP from a North African background expressed concern over the prospect of an unwarranted and heavy-handed imposition of European political norms on the region, the cautious nature of European policy up to 2002 appeared to have rendered such fears misplaced. While European strategy seemed consistent with theorists' advocacy of external initiatives based on the need to generate normative 'consent' in relation to the development of democratic norms, the EU's execution of this approach undoubtedly left considerable room for improvement. While the eschewal of overtly punitive top-down democratic conditionality might widely be seen as not entirely inappropriate, it would be reasonable to suggest that a degree of micro-level pressure could have succeeded in opening up scope for a profile of political work aid less likely simply to exacerbate existing imbalances between civil and political society. Economic policy could have been far more closely harnessed to the democracy promotion agenda, as the complex nexus between these two domains received insufficient analytical attention from European policy-makers. The much heralded engagement with political Islam, the essential driving force behind the EU's whole Mediterranean policy, remained at the level of nebulous generality, the EMP's moderating influence assumed too easily to flow from its general attractiveness more than its concrete forms of purchase. It must be legitimate to suggest that these weaknesses undermined the very dynamics of socialization and inter-issue linkages upon which EU policy was predicated. Even if the EMP is seen to have helped begin in a modest way laying the cognitive and socio-economic foundations for democracy to take root – which some might judge as no limited achievement – its potential was manifestly far from being realized.

The attitudes of many in the Mediterranean towards the West and western values clearly remained conditioned in a less-than-favourable fashion by different historical patterns of state formation, and there was little evidence that political elites, economic actors or civil society had unequivocally come to perceive democratization as either an apposite or a necessary prerequisite to achieving a more symmetrical partnership with the EU. There were good grounds for arguing that precisely this had occurred in relation to attitudes towards basic human rights, but this dynamic showed little sign of extending to the broader question of democracy. Developments in Morocco might reasonably have been interpreted as a more successful EU-assisted dissemination of democratic norms, but this case also presented the EU with a crucial challenge for the future: namely, to decide whether its agenda in the Mediterranean was, whether by choice or not, in practice to be limited to achieving partial reform rather than full political pluralism.

NOTES

1. In outlining the perspectives of European and Mediterranean actors, the article is based on information obtained from over 30 interviews, with: EMP desk officers in the French, German, Spanish, Italian, British, Danish, Algerian, Jordanian and Tunisian delegations to the EU in Brussels; officials in the European Commission and the Council Secretariat; foreign ministry officials in London, Paris and Madrid; representatives of the French, Spanish, British, European Commission and US embassies in Morocco and Egypt; non-governmental organizations (NGOs) in Morocco (Transparency International, *Espace Associative*, as well as the National Democratic Institute) and London (Amnesty International); and, in relation to economic-investor interests, interviews with UNICE in Brussels, national employers' organizations, European and US companies, and commercial officers in both Morocco and Egypt.
2. For examples of this interpretation of political Islam, see J. Esposito, *The Islamic Threat* (Oxford: Oxford University Press, 1992); J. Esposito and J. Piscatori, 'Democratization and Islam', *Middle East Journal*, Vol.45, No.3 (1991), pp.427–40; G. Joffé, 'Democracy, Islam and the Culture of Modernism', *Democratization*, Vol.4, No.3 (1997), pp.133–51; B. Roberson, 'Islam and Europe: An Enigma or a Myth?', *Middle East Journal*, Vol.48, No.2 (1994), pp.288–308; F. Halliday, *Islam and the Myth of Confrontation* (London: I.B. Tauris, 1996); and G. Martín-Muñoz, 'Political Reform and Social Change in the Maghreb', in A. Vasconcelos and G. Joffé (eds.), *The Barcelona Process: Building a Euro-Mediterranean Regional Community*, special edition of *Mediterranean Politics*, Vol.5, No.1 (2000), p.97.
3. For example, A.R. Norton, 'Political Reform in the Middle East', in L. Guazzone (ed.), *The Middle East in Political Change* (Basingstoke: Macmillan, 1997); M. Salla, 'Political Islam and the West: A New Cold War or Convergence?', *Third World Quarterly*, Vol.18, No.4 (1997), pp.729–42; and D. Kibble 'Monarchs, Mosques and Military Hardware: A Pragmatic Approach to the Promotion of Human Rights and Democracy in the Middle East', *Comparative Strategy*, Vol.17 (1998), pp.381–91.
4. R. Edis, 'Does the Barcelona Process Matter?', *Mediterranean Politics*, Vol.3, No.3 (1998), pp.97–9.
5. *Agence Europe*, 2 Oct. 1998, pp.13–14; 18 July 1998, p.9; 17 April 1997, p.14.
6. Commission of the European Communities, *The MEDA Regulation*, Note de Dossier, Jan. 2000.
7. R. Youngs, 'The Barcelona Process after the UK Presidency: The Need for Prioritization', *Mediterranean Politics*, Vol.4, No.1 (1999), p.14.
8. *Agence Europe*, 19 April 1999, p.15.
9. M. Köhler, *The Mediterranean Policy after the Conference of Barcelona*, European Parliament, Working Document 103 (1998), p.37.
10. Among the many critiques of the economic elements of the EMP are J. Marks, 'High Hopes and Low Motives: The New Euro-Mediterranean Partnership Initiative', *Mediterranean Politics*, Vol.1, No.1 (1996), pp.1–24; T. Parfitt, 'Europe's Mediterranean Designs: An Analysis of the Euromed Partnership with Special Reference to Egypt', *Third World Quarterly*, Vol.18, No.5 (1997), pp.865–81; V. Nienhaus, 'Promoting Development through a Euro-Mediterranean Free Trade Zone?', *European Foreign Affairs Review*, Vol.4 (1999), pp.501–18; A. Aghrout and M. Alexander, 'The Euro-Mediterranean New Strategy and the Maghreb Countries', *European Foreign Affairs Review*, Vol.2, No.3 (1997), pp.307–28; and N. Salah, 'Global Euro-Mediterranean Partnership', *Journal of North African Studies*, Vol.3, No.2 (1998), p.44. Those pointing more specifically to the political management of the FTA preparations include E. Kienle, 'Destabilization Through Partnership? Euro-Mediterranean Relations After the Barcelona Declaration', *Mediterranean Politics*, Vol.3, No.2 (1998), pp.1–20; J. Cassarino, 'The EU–Tunisian Association Agreement and Tunisia's Structural Reform Programme', *Middle East Journal*, Vol.53, No.1 (1999), pp.59–74; and B. Dillman, *Global Markets and Democratization in North Africa*, paper presented to XVIII IPSA

World Congress, Quebec, Aug. 2000.

11. The information on democracy assistance presented here is taken from Commission of the European Communities, *Report on the implementation of measures intended to promote the observance of human rights and democratic principles 1996–99* (Brussels: European Commission, 2000); Commission Delegation to Morocco *The MEDA Democracy Initiative* (Rabat: European Commission, 1999); Euronet Consulting, *Evaluation of the MEDA Democracy Programme* (Brussels: Euronet, 1999); and personal interviews.
12. *Economist*, 20 March 1999, p.17; *Financial Times*, 10 May 2000, Survey, p.xv.
13. *Agence Europe*, 17–18 April 2000, p.5.
14. *Agence Europe*, 26 April 2000, p.13.

International Markets and Partial Economic Reforms in North Africa: What Impact on Democratization?

BRADFORD DILLMAN

In the last 15 years, governments in Morocco, Algeria, Tunisia and Egypt have adopted a variety of economic reform programmes in the face of contradictions in earlier development strategies and pressures from the European Union and the United States. A comparison of the four North African cases calls into question conventional arguments that economic liberalization is strongly correlated with political liberalization. With the exception of Morocco, economic reform has been associated with the maintenance of a high degree of political authoritarianism. The region's two early economic adjusters, Morocco and Tunisia, followed different political routes in the 1990s. Morocco's King Hassan II bolstered pluralism, enhanced respects for human rights, and permitted an opposition-led government to form, while Tunisia's President Zine el Abidine Ben Ali reinforced corporatist authoritarianism by crushing Islamist and secular opposition. Of the late economic adjusters, Algeria almost witnessed a democratic transition in 1991. Yet a coup d'état followed by almost a decade of severe civil strife has left the country with military dominance over a truncated, semi-pluralistic party system. Egypt, another late economic adjuster, underwent some political liberalization under President Hosni Mubarak in the 1980s, but in the 1990s there was a deep erosion of the rights of civil society and a virtual exclusion of the political opposition from parliament.

Why has North Africa experienced little political liberalization despite undergoing significant economic liberalization? Answering this question requires an analysis of the specific nature of economic reforms and their effects on key economic actors. Moreover, it requires an analysis of how state elites have adapted to international market forces while implementing reform policies. This article argues that state elites have accessed resources from the international economy to implement partial economic reforms that sustain their distributional coalitions and thereby inhibit far-reaching political reform. The global economy and western governments impose constraints on would-be state reformers, but also offer them opportunities. To the extent that elites can tap and control international resource inflows as they undertake structural adjustments that more deeply integrate their economies into global markets, they can strongly shape the nature and extent of internal reforms, as well as the winners and losers from change. By preserving their states as the necessary intermediary between international and domestic economic actors, they have been able to construct and reshape patronage networks in such a manner as to maintain, if not reinforce, their own economic and political power. The ability of state elites to sustain and control large distributional coalitions during economic reform relieves pressures for political liberalization from key domestic constituencies. This article examines how state elites access resources from the European Union – North Africa's main economic partner – and manage patronage networks during selective economic liberalization.

Neo-Liberal Economic Reforms and Democratization

The democratization literature has not had a stellar ability to explain political change in the Middle East and North Africa (MENA).[1] This weakness stems in part from the tendency of democratization theorists to choose their cases on the dependent variable and thereby to neglect to test their explanatory frameworks on countries that have not experienced a democratic breakthrough. Most analyses of democratization in the MENA focus on domestic variables that are presumed to have inhibited far-ranging political liberalization, such as political culture, religion, the level of socio-economic development, and weakness in civil society. Factors internal to North African states, such as elite willingness to engage in high levels of coercion, the lack of democratic credentials of the opposition, and the lack of a large industrial working-class, might also prevent democratization.[2] Sometimes invoked are international geopolitical variables such as war and war preparation, transnational ideological rivalries in the MENA, and western indulgence of friendly authoritarian rulers.[3] Arguably, some states have been spared some democratization pressures owing to the unwillingness of advanced capitalist states to push the human rights issue in the face of conjunctural security problems such as the Gulf War and extremist Islamist movements. The rentier state literature has proved more useful in tying together structural variables at the national and international levels.[4]

Some theorists claim that international forces during the third wave of democratization created an international democratic conjuncture. North

Africa has been as deeply exposed to many of these international forces as Latin America, sub-Saharan Africa and eastern Europe. For example, it has been affected by: reductions in external rents that have caused economic crises and capital flight; deep dependence on trade with advanced capitalist democracies;[5] conditionality attached to International Monetary Fund (IMF) and World Bank loans and US and EU aid; exposure to western satellite-based media; proximity to Europe and direct experience in Europe through migration and elite education; and reductions in regional interstate conflicts in the 1990s. Yet the democratization literature does not adequately account for why these variables apparently had little effect on the prospects for political liberalization in North Africa.

The political economy literature has also addressed the issue of democratization by examining the impact of changes in the global economy on economic reform and political change. Much of the literature focuses on the pressures that states face from the rise of new economic actors, changes in technology and trade, and the demands of leading capitalist nations. Authoritarian governments in developing countries must adapt to these global and domestic pressures by, among other things, liberalizing the economy, encouraging foreign investment and paring down the public sector. To the extent that these types of policy reforms foster greater transparency, accountability and a rule of law, the prospects for democratization should increase.

The political economy literature on internationalization has theorized about the domestic political effects of greater economic openness and cross-border economic transactions.[6] It is dominated by an economic pluralist approach to understanding economic reform that asserts that exogenous changes in the international economy such as price fluctuations, financial flows and trade patterns place constraints on social forces, who in turn place demands on state elites. The result is new policy preferences, new political coalitions and new domestic political institutions.[7] This approach views economic reform policies as the outcome of lobbying by private sectoral interests, whether private companies, business associations, organized labour or political parties. This approach generally fails to acknowledge that state elites have their own autonomous preferences and interests when it comes to mediating the impact of external forces on business and labour. The approach's explanatory power in North Africa is relatively weak, given the characteristics of the private sector and political institutions. The private sector has limited structural power. Private businesses have historically not accounted for the largest share of gross domestic product (GDP) and have been excluded from strategic sectors of the economy. Partly as a legacy of colonialism and of post-independence economic *dirigisme*, private sector claimants tend to be weak and poorly organized. By contrast, public enterprise cadres and public sector workers are key economic actors who can affect state policy-making. Moreover, North Africa lacks well-developed party systems and mass-based political parties that articulate clear economic policies, particularly neo-liberal policies. Because most elections have been unfree and unfair, state decision-makers have faced no significant voter sanction, except in Algeria in 1991. Thus we cannot assume that state economic policy is formed on the basis of a rational calculation of voter behaviour.

The European Union has based its policies in North Africa on a number of problematic assumptions that are evident in the democratization and political economy literature. One of these assumptions is that economic development will lead to more political liberalization, and eventually democratization. By accelerating economic progress, the EU hopes to open up political processes. As Brynjar Lia notes, 'Curiously, there seems to be a certain degree of Marxist historicism underlying European thinking on Mediterranean security challenges in the sense that one presupposes political liberalization to take place only when the economic "basis" has been put in order'.[8] Yet, the EU is sensitive to the argument of many southern Mediterranean regimes that if it presses too forcefully for rapid economic change, it may actually undermine the prospects for political liberalization. Shock therapy, many argue, would alienate potential supporters of political pluralism and embolden anti-liberal and extremist forces. Thus, the EU, like the US, has adopted an incrementalist-developmentalist approach to democracy building. It presumes that economic incentives and moderate pressure on governments to enact economic reforms based on the 'Washington consensus' will slowly but inexorably reduce government power, expand the influence of the private sector, and enable the promotion of a rule of law. But as Stephen Larrabee observes, 'EU influence on democratization and other social issues is tenuous at best and likely to bear fruit only in the long run'.[9] The approach may unwittingly play into the hands of authoritarian rulers who are able to sustain a slow, uneven reform process. The risk is that incomplete economic reforms will fail to produce the social-structural conditions that are presumed to be the basis for a democratic transition.

Since 1995, the European Union has placed great hope in its ability to foster change in North Africa via the Euro-Mediterranean Partnership (or Barcelona Process). Yet given that the promotion of democracy and civil society has a low level of priority compared to the promotion of political and security co-operation and economic development, the Barcelona Process may not produce the kinds of political changes in the Mediterranean basin that the EU desires. In June 2000, the European Council adopted a Common Strategy on the Mediterranean Region, in which it pledged to 'promote the strengthening of democratic institutions and the rule of law', 'support and encourage efforts to promote good governance', and 'stress the importance of promoting and protecting human rights'. Promotion of 'good governance' is seen as a method of reinforcing the 'rule of law' so necessary to a potential democratic regime. To the extent that a stronger judicial system, a more transparent customs regime and a more efficient and predictable bureaucracy can be nurtured, better governance will presumably facilitate private investment, expand the availability of information and reduce opportunities for corruption. While the intent is laudable, there is little evidence that modest EU efforts have had or will have much impact on overall administration, which is profoundly tied to the nature of a country's political culture, social structure and political system. Moreover, as Jacqueline Coolidge and Susan Rose-Ackerman have pointed out, where countries are ruled by autocratic rent-seekers, partial administrative reforms such as those related to taxes and customs may simply increase the efficiency of rent-seeking and hamper growth, particularly when the state controls key domestic natural resources and access to foreign aid.[10] Good governance, which is profoundly difficult to define or assess, is a problematic policy in that it is based on a presumption that one can significantly alter a process of governing before changing governors themselves. The risk is that the EU may have underestimated the resilience of existing political elites and may be promoting a policy that is simply a euphemism for working with more efficient authoritarian regimes.

That the EU has not pressed forcefully for democratization can be seen in Algeria, Tunisia, Egypt and in the Palestinian Authority. What progress toward political reform that has occurred in Morocco, Lebanon and Jordan has much less to do with Europe than with purely domestic dynamics in these countries. The democratization deficit in Europe's Mediterranean policies has a number of causes. Southern European countries in particular are willing to tolerate the authoritarian excesses of some southern Mediterranean regimes. Presently, EU association agreements are in practice delinked from human rights progress. The EMP's state-to-state framework excludes Islamists from participation in dialogue. Moreover, European governments have for years been arresting Islamist activists in exile in Europe. Like many of their southern partners, European states are afraid that democratic elections would lead to Islamists gaining significant power in political systems. Instead, they want a 'status quo oriented policy that aims at securing the "stability" of pro-Western regimes, a policy reminiscent of US containment policies in the Third World during the Cold War'.[11]

The Barcelona Process can be seen as part of Europe's response to American hegemony in the Middle East. The US–European geopolitical rivalry in the Middle East has a long history, and was particularly apparent during the 1956 Suez crisis and the Algerian war of independence. In the 1990s, tensions emerged over a range of issues, including US dual containment of Iran and Iraq, arms sales, sanctions, Israel's 1996 'Grapes of Wrath' campaign in Lebanon, the Helms-Burton Act imposing trade sanctions and other American efforts at extraterritoriality. 'Atlanticists' in the EU have faced a challenge from 'Nationalists' who want to resist US unilateralism and exclusionism, find a more independent foreign policy, and reconstruct 'their former colonial empires in the image of the US informal empire in Latin America'.[12] France, which fears being displaced in the MENA, has been the leading force for exerting European influence in the region. Spain and Italy have also pushed hard for expanded European economic influence.

In sum, the EU's democracy promotion policies may have important limitations in North Africa. To the extent that rivalry with the United States and other geopolitical considerations undergird the EMP, the EU may have more interest in regime stability than change. The promotion of a rule of law and human rights has generally been a residual interest subordinate to the promotion of economic development and European economic interests. Moreover, the EU may have a misplaced faith in the ability of incremental, partial economic reform to induce democratization, given the continued weakness of the region's private sector, the manipulation of elections, and elite willingness to use large-scale coercion. Fortunately, Morocco is becoming something of an exception. Finally, it appears that the effects of the EU's specific democracy promotion initiatives have been largely counterbalanced by the structural impact of its official economic policies and the policies of its leading market actors. European investors and governments have assiduously avoided supporting the most powerful domestic forces (including mainstream Islamists) demanding economic transparency and political accountability. Not only have individual European governments often pursued bilateral policies with North Africa at odds with the declared political goals of the Union as a whole, but Europe's private companies and investors have pursued individual interests whose collective impact may not be supportive of the democracy-promoting goals of the Union.

Partial Reforms and International Resource Inflows

From a theoretical perspective, one can explain some of the limits to the EU's approach to democratization by examining the range of opportunities available to North African policy elites to extract advantages from the international system and thereby patch together supportive and dependent political-economic coalitions during partial economic reform. International economic forces alter the structure of constraints and opportunities facing policy-makers. State elites seek to use resources available from the international economy to shape and sustain a coalition of winners from economic reform whose members may not have an interest in political democratization. Moreover, to explain the process of economic policy outcomes, it makes more sense in North Africa to start with a focus on supply-side forces, that is the preferences and calculations of top government decision-makers, rather than social, demand-side forces. State elites appear to be motivated by the desire to maximize economic resources available to the state budget and extra-budgetary resources over which they have discretionary power. Moreover, they seek to maintain dependent distributional coalitions that are large enough and cohesive enough to prevent threats to the political power of these elites. Top decision makers are motivated less by the desire to minimize the number of losers from economic change than to maintain a set of economic winners that is politically loyal.

Joel Hellman's analysis of post-communist transitions in eastern Europe and the former Soviet Union provides important insights into the relationship between partial economic reforms, political change and international inflows that one also sees in North Africa.[13] As opposed to comprehensive reforms or an absence of reforms, partial economic reforms initially create the largest concentrated gains for winners and largest diffuse losses for most of society. Transition from a command to market economy produces enormous rent-seeking opportunities, as there are market distortions and continued misallocation of resources. People in a position to arbitrage between the reformed and unreformed sectors of the economy make large gains. Over time, the concentrated gains of winners should decrease steadily as the market, bolstered by price liberalization, hard budget constraints on state enterprises, privatization and better public sector governance, eliminates arbitrage opportunities and spreads welfare gains to society.

However, winners during initial stages of reform in post-communist states seek to prevent further reform that would diminish their concentrated gains. They try to block policies that eliminate market distortions that form the basis of their rents. Winners from early market reform who are shielded from the electorate serve as veto players over further reforms, producing lower GDP growth rates and higher inequality in the long term. This inefficient outcome may be sustained for some time if winners have access to external resources. Their stripping of the assets of state enterprises, which may cause social losses as purchasing power is undermined, can be compensated by the attraction of foreign joint venture partners with cash, technology and access to export markets. Rent-taking from stock markets and privatization is facilitated by sufficient foreign direct investment (FDI) and portfolio equity flows. Official concessionary loans help foreign contractors build infrastructure that serves the needs of winners. Also, official and commercial loans that pump money into the state-dominated banking system help state banks continue to provide credits to winners during incomplete reform. If the veto power of winners over policy cannot be broken at the ballot box, and slow reform creates relentless structural pressures and high social costs, elites can sustain this inefficient outcome through a mix of coercion and supplementary external resources that allow governments to support subsidies and minimal social needs, continue public infrastructure investment and maintain banking solvency.

On a continuum of choices ranging from no reform to comprehensive neo-liberal reform, North African leaders have mostly pursued partial reform. In none of the North African states have radical policy reform movements emerged to carry out the kinds of deep, rapid, co-ordinated economic reforms seen in eastern Europe and Latin America. Despite some devaluation, debt-rescheduling, gradual tariff reductions and a freeing of prices, there has been no far-reaching banking reform, public sector restructuring or privatization. In recent country reports, the IMF has circumspectly criticized North African regimes for stalling on deeper liberalization.[14]

Partial market-oriented reforms, even when imposing losses on large segments of society as in Egypt, Algeria and Morocco, can serve the economic and political objectives of North African elites as much as populist and state socialist policies did in the 1960s and 1970s. These elites have sought access to European and other international economic resources that can be injected into the patronage networks that they manage. By determining the winners in a distributional coalition, they have sought to affect the desire and capacity that winners have to pursue political change. Winners during North African reform have managed to garner concentrated gains due to direct government transfers, state-provided rent-seeking opportunities, shielding from external economic competition, tolerance of illegality, and other government-granted privileges.[15] Ruling elites have sought to insure that winners do not have a significant interest in democratization or comprehensive economic reforms. Threatening to withhold state support from members of a distributional coalition can sometimes generate as much loyalty as distribution of aid itself. Eva Bellin finds that in late-developing countries where the private sector's profitability is highly subject to the state's discretionary support and where the private sector fears political mobilization by the poor (for example via Islamist movements), private capitalists have little enthusiasm for democratization.[16] In these same countries, where organized labour is highly dependent on the state and has an 'aristocratic position' (as is true in Egypt, Algeria and Tunisia), it is not committed to democratization. Until state dominance of credit allocation through the banking system is significantly reduced in North Africa, private sector enthusiasm for deep political reform will likely remain limited.

Although partial reform is economically not ideal, it has been a dominant strategy, as comprehensive reform would create higher social costs in the short term, provoke serious divisions between regime members, and create autonomous sources of economic power. North African regimes (except Algeria's) have been able to generate reasonably high growth rates and attract sufficient external resources to expand distributional coalitions and co-opt potential troublemakers. Moreover, partial reform has not substantially decreased the state's discretionary authority over economic privileges. In other words, economic liberalization has not limited the government's ability to use selective distribution of economic privileges and punishments as an instrument of political control. A strong, autonomous private sector and solid market institutions have yet to emerge.[17] Moreover, those neo-liberal reforms that are actually implemented provide political incumbents with an opportunity to re-regulate by creating new market-governance institutions.[18] After implementing reforms, incumbents have created new mechanisms to regulate actors, expand regime power and expand coalitions. Unless the European Union can substantially increase the capacity of North African social actors to contest re-regulation strategies, neo-liberal reforms may simply bolster governance of the market by authoritarian elites.

European Resource Inflows

While Europe is not the only source of external resources for Egypt and the Maghreb, the European Union collectively has been the predominant source of capital inflows and the main trading partner of its southern Mediterranean neighbours. Its dominant structural impact on North Africa is for the most part complemented by the United States, Japan and Arab states. Data from the World Bank's *Global Development Finance* provide important indicators of the level of net resource flows into North Africa.[19] The World Bank measures net long-term resource transfers as loan disbursements plus net foreign direct investment (FDI), equity flows and grants, minus loan repayments. The transfer figures indicate the level of international resources that have flowed into or out of a country in a given year. There is significant variation across the four North African countries. Algeria has fared the worst. From 1990 to 1998, net transfers amounted to a staggering \$-15.5bn, mostly due to repayments of private commercial debt. The country gained almost nothing from private net FDI and portfolio equity flows.[20] Before 1997, net transfers from official sources (countries and multilateral institutions) were either positive or only slightly negative, meaning that new official loan disbursements and grants were offsetting large repayments on commercial loans.

From 1990 to 1998, Morocco's net transfers were \$-4.6bn, mostly due to repayments of official debt since 1992. While private net transfers were \$–1.2bn in 1992, they were highly positive in 1997 and 1998. Net FDI and portfolio equity flows from 1990 to 1998 were \$5bn, while grants over the same period totalled \$4.8bn. Egypt has fared very well in terms of net transfers, which totalled \$17bn from 1990 to 1998, owing to official debt forgiveness and high private inflows. Net FDI and portfolio equity flows were \$9.9bn, while grant inflows were \$23bn. Tunisia also had modestly positive net transfers from 1990 to 1998 of \$879m, and positive private resource inflows offset net repayments on official debt. Net FDI over the period was \$3.3bn but there were no portfolio equity inflows. Grants amounted to \$1.9bn.

In aggregate terms, Algeria and Morocco have been burdened with high debt repayments, which in Morocco have been partly offset by considerable private inflows from Europe. Yet Algeria has had trouble attracting compensating private inflows. Interestingly, these two countries with the greatest resource inflow constraints have experienced more political liberalization. Egypt and Tunisia have been spared a high debt burden, and while both are attracting considerable private and official flows, Egypt has benefited enormously from official grants. In these two cases, little political liberalization has occurred in a context of positive inflows. It would seem that positive net transfers better allow Egyptian and Tunisian elites to sustain large distributional coalitions. Nevertheless, what is common across all four countries is that the bulk of official and private inflows are filtered through the hands of government elites. Foreign aid, loans, official concessionary finance, foreign direct investment, remittances and tourism receipts from Europe are potentially important resources that governing elites can access or channel. Debt rescheduling, debt forgiveness, and debt-to-investment conversions organized by western governments, the IMF and World Bank, and the Paris and London Clubs, can also provide large concentrated benefits to regimes and their economic allies.

Grants from the European Union through the MEDA I programme (1995–99) were significant but disbursement was slow. Of total commitments to the four North African countries of €1.9bn, only €482m (a quarter) was actually paid out during the period.[21] If the new MEDA II credits (2000–06) are administered like MEDA I aid, they will primarily finance public infrastructure, public administration reform, public sector reform and social development projects. Existing political elites in the south have much to gain from MEDA, even if the use of the funds for graft and patronage can be minimized. Moreover, it is political elites that will determine how the relatively small amount of MEDA credits that reach the private investors is distributed.[22] Europe has yet to operationalize the political conditionality associated with its MEDA credits. In effect, partial economic liberalization and market reforms backed by EU MEDA grants and associated loans from the European Investment Bank may have illiberal effects on southern Mediterranean economies, leading to a re-concentration of economic power.

European governments have played a leading role in helping regimes deal with debt burden by supporting rescheduling, forgiveness and debt-to-investment conversion, and extending large trade credits. After the 1991 Gulf War, the Paris Club of bilateral donors agreed to forgive a large proportion of Egypt's debt to official creditors. Spain, like other European countries, has extended large commercial credits, including $900m to Algeria in 1996 and $1bn to Morocco from 1996 to 2001.[23] France played a leading role in refinancing Algeria's short-term debt in the early 1990s. In addition to major commercial credits extended to Algeria in the 1990s, the French government helped persuade the IMF in 1995 to extend a $1.8bn extended credit facility. It also lobbied the Paris and London Clubs (for commercial debt) in 1995 and 1996 to reschedule debt worth $10bn. As Philip Naylor points out, 'French intervention in multilateral financial circles, even if self-serving given the size of its own loans, prevented Algeria's economy from suffering a meltdown'.[24] Most recently, Spain converted some Moroccan debt to equity held by Spanish companies. France agreed to convert $61m of Algerian debt to French investment, and Algeria began negotiating with Spain and Italy to convert some of its debt into foreign investment. In 2000, Italy converted $100m of Moroccan debt to investment, while France converted FF 700m. In 2001, Germany converted $34m of Egyptian debt for investment in water projects.

European foreign direct investment is often made through joint ventures between multinational companies and public enterprises, bolstering the resources, if not the solvency, of ailing state companies.[25] Moreover, a considerable amount of foreign portfolio investment has flowed to state companies and financial institutions listed on stock markets. Large direct investors have generally preferred joint ventures with public entities rather than with domestic private capitalists. French, Italian, Spanish and German companies have been the dominant European investors in North Africa. By 2000 there were some 700 Spanish companies in Morocco; at the same time Italy had become the second most important source of FDI in Tunisia after France, and there were more than 600 Italian firms in Tunisia. Investments in Algeria by Italy's ENI alone will amount to $500m by 2004. Germany's MAN AG has also taken an interest in Algeria, setting up a joint venture in 2000 with Algeria's state company Asmidal and an American petrochemical company to invest $370m in an ammonia plant. In the same year, Germany's Henkel invested $15m in a joint venture with Algeria's state-owned Enad to produce detergent. This later type of medium-sized investment has been replicated throughout the region between European companies and state companies in pharmaceuticals and consumer goods sectors. Not uncommonly, the joint ventures have dominance over their market sectors, generating important gains for state enterprises and increasing the price of market entry for domestic private investors.

European investment in the tourism sector has also been quite significant in the last decade and is set to expand further. Some of this investment has been in conjunction with state-owned companies or quasi-public entities. The Egyptian, Moroccan and Tunisian governments have benefited directly and indirectly through an expanded tax base, revenues to state-owned airlines and balance of payments support. In the late 1990s, Morocco attracted tourism investment projects worth $900m, and most of the projects were led by foreign investors.[26] In 1999, tourism receipts rose to $2bn. Tunisia's and Egypt's tourism receipts had reached $1.6bn and over $3.5bn respectively by the same year.

The majority of private international investment inflows to Algeria, Egypt and Tunisia in the 1990s were in the hydrocarbon sector. The European fixation with oil and gas is likely to continue for the next decade. The direct rents to governments and state oil companies in these three countries have been enormous. Since 1986, Algeria has signed at least 46 partnership agreements with world oil companies, many of which are Anglo-American. In many cases, companies have made advance payments to the state for oil and gas exploration rights. The Algerian government in early 2001 drafted legislation that would open up the hydrocarbons sector to even more foreign investment. In 2000, Sonatrach's revenues reached $22bn. Investments and agreements in 2000 and 2001 give an indication of the increasing importance of European hydrocarbon investments. BP-Amoco announced it would invest $1.6bn in an Algerian gas field in partnership with Sonatrach. France's BNP Paribas opened a $87m credit line to Sonatrach for imports of French goods. Sonatrach and France's Gaz de France (GDF) committed themselves to a 13-year partnership. Sonatrach already supplies 25 per cent of France's gas needs. Sonatrach, GDF and Malaysia's Petronas signed a $2bn agreement on gas exploration, development and production sharing, preceded by payments of $45m by GDF and Petronas simply for access rights. Sonatrach also formed a joint venture with six European energy giants – Cepsa, GDF, Endesa, ENI, TotalFinaElf and BP – to develop a new gas pipeline from Algeria to Spain. Finally, a top adviser to the Irish president claimed that Ireland was willing to invest $2bn in Algeria's hydrocarbon sector.

Tunisia and Egypt have not escaped the interest of European hydrocarbon giants since the mid-1990s. In 2000, British Gas announced that it would invest $450m in an extension of Tunisia's Miskar gas field, where it had already invested some $600m in the 1990s.[27] In 2000, the Egyptian government announced a $10bn plan to expand petrochemical production over 20 years with the help of foreign investors.[28] State-owned companies are already the major petrochemical producers in Egypt. Royal Dutch Shell signed a $2.5bn agreement with the state-owned Egyptian General Petroleum Corporation (EGPC) to develop gas fields and build a gas liquefaction plant, and it was considering another project worth $1.7bn.[29] BP and ENI agreed to construct a $2bn liquefied natural gas plant in association with EGPC.[30] Moreover, Egypt negotiated with international oil companies to change the pricing of gas supplied to EGPC under production-sharing agreements, saving the government a projected $250m a year.[31]

Since 1999, telecommunications has joined hydrocarbons as a major sector for European investment. Privatization receipts and sales of cellular phone licenses are pumping large amounts of money directly into the hands of state elites. In 1999, Méditel, a consortium of Spain's Telefónica, Portugal Telecom and Moroccan investors, paid $880m for Morocco's second GSM mobile telephone licence. Méditel has since proceeded to raise $616m in project financing with loans from the International Finance Corporation and export credit agencies in Sweden and Spain.[32] Mostapha Terrab, head of Morocco's National Telecommunications Regulation Agency, has publicly complained that his government is using telecoms licence revenue as a 'cash cow' rather than reinvesting profits.[33] In late 2000, the French-Canadian media giant Vivendi paid $2.1bn for a 35 per cent share of Morocco's partially-privatized Maroc Télécom, allowing the government to maintain its 2001 budget targets. Since 2000, Egypt has been preparing to sell off 20 per cent of TelecomEgypt through an initial public offering expected to raise up to $1.4bn in privatization revenue for the state treasury. By early 2001, France Telecom had acquired a 71 per cent majority stake in the Egypt's MobiNil, the country's largest mobile phone operator. By the same time, Tunisia had contracted with France's Société de Banque Française et Internationale (SBFI) to prepare a tender for a second GSM mobile network. Algeria also sought help from France's BMP-Paribas to prepare an international tender for a GSM licence.

While a significant portion of European FDI is in conjunction with public enterprises, another fact often overlooked is that a large proportion of North Africa's FDI is actually privatization receipts. Unlike 'traditional' FDI, investment through privatization sends money directly into the state's coffers and has relieved North African governments of the burden of financing some infrastructure projects, particularly in power generation and telecommunications. A World Bank official noted recently that 60 per cent of all FDI in the MENA is coming in the form of privatization revenues, and only 10 per cent of the region's privatization potential of $100bn has been tapped by governments.[34] In Tunisia, for example, 40 per cent of the estimated FDI of $650m in 2000 came from the privatization of a state cement company.[35] Starting in 2001, Tunisia intends to privatize 41 public enterprises worth some $1.3bn. Egypt, Morocco and Algeria have also announced ambitious privatization strategies for 2001. The upshot is that through FDI in the form of privatization, the mostly unaccountable governing elites in the region will continue to have large amounts of rents to distribute to loyal coalitional members.

While FDI, loans, grants and privatization receipts are the dominant sources of resource inflows, states have also tapped several other sources. Oil, gas and phosphate exports by state monopolies are important sources of budget revenue. Tunisia and Egypt have also turned recently to sovereign bond issues. In 2000, the Tunisian government raised Td 600m in a bond issuance in Japan. Half of the investors were European or American.[36] In late 2000, the Egyptian government began preparations to launch a $500m Eurobond offering with the help of major European banks. Worker remittances, which in the Maghreb mostly come from Europe, have also provided indirect benefits to governments in that they help with the balance of payments, and a proportion of the remittances placed in North African banks have been used to finance government debt. From 1990 to 1998, worker remittances averaged about $2bn a year in Morocco, well over $3bn a year in Egypt, and rose from a yearly average of $500m to $700m in Tunisia. In 1999, Tunisia's worker remittances reached $858m. Since 1994, remittances to Algeria have averaged over $1bn a year.

The Risks of Partial Reform

Accessing external resources is not without risks for North African elites. Most importantly, the international economy may not provide enough resources to maintain broad and viable distributional coalitions. There can be large contractions in external resources due to changes in the international system as a whole. Large-scale defection by domestic actors via capital flight can also reduce the capacity of elites to manage the economy. Many exogenous factors have at various times reduced resource inflows, placing constraints on budgets and forcing negotiations with creditors and European governments. The vagaries of oil prices, the Asian financial crisis, swings in the value of the dollar, and conditions in international capital markets are but a few of the market constraints. The United States and Europe, at the bilateral and multilateral levels, have sometimes threatened resource penalties to force policy changes. Available rents, especially FDI, have at times been reduced due to a state's failure to reform or implement reforms well. Moreover, in comparison to its investment flows to all developing countries, European FDI to the MENA has been very limited. For example, in 1998 FDI inflows to North Africa from all countries were only 1.6 per cent of all inflows to developing countries. In the same year, FDI inward stock in North Africa was only 2.4 per cent of total stock in developing countries.[37] While European FDI generally helps regimes, the continuing inability of North African elites to redirect a significantly higher proportion of international investment to their economies reduces their incentive to reform.[38]

States have also faced a number of problems in their strategies to manage winners and losers during partial reform. They have faced unmitigated pressures to cut expenditures, lay off workers, reduce subsidies, expose companies to foreign imports, and shed some rent-taking opportunities through regulatory reform. All of these types of measures penalize sectors of society that may have the capacity to generate significant political opposition. While elites have sought controllable winners, they have also tried to avoid creating large, concentrated losers from economic reform that have the will and capacity to mobilize politically. To the extent that 'outcasts' from a distributional coalition have been able to find allies in the government or the military, they have sought to thwart reforms and challenge segments of the state elite. This scenario has created regime divisions that private actors and social forces have sought to take advantage of to extract concessions from government officials.

Excessive concentration of gains (rent-taking) amongst winning members of distributional coalitions continues to endanger macro-economic growth and the ability to access external resources in the future. Moreover, partial reforms may ultimately be unsustainable in the face of continuing fiscal crisis. Regimes in North Africa have faced fiscal problems measured in terms of high budget deficits that result from excessive expenditures and strict limits on revenue collection. Customs revenues are set to decline steeply as the Euro-Mediterranean free trade area comes into existence. To the extent that unresolved fiscal constraints force governments to raise alternative revenues and cut spending more, divisions in distributional coalitions should emerge.

The severity of risks has varied across the region and over time, depending on which groups have remained in distributional coalitions and which outcasts have faced the largest concentrated losses. Algeria's military regime has faced great risks from contractions in external resources and from a reform strategy that has produced great economic decline. Social losses have been high, with large numbers of outcasts amongst public sector cadres, public sector workers and small businesses. Morocco has also faced resource constraints and a mixed growth rate due to periodic drought. Despite the *makhzen*'s ability to sustain a stable distributional coalition amongst reform winners, civil servants and labour have faced losses, and small businesses are coming under pressure from the looming import competition from Europe via the Euro-Mediterranean Partnership.[39] Egypt has been fortunate to have large positive transfers from the international system and strong economic growth, reducing the number of outcasts from reform and allowing for some new groups to be brought into the distributional coalition. Nevertheless, the Islamic banking sector was shut down, and segments of public sector labour, civil servants and small businesses are under threat of large losses. Tunisia has fared quite well, with sufficient external resources, manageable debt and sustained high growth. Outcasts are not concentrated in major social sectors, and their losses are selective and smaller than elsewhere in the region. Large gains to society have significantly limited social mobilization. In all of the countries, winning members of distributional coalitions tend to be military officers, private sector oligopolists, public sector joint venture partners of foreign investors, exporters, importers and public sector cadres who have arbitrage opportunities. Nevertheless, each country has also had losers within these groups, as well as within the public bureaucracy and the import-substituting private sector. The greatest pressures for political change have come from some of the biggest losers: Islamists, low ranking civil servants, public sector workers, the urban lumpenproletariat and small- and medium-sized businesses hurt by trade liberalization, credit restrictions and exchange rate changes. Many of these groups have been subject to large-scale state coercion and repression for well over a decade.

How have Egyptian and Maghrebi elites dealt with political risks posed by limits on international resource inflows, reaction by reform losers (outcasts) and fiscal constraints in general? One strategy to avoid large losers has been to proceed slowly and selectively with reforms. Ideally, economic growth will allow losers to find compensating economic activities. Elites have also tried to disperse losses during economic reform as widely as possible throughout society. Outcasts from state patronage networks – whether individuals, companies or sectors – have sometimes been counterbalanced by new groups – whether offshore exporters, new commercial bankers, investment fund managers or new private entrepreneurs – admitted into distributional coalitions. In other words, specific economic groupings can be sacrificed as long as overall distributive coalitions remain viable through the extension of privileges to new entrants. To the extent that regimes are not beholden to any specific sectors, elites can rearrange privileges as long as systemic clientelism is maintained.

Private sector elites have a limited capacity to threaten the political privileges of incumbent reformers. Egypt's private sector, based on a crony capitalist model of co-optation and oligopolies, has seen its political power diluted by its weak industry associations and vulnerability to the still large public sector. Facing a state-controlled banking system and corporatist organization, the Tunisian business class has been prepared to remain very quiet as long as President Ben Ali's policies have successfully promoted economic growth. Algeria's employers' associations are weak and fragmented, while businesses in general are at the mercy of the state-controlled banking system. Only Morocco's business class has built up enough autonomy to challenge the regime on key policies, and many of its members have gained seats in the legislature in the most recent elections.[40] The Confédération Générale des Entreprises du Maroc, reflecting the views of modernist businessmen in medium-sized firms, has lobbied with some success for administrative reform and greater economic transparency.[41] Employers' associations in the other countries have an increasing incentive to seek political change, and many of their members lobby the government over specific issues like customs, taxation, credit and exchange rates. There are a growing number of businessmen who are 'outsiders' in relation to traditional employers' associations. They include emigrant-returnees, some exporters, medium-sized firm owners, and Islamist-leaning businessmen who have emerged out of liberalization programmes. Yet in the case of Tunisia's new returning emigrants, their clear disaffection with the Ben Ali regime is 'hidden' and they tend to avoid political activity or participation in business associations.[42]

Many private and public players, both winners and losers, have accepted loyalty and quiescence in exchange for side payments or in the hope of future patronage. North Africa's *mise à niveau* (industrial upgrading) programmes, backed by EU and World Bank funds, are examples of the kinds of side payments given to businesses in return for their acceptance of regime policies, especially lower tariff barriers with the EU. These programmes can make or break businesses, and they extend state involvement in the affairs of many private businesses. Tunisia has been the most aggressive in its upgrading programme.[43] By late 2000, 70 per cent of export-oriented firms were in the programme compared to 23 per cent of large, non-exporting businesses.[44] The Tunisian government claimed that 63 per cent of small- and medium-sized businesses had signed up for the upgrading programme and that Td 1.6bn had been invested in 1,609 businesses.[45] From 1995 to 1999, the EU pledged €250m to Egypt's Industrial Modernization Programme, through which the Ministry of Industry will help some 5,000 companies become more competitive. Morocco's upgrading programme only started in 1998, and by late 2000 27 proposals worth Dh 156m had been approved. In early 2001 the Algerian Ministry of Industry and Restructuring announced plans to start a corporate upgrade programme for small- and medium-sized businesses.

There are many other types of side payments, rents and compensations that states can distribute to ensure the viability of a winning coalition and dampen reaction from losers or potential losers. These resources are generated by government decisions and feed clientelistic networks in a context of incomplete market reform. Some are largely independent of the official budget and are controlled by a small handful of people. As such, measuring fiscal constraints or crises simply in terms of yearly budget figures does not provide a full picture of the resources over which elites have discretionary power. These resources include investments of state enterprises, state bank credits, bribes and advance payments by foreign investors, elite revenues and commissions derived from government spending, stakes of political elites in private businesses, social funds controlled by leaders, military grants and other funds not recorded in the state budget, and proceeds of legal and illegal importing.

These resources have been relatively large in North Africa and have been somewhat immune to the economic reforms pushed by the European Union. For example, Morocco's Hassan II Fund for Economic and Social Development, controlled by the central bank governor and Mohammed Kabbaj, one of the king's advisers, announced in 2000 that it would grant Dh 16bn for various social projects. This huge 'slush fund' controlled by the *makhzen* received more than Dh 7bn from the sale of the second GSM licence and will get money from the partial privatization of Maroc Télécom.[46] Tunisia has a Fonds de Solidarité Nationale (FSN) to which workers and enterprises contribute annually on a semi-involuntary basis. Used ostensibly to fund anti-poverty projects, the FSN is controlled by President Ben Ali through a secretary of state without oversight by the cabinet, government or judiciary.[47]

More importantly, public banking systems have remained the locus of clientelism and control of economic actors. From 1991 to 1997, Algeria pumped massive resources equal to 15 per cent of GDP into the public banking system to recapitalize banks and cover foreign exchange losses.[48] In late 2000, Algeria's minister of privatization, Hamid Temmar, and Central Bank Governor, Abd al-Wahab Keramane, admitted that some $10.3bn, equal to 23 per cent of GDP in 2000, had been spent on support for government enterprises, whose total bad debt still amounted to 85 per cent of GDP.[49] After a decade of financial restructuring, which was essentially an exercise in massive clientelistic resource distribution, state enterprises were still unprofitable and sustained by overdrafts from state banks, which still controlled 95 per cent of the financial system's total assets and deposits. In Tunisia, the state-owned Banque de l'Habitat still provides 80 per cent of home mortgage lending.[50] Despite a restructuring of public banks and an associated clean-up of public enterprise debt begun in 1999, Tunisia's public banks still control 60 per cent of total banking assets. Plans in early 2001 to merge and partly privatize three Tunisian banks would leave half of the new bank's stock under government control, and the new entity would still account for 28 per cent of the country's banking activity.

Morocco's mostly state-owned real estate and tourism bank, Crédit Immobilier et Hôtelier, was recently subject to a government investigation into corruption. The bank had lost some $1.3bn in bad loans, many of whose recipients, according to a list published by parliament, were senior politicians, trade union leaders and associates of the late King Hassan II.[51]

In 2000 the government was forced to launch a Dh 5bn rescue package. Egypt's massive public sector banks, insurance companies, and other public agencies have significant stakes in joint venture banks that have domestic and foreign private investors. Although in 1994 the government had ordered public banks to reduce their stakes in joint venture banks to below 20 per cent, in 2000 the Central Bank permitted them to increase holdings.[52] This is part of Egypt's re-regulation strategy that preserves a state role in governing semi-private financial actors.

Challenges for the European Union

This article has argued that with access to European Union and international resources, regimes in North Africa have undertaken partial economic reforms that have not led to deep political change. When regimes maintain direct or indirect control over large capital inflows during structural adjustment, they appear capable of resisting demands for a truly transformative political pluralism. While Algeria and Morocco, facing more significant resource inflow problems in the 1990s, have faced the greatest pressures for democratic politics, they, like their more fortunate neighbours Tunisia and Egypt, have been able to sustain distributional coalitions and suppress often considerable challenges from society.

Global markets and European governments pose challenges, but they also offer opportunities. External resources channelled through governments, state-controlled institutions or state allies in distributional coalitions have generated new sources of rent, allowed many ailing public enterprises to offset otherwise fatal structural problems, and facilitated the task of re-regulation of economic actors disguised as liberalization. With outside help, executive authorities have had a higher capacity to limit the growth of private sectoral interests and relative autonomy that would encourage both private and public sector actors to switch from being co-opted allies of authoritarianism to demanders of inclusive pluralism and democracy.

The European Union faces a quandary in its attempts to promote democracy in North Africa. Its incrementalist-developmentalist approach to democracy-building, based upon offering economic carrots with little political conditionality, may serve to perpetuate existing regime structures. Neo-liberal economic reforms promoted by the EU may be beneficial for the region over the long term, but their incomplete implementation has allowed a re-concentration of economic power and continued government domination of the market. As Joel Hellman has discovered in post-communist states, where the winners from initial reform are shielded from mass politics and the demands of losers, there are less comprehensive reforms and fewer social gains.

An important lesson seems to be that political reform prior to economic reform would allow North African society to tame winners better and prevent monopolization of external resources by governing elites. Exposing existing distributional coalitions to mass politics and electoral pressures would be likely to make economic reforms more comprehensive and equitable. The EU might best promote the long-term success of democracy in the region through a 'big bang' approach to political reform based on a push for free, fair and inclusive elections. Arguably one lesson from eastern Europe and much of Latin America is that competitive elections, which fundamentally change the composition of policy-makers, are the necessary precondition for successful market-oriented reform and civil society development. This 'politics first' approach to reform is fraught with risks for the EU and its partner regimes in the southern Mediterranean. Incumbents would strenuously resist pressures for political reform, and the biggest initial winners from true liberalization would probably be mainstream Islamists. Europe's interest in stable hydrocarbon supplies, reduced immigration and greater security might be at stake. A fundamental political transformation appears unlikely unless the EU begins to show more serious concern about southern regimes when they stage sham elections. To date, conspicuously absent from EU policy is a focus on the role of elections in democratization. Political conditionality through the new MEDA II credits, an expanded role for the European Parliament, support for human rights groups, and official European dialogue with secular and Islamist opposition parties are all political measures which would further reform. Fake political reform as witnessed in Egypt and Tunisia for over a decade does not deserve European support or encouragement. But when genuine reform is initiated from within the region, as in Morocco since the early 1990s and in Algeria from 1988 to 1991, Europe must be a more active supporter, which also makes credible the threat of massive economic penalties for a reversal of political liberalization. While the big bang of democratization is mostly a complex internal process, European political pressure can provide important support.

The Euro-Mediterranean Partnership has proven to be an inappropriate framework for promoting political reform and deep economic reform, partly because its aims are too disparate and ambitious. A continuation of this 'economics first' approach may have a counterproductive effect on Algeria, Egypt and Tunisia. It is unrealistic for the EU to believe that its limited official economic assistance, channelled mostly through North African governments, will have any significant impact on socio-economic change. The promotion of free trade, European investment and debt relief, without a credible EU interest in democratization, are prescriptions for incomplete, inequitable reform.

Perhaps the most realistic strategy for the European Union is a combined emphasis on both economic and political change. Through its self-generated political opening, Morocco has provided an opportunity for the European Union to utilize co-ordinated policies and resources to help bring the country to full democracy. Morocco deserves special consideration and much more political devotion from the European Union. On the other hand, intransigent elites in Algeria, Egypt and Tunisia are unlikely to change without more economic and political 'sticks' in the European policy repertoire. Individual European states cannot promote political reform simply through their bilateral relations with North Africa and without associated pressure from the US, whose economic and political interests in the Maghreb are similar to those of Europe. The EU needs a co-ordinated policy that ties the flow of economic resources from individual states to the overall political aims of the EU. Aid needs to be channelled more directly to private actors. Considerable pressure should be exerted on Tunisia, Egypt and Algeria for fundamental reform of the banking sector, which, if successful, would unravel clientelistic networks, empower private actors, accelerate reform of public enterprises and facilitate privatization. Moreover, a credible commitment to dramatically lowering barriers to North African agricultural exports would accelerate economic growth while enhancing the EU's bargaining power over southern regimes. Europe must convince North African regimes that it is willing to sacrifice some of its short-term economic interests for the sake of promoting democracy. If it continues its passive, muted response toward controlled electoral campaigns, rigged elections and the suppression of some of the biggest opposition parties in Algeria, Tunisia and Egypt, southern regimes and opposition parties will not be convinced of the credibility of its democracy promotion policies.

NOTES

1. See Lisa Anderson, 'Democracy in the Arab World: A Critique of the Political Culture Approach', in Rex Brynen, Bahgat Korany and Paul Noble (eds.), *Political Liberalization and Democratization in the Arab World: Volume I Theoretical Perspectives* (Boulder, CO: Lynne Rienner, 1995).
2. Many analyses assume that mainstream Islamist parties promote beliefs that are incompatible with democracy. Yet some mass-based, deeply-rooted Islamist parties share characteristics with early pro-democracy movements in Latin America, eastern Europe, and the former Soviet Union: they engage in extensive patronage activities; promote a rule of law and human rights; and stress the importance of fair elections.

3. European support for (and indulgence of) authoritarian regimes in North Africa is stressed in François Burgat, *L'islamisme en face* (Paris: La Découverte, 1996); Nicolas Beau and Jean-Pierre Tuquoi, *Notre ami Ben Ali: l'envers du 'miracle tunisien'* (Paris: La Découverte, 1999); and Gilles Perrault, *Notre Ami le Roi* (Paris: Gallimard, 1992).
4. See Kiren Aziz Chaudhry, *The Price of Wealth: Economies and Institutions in the Middle East* (Ithaca, NY: Cornell University Press, 1997); Dirk Vandewalle, *Libya since Independence: Oil and State-Building* (Ithaca, NY: Cornell University Press, 1998); and Terry Lynn Karl, *The Paradox of Plenty: Oil Booms and Petro-States* (Berkeley, CA: University of California Press, 1997).
5. Since 1991, the EU's share in the total trade of the Maghreb has been over 65 per cent, higher than its share for Latin America and eastern Europe or any other region. See Roberto Aliboni, 'Change and Continuity in Western Policies Towards the Middle East', in Laura Guazzone (ed.), *The Middle East in Global Change: The Politics and Economics of Interdependence versus Fragmentation* (New York: St. Martin's Press, 1997).
6. See Helen Milner and Robert Keohane, 'Internationalization and Domestic Politics: An Introduction', in Robert Keohane and Helen Milner (eds.), *Internationalization and Domestic Politics* (New York: Cambridge University Press, 1996), pp.3–24.
7. Examples of this approach include Ronald Rogowski, *Commerce and Coalitions: How Trade Affects Domestic Political Alignments* (Princeton, NJ: Princeton University Press, 1989); Jeffrey Frieden, *Debt, Development, and Democracy: Modern Political Economy and Latin America* (Princeton, NJ: Princeton University Press, 1991); and Stephen Haggard and Sylvia Maxfield, 'The Political Economy of Financial Liberalization in the Developing World', in Keohane and Milner, op. cit., pp.209–39.
8. Brynjar Lia, 'Security Challenges in Europe's Mediterranean Periphery – Perspectives and Policy Dilemmas', *European Security*, Vol.8, No.4 (Winter 1999), p.33.
9. F. Stephen Larrabee, *NATO's Mediterranean Initiative: Policy Issues and Dilemmas* (Santa Monica, CA: RAND, 1998), p.33.
10. Jacqueline Coolidge and Susan Rose-Ackerman, 'High-Level Rent Seeking and Corruption in African Regimes: Theory and Cases' (Washington, DC: The World Bank, 1997), pp.46–8, www.worldbank.org/wbi/governance/pdf/wps1780.pdf [accessed 19 March 2001].
11. Lia, op. cit., p.48.
12. James Petras and Morris Morley, 'Contesting Hegemons: US–French Relations in the "New World Order"', *Review of International Studies*, Vol.26, No.54 (2000), pp.49–67.
13. Joel Hellman, 'Winners Take All: The Politics of Partial Reform in Postcommunist Transitions', *World Politics*, Vol.50, No.2 (1998), pp.203–34.
14. See International Monetary Fund, 'Algeria: Recent Economic Developments', IMF Staff Country Report No.00/105 (Washington, DC: International Monetary Fund, 2000); International Monetary Fund, 'Tunisia: Staff Report for the 2000 Article IV Consultation', IMF Country Report No.01/36 (Washington, DC: International Monetary Fund, 2001); and International Monetary Fund, *Egypt: Beyond Stabilization, Toward a Dynamic Market Economy* (Washington, DC: International Monetary Fund, 1992).
15. Oliver Schlumberger stresses this point in describing the resilience of patrimonialism and the '*wasta*' system in Arab economies. See Oliver Schlumberger, 'Arab Political Economy and the European Union's Mediterranean Policy: What Prospects for Development?', *New Political Economy*, Vol.5, No.2 (2000), pp.247–68.
16. Eva Bellin, 'Contingent Democrats: Industrialists, Labor, and Democratization in Late-Developing Countries', *World Politics*, Vol.52, No.2 (2000), pp.175–205.
17. Similar arguments are found in Béatrice Hibou and Luis Martinez, 'Le Partenariat euro-maghrébin: un marriage blanc?', *Les Etudes du CERI*, No.47 (Nov. 1998), pp.1–39.
18. This argument is developed in Richard Snyder's analysis of Mexico's re-regulation dynamics. See Richard Snyder, 'After Neoliberalism: The Politics of Reregulation in Mexico', *World Politics*, Vol.51, No.2 (1999), pp.173–204.
19. The following data come from: *Global Development Finance 2000 CD-ROM*, Vol.2, Country Tables (Washington, DC: The World Bank, 2000), pp.66, 214, 394, 554; *Global Development Finance: Country Tables* (Washington, DC: The World Bank, 1999), pp.56, 56, 204, 388, 548.

20. The IMF contradicts World Bank data on direct investment. It estimates that from 1996 to 1999, FDI to Algeria amounted to $1.5bn. See IMF, 'Algeria', p.84.
21. Commission of the European Communities, 'Annual Report of the MEDA Programme 1999' (Brussels, 2000), p.8, http://europa.eu.itn/comm/external_relations/med_mideast/euro_med_partnership/meda/report 1999_en.pdf [accessed 15 Feb. 2001].
22. Schlumberger, op. cit., pp.261, 268.
23. Jesús A. Nùñez Villaverde, 'The Mediterranean: A Firm Priority of Spanish Foreign Policy?', *Mediterranean Politics*, Vol.5, No.2 (2000), p.136.
24. Philip C. Naylor, *France and Algeria: A History of Decolonization and Transformation* (Gainesville, FL: University Press of Florida, 2000), p.246.
25. EU investors often choose joint ventures with public enterprises out of necessity. In many sectors there are simply no domestic private companies of any significance. Public companies are also better able to contribute investment capital. Most importantly, public partners minimize risks to foreign investors from arbitrary ministerial decisions, bureaucratic blockages and haphazard judiciary outcomes.
26. *Maghreb Weekly Monitor*, No.97 (24 Dec. 2000), p.19.
27. *Jeune Afrique/L'Intelligent*, No.2095 (6–12 March 2001), p.80.
28. *Middle East Economic Survey*, Vol.43, No.46 (13 Nov. 2000), p.A7.
29. Ibid., p.A18.
30. *Middle East Economic Survey*, Vol.44, No.13 (26 March 2001), p.A20.
31. *Middle East Economic Survey*, Vol.43, No.39 (25 Sept. 2000), p.A15.
32. *Middle East Economic Survey*, Vol.43, No.43 (23 Oct. 2000), p.B7.
33. *Maghreb Weekly Monitor*, No. 99 (18 Jan. 2001), p.7.
34. *Middle East Economic Survey*, Vol.43, No.48 (27 Nov. 2000), p.B5.
35. IMF, 'Tunisia', p.13.
36. *Maghreb Weekly Monitor*, No. 92 (22 Sept. 2000), p.10.
37. Economic Research Forum, *Economic Trends in the MENA Region, 2000* (Cairo: Economic Research Forum, 2000), ch.2, www.erf.org.eg.html/economic_00/html/table2_13.html and www.erf.org.eg.html/economic_00/html/table2_14.html [accessed 15 Jan. 2001].
38. Southern Mediterranean regimes are unlikely to attract much more FDI without addressing socio-political factors such as independent legal systems, foreign property rights and good governance (which rests upon political participation and accountability). See George Joffé, 'Foreign Investment and the Rule of Law', *Mediterranean Politics*, Vol.5, No.1 (2000), pp.33–49.
39. The *makhzen* refers to the de facto power structure in Morocco, associated for many years with the role of Driss Basri at the head of the interior ministry. See also Haddadi, this collection, p.159.
40. See Myriam Catusse, 'Les entrepreneurs marocains, nouveaux défenseurs du trône? Sur la construction sociale et politique d'une catégorie libérale', paper presented at the XVIIIth World Congress of the International Political Science Association, 1–5 Aug. 2000, Quebec, Canada.
41. Guilain Denoeux, 'The Politics of Morocco's "Fight Against Corruption"', *Middle East Policy*, Vol.7, No.2 (2000), pp.165–90.
42. See Jean-Pierre Cassarino, *Tunisian New Entrepreneurs and Their Past Experience of Migration in Europe* (Aldershot: Ashgate, 2000).
43. For a comprehensive overview of this programme and how the Tunisian regime has used it to re-regulate the private sector, see Cassarino, ibid.
44. *Maghreb Weekly Monitor*, No.93 (13 Oct.2000), p.7.
45. *Maghreb Weekly Monitor*, No.95 (2 Dec. 2000), p.8.
46. *Maghreb Weekly Monitor*, No.92 (22 Sept. 2000), p.6.
47. Beau and Tuquoi, op. cit., pp.148–9.
48. IMF, 'Algeria', p.38.
49. *Middle East Economic* Survey, Vol.43, No.46 (12 Nov. 2000), p.B6.
50. IMF, 'Tunisia', p.9.
51. *Middle East International*, No.643 (9 Feb. 2001), p.18.
52. *Middle East Economic Survey*, Vol.43, No.44 (14 Aug. 2000), p.B6

From the Bottom to the Top: Civil Society and Transnational Non-Governmental Organizations in the Euro-Mediterranean Partnership

ANNETTE JÜNEMANN

The Euro-Mediterranean Partnership (EMP) is based on the assumption that the deepening of interregional relations cannot be achieved through governmental agreements alone, but requires popular participation. Against the background of mutual prejudices and misperceptions between the South and the North, co-operation at the level of civil society contributes to intercultural understanding. Furthermore, as the lines of conflict run not only between North and South, but exist also within each of the two regions – between Israelis and Palestinians, Greeks and Turks, Turks and Kurds – civil society co-operation can be particularly important in facilitating the reconciliation of conflict. This positive potential of civil society is recognized by all members of the EMP, and the Barcelona Declaration (1995) stresses 'the essential contribution civil society can make in the process of development of the Euro-Mediterranean Partnership and as an essential factor for greater understanding and closeness between the people'.[1]

The EU, however, also adheres to a less consensual goal in supporting civil society initiatives within the EMP, namely the promotion of democratization in the Mediterranean Partner Countries (MPC). The EU's post-cold war focus on democracy includes the promotion of institutional reform, the rule of law and good governance, but also complements this classical top-down approach to democratization with a bottom-up strategy, based on the assumption that democratization is inseparable from greater respect for human rights and a strong civil society.

Authoritarian regimes in the southern Mediterranean are aware of this hidden agenda. To the extent that civil engagement can undermine authoritarian structures, these governments feel threatened by European support for civil society actors. Beneath the superficial consensus concerning civil society's importance to the EMP, as laid out in the Barcelona Declaration, there exist strong reservations amongst MPCs. The latter accepted the civil society dimension only because it was essentially imposed upon them by the EU, in exchange for the promise of deeper economic co-operation and enhanced financial assistance. To reduce the risk that civil society might endanger present power structures, some authoritarian MPCs insisted on the insertion of a formula into the Barcelona Declaration specifying that civil society projects must be 'within the framework of national law'.[2]

Civil society not only challenges authoritarian regimes in the South. Respected human rights non-governmental organizations (NGOs) like Amnesty International also criticize the EU and its member states, for example over European migration and political asylum policies.[3] Furthermore, representatives of civil society have also criticized the lack of a social dimension and the neglect of environmental considerations within the EMP. The major reproach against the EU concerns the unbalanced commercial interdependence between the MPCs and the EU, developed strongly to the latter's advantage. As the concept of the EMP was elaborated predominantly by the European side, these criticisms are directed mainly against the EU.[4] For the EU itself, civil engagement is, in sum, a double-edged sword.

Authoritarian MPCs openly oppose civil society co-operation and/or try to undermine it through various hidden strategies. While the EU is more generally supportive towards the role of civil society, it has been ambivalent over the extent of its support for civil society initiatives. The reason for the EU's ambivalence is less the fear of being challenged by European civil society actors than concern over the potentially destabilizing effects of civil society support within the MPCs. The EU's goal of promoting democratization can, at least during periods of transition, conflict with the EU's predominant goal of stabilization. In most of the MPCs, processes of democratization will most probably lead to extremely unstable transition periods, with the risk of violent upheavals or even civil wars.[5] Consequently, the EU aims to promote only a gradual process of democratization under the strict control of ruling elites. This caution is advocated especially strongly by France and Spain, owing to these states' special relations with their respective former colonies and protectorates in North Africa. In contrast, the Commission, with no direct interests in the region, has been more ambitious in its attempts to encourage democratization in co-operation with civil society. The strongest supporter of civil society in the Mediterranean has been the European Parliament (EP), but the EP is a relatively weak player within the predominantly intergovernmental EMP.[6]

This account analyses civil society work undertaken within the framework of the EMP. It begins with some basic reflections on the theoretical conceptualization of civil society. The second section outlines and evaluates the various instruments and programmes set up by the EU to support Euro-Mediterranean civil society co-operation within the EMP. The account then analyses the political impact of transnational NGOs, in particular by examining the work of the Euro-Mediterranean Human Rights Network. Finally, a brief assessment is offered of the future prospects of the EU's bottom-up approach to democratization.

Contrasting Views of Civil Society

Civil society is a European concept based on Enlightenment concepts of reason and rationality, and supposing there to be a basic separation and tension between (civil) society, economy and the state.[7] There has never been a universally accepted definition of civil society, even within the western world. Civil society has remained a normative and value-laden concept:

> The values involved are those relating to liberty, to civilized or civilizing behaviour, and to a set of ethics relating to work, social relationships, respect for human rights and so on. The emphasis on one or another aspect may vary from definition to definition, yet liberty must always be at the centre. Descriptive definitions which focus on pluralism or on a realm that is simply distinct from the state miss the point. There are pluralistic societies in which civil society does not exist; they are little more than fragmented societies if liberty does not transcend the various groups.[8]

There is general agreement that civil society organizations should properly exhibit a number of characteristics, and that these help to describe – rather than define – civil society:[9] participation in the political and social development of the country; tolerance and a rejection of violence; democratic internal structures.[10] Beyond this, however, there is a wide range of different forms of civil society, depending on the historical, cultural and religious background of a society and also on the nature of the political system.[11] Consequently, other criteria often seen as central to civil society organizations are highly controversial: independence from the state; independence from private business; independence from primordial structures.

Independence from the State

The most controversial aspect of defining civil society concerns the relationship between civil society and the state. In this respect there have been two competing perspectives: a 'dichotomous' view, going back to the English philosopher John Locke (1632–1704); and an 'integrative' definition going back to the French thinker Montesquieu (1689–1755).[12] According to the dichotomous concept, civil society is completely independent of the state and its primary function is to control the latter. The relationship between civil society and the state is thus conflictive and polarized, and civil society is legitimately concerned with undermining authoritarian regimes. In contrast, the integrative concept sees civil society as part of a political system, with no clear-cut divisions existing between the state and civil society. According to the integrative concept, civil society's function is both to control the state and to enhance the latter's legitimacy through civic participation.

The European Commission has not favoured co-operation with representatives of the dichotomous concept of civil society such as would bring the EU into conflict with southern Mediterranean governments. Clear preference has been given to representatives of the integrative concept, in accordance with the EU's long-term interest of supporting no more than a carefully controlled process of gradual political reform. From a theoretical perspective, the preference given to the integrative concept of civil society is problematic in the context of the Mediterranean basin, given that this concept presumes the existence of a *democratic* political system. In practice, the difference between the dichotomous and integrative concepts is not as clear-cut as the theoretical model implies. In most contexts, civil society's relations with the state are in practice situated somewhere between the two poles of (dichotomous) anti-system opposition and (integrative) mediation. Civil society actors can fluctuate between these two poles. This complicates the EU's selection of essentially integrative civil society partners and, as examined below, affects the composition of transnational NGOs.

The classification of an NGO in the wide spectrum between dichotomous and integrative civic engagement depends very much on the issue it addresses. Human rights NGOs have a mainly conflictive, dichotomous relationship with regimes in the Mediterranean. Their antagonism towards these regimes is so strong that it leaves little room for mediation. In contrast, environmental NGOs and trade unions have slightly more room for manoeuvre: as long as they do not openly question the political system as such, they can function as both critical watchdogs and integrative mediators. They can push political reforms forward within the confines of an autocratic system, using a mixed strategy of political pressure and professional consultancy. Regimes have an incentive to work with such actors, as a means of enhancing their own domestic legitimacy. However, the experience of eastern European states demonstrated that these seemingly less political actors can help 'open the doors' to democratization. Authoritarian regimes in the Mediterranean have been sensitive to this and have sought to suppress, infiltrate or co-opt trade unions and integrative NGOs. From the point of view of EU strategy, this has made the support of civil society a difficult and risky task in all spheres.

Independence from Private Business

Another debate concerns the question of whether private business is part of civil society or whether it should be regarded as a separate sphere.[13] While trade unions are widely accepted to be part of civil society, the classification of private entrepreneurship is less clear. Having set up the MED-Invest programme to promote exchanges between small- and medium-sized enterprises within the framework of the EMP, the EU clearly sees private entrepreneurs as being part of civil society. Indeed, there are two reasons why their inclusion is seen as important in the context of the EMP. First, private trade accelerates interregional and intraregional *rapprochement*; second, private entrepreneurs are seen as reducing the dominant role of the state sector and thereby undermining the structure of authoritarian regimes.

Nevertheless, the EU's inclusion of the business sector within its conceptualization of civil society is not without its problems. This is so in particular with regard to the high priority that the EU attaches to privatization processes within the economic basket of the EMP. Some theorists warn that Europe's focus on privatization 'may increase the power of groups in society that are connected to the political establishment',[14] and thus actually undermine the cause of democratization in authoritarian countries. As entrepreneurs depend on stable political structures to run their business, they have no interest in directly challenging the state. Thus, entrepreneurs often tend to side with the state, even if it is authoritarian, rather than with the democratic forces of civil society:

> If we wish to treat civil society as that realm which stands against the political despotism of the state, then we should ... leave the economy out, because entrepreneurs, merchants and firms will not fight the state politically but only in defence of their economic interests, and

> the pursuit of these interests may well lead to alliances with the state that reinforce its political authority and its despotic tendencies.[15]

Hence, entrepreneurs should be acknowledged as part of civil society only if they stand for political and social goals that go beyond their private economic interests. Thus, in contrast to the apparent belief of many officials – in Brussels and national capitals – the encouragement of privatization is not on its own sufficient to promote political change in the MPCs. Privatization might be important for economic development, but does not necessarily constitute a positive contribution in support of democratization.

Independence from Primordial Structures

Likewise it is difficult to answer the question of whether groups that are organized according to primordial structures of society such as the family, clan or tribe should be seen as being part of civil society. As religious institutions also belong to the category of primordialism, the political sensitivity of this question concerns the problem of how to deal with Islamist associations. Do Islamist associations meet the theoretical categories defining civil society?

> Some Islamist thinkers reject the concept of *civil society* (*al-mutjama al-madani*) because of its western roots. They argue that the acceptance of the term already implies the acceptance of a western model of society. So they developed the alternative concept of *citizen society* (*al-mutjama al-ahli*), meaning primordial structures of society such as the family, clan and especially the religious institutions. These are not seen as (second best) equivalents to civil society, but as authentic structures in the context of a Muslim state.[16] [original emphasis]

The values of citizen society do not necessarily contradict the values that constitute civil society. Yet many intellectuals in Europe and the Arab world, especially those within the secular sphere of society, refuse to accept citizen society as an equivalent to civil society, as their understanding of civil society is based on individual rights and freedoms, not those of groups or clans. It is argued that primordial institutions should not be accepted as parts of civil society as they are not based on the free and rational will of their individual participants. Some also reject the idea that political Islam is capable of tolerance. Against the background of Algeria's civil war, some analysts draw the decisive line not between society and the state, but between secularism and Islam.[17]

The European Commission has not included primordial associations in its civil society projects, in order to avoid conflict with both secular NGOs and MPC governments (especially in Tunisia, Algeria and Turkey). MPC governments fear that Islamist groups persecuted in their home countries might gain international recognition in the framework of religious dialogue projects initiated by the Europeans. Due to these reservations of the MPCs, the EU has reduced its support for religious dialogue projects to a minimum and the few projects that are organized involve only those representatives of Islam that are loyal to their governments. Many governments in the southern Mediterranean have co-opted sectors of political Islam to counterbalance the growing popularity of anti-system political Islam. Algeria and Egypt, for example, made far-reaching concessions to political Islam in the realm of civil law – concessions that are passionately combated by women's rights activists.

The vast majority of participants in civil society programmes are secular intellectuals, many with a western-influenced education and socialization. Although it is much easier for Europeans to co-operate with partners who share a similar political background, there is a growing awareness that the problem of how to integrate Islamists has to be addressed, as the secular segments of civil society taken alone are not fully representative of societies in the MPCs.[18] Most Islamist associations have deep roots in society, not least because of their charitable engagement that has compensated for incompetent or corrupt government. The difficulty for the EU in choosing dialogue partners within the heterogenous spectrum of political Islam lies in the inscrutable links that often exist between radical and moderate groups.[19] It would, however, be a severe misperception to reduce Islamism to its radical segments and ignore its manifold non-violent components.

> So long as religious based parties and associations accept the principle of pluralism and observe a modicum of civility in behaviour toward the different 'other', then they can expect to be integral parts of civil society. In this respect, even the Islamists may evolve into something akin to the Christian Democrats in the West or the religious parties in Israel. There is nothing intrinsically Islamic that contradicts with the codes of civil society or democratic principles.[20]

The integration of non-violent Islamist associations into Euro-Mediterranean civil society networks would help generate a better understanding between Muslims and non-Muslims both within Europe and across the Mediterranean. It would also make these networks more representative and thus enhance their legitimacy.

EU Support for Civil Society Co-operation

Basket III of the EMP – the Partnership in Social, Cultural and Human Affairs – comprises a variety of civil society initiatives. The MED programmes were the first to be launched, promoting Euro-Mediterranean dialogue at the level of universities, the media and local authorities.[21] The distinctive feature of the MED programmes was that European organizations could choose their partners without consulting the government of the country concerned, this being seen as key to the strengthening of genuinely independent civil society structures. The MED programmes were taken up very positively by associations in the MPCs. Many significant projects were initiated – in fact, so many that these initiatives overstretched the capabilities of the Commission's administration, which had not anticipated such a strong interest. For the first year of the EMP it seemed, therefore, that the MED programmes were highly successful. Unfortunately, an inspection of the MED programmes by the Court of Auditors in 1996 revealed significant funding abuses in the period between 1992 and 1994.[22] European participants had benefited far more from many projects than their Mediterranean partners. Other projects were criticized because they had failed to respect co-financing rules. The Commission accepted mismanagement in the MED programmes but also complained that the Court had overstretched its competences, evaluating not only the management of funds, but also the political content of the programmes.[23] Indeed, the Court evaluated only the financial administration procedures and was not able to judge the undoubtedly positive effects of the MED programmes. The Court's report led to the suspension of all MED programmes in September 1996. The Commission tried for several years to reinstall these programmes, before these again became an issue within the corruption scandal at the Commission in 1999.

Unsatisfied with the limited approach of the MED programmes – which did not offer support for NGOs – the EP pushed in 1996 for an additional instrument to support democratization at the level of civil society. Threatening the Commission and the Council that it would refuse approval of the EMP's financial protocol (MEDA), the European Parliament secured the establishment of MEDA Democracy. This was to be a programme that:

> grants subsidies to non-profit-making associations, universities, centres of research and to public bodies to implement projects which aim to promote democracy, the rule of law, freedom of expression, of meeting and of association, to protect target groups (women, youth, minorities) and to increase the awareness of socio-economic rights.[24]

MEDA Democracy[25] was more challenging for the governments of the MPCs, as it potentially covered groups representing the dichotomous concept of civil society, such as human rights NGOs. From the perspective of southern NGOs, it was the most important instrument in the framework of the EMP. Participation in MEDA Democracy projects has, however, been criticized by civil society representatives as being unduly complicated by an extremely slow flow of funds and opaque application and selection procedures.[26] This helps explain how it was possible for the Tunisian government to block the funding of projects that were eligible and already approved within the framework of the MEDA Democracy programme.[27] The severest setback for MEDA Democracy was in June 1998, when the Commission froze all projects following a ruling of the European Court of Justice. This ruling concerned the lack of a legal basis for a relatively minor budget line dealing with an anti-poverty programme, but its consequence was the freezing of all projects within the European Initiative for Democracy and Human Rights (EIDHR), including MEDA Democracy projects.[28] There followed a period of considerable uncertainty for civil society activists, until later in 1999 the Council adopted two regulations providing the missing legal basis.[29] Uncertainty has since returned as the administration of democracy projects in the Mediterranean was in 2000 transferred to a new Democracy and Human Rights Department in the Commission and has been subject to an unsettling ongoing process of reform.

The abolition of the MED programmes and the temporary freezing of MEDA Democracy projects added up to a severe setback for the EU's bottom-up approach to democratization. The programmes within the third 'basket' that have proceeded less problematically, such as Euromed Heritage[30] and Euromed Audiovisual,[31] are valuable in their own field and generate transnational contacts between the North and the South, but are politically less ambitious. In contrast to the MED Programmes and MEDA Democracy, these do not exclusively target civil society, but also include the public sector and require projects to be approved by recipient governments. Only the Euromed Youth Action Programme[32] is clearly and explicitly oriented to EU democratization policy in the region.

Against the background of these limitations to EU co-operation programmes, civil society actors have attached more importance to the Civil Forum, which has met alongside ministerial conferences. Meetings of the Civil Forum are part-financed by the Commission and organized in co-operation with the country hosting the official Euro-Mediterranean conference. The incorporation of the Forum into EMP events has had ambivalent effects. The Forum is too far away from the decision-making process to be effective in influencing EMP policies, but too exposed to the political influence of the member states hosting its meetings to fulfil an external, critical 'watchdog function'.[33] Governmental interference was especially strong during the Civil Forums in Barcelona in 1995 and in Marseille in 2000, because the Spanish and French governments wanted to protect the North African participants of the ministerial conference from too much embarrassment through the civil society activists.[34]

Only once, at Stuttgart in 1999, did the Forum manage to show its teeth, by organizing a conference dedicated exclusively to human rights, a taboo at all previous Forums.[35] Some of the MPCs tried to block this conference, but, having adopted the Barcelona Declaration and thus a commitment to the principles of human rights, could not openly do so. Behind the scenes, however, they put considerable pressure on the organizers, trying to influence the agenda and the list of participants. Germany's Friedrich Ebert Stiftung, hosting the conference, did everything to protect the participants from the pressure of their governments and invited only genuine and trustworthy NGOs.[36] This could not prevent the appearance of some North African 'GONGOs', organizations parading as NGOs but in reality linked to and controlled by governments. Despite this, the human rights conference at Stuttgart gained considerable public interest and media attention, indeed almost as much as the Euro-Mediterranean ministerial conference.[37]

One year later at the Marseille Civil Forum there was also a human rights workshop, but it was downgraded at the behest of the French government. A lot of lobbying was necessary in the run-up to the workshop and many compromises had to be accepted. For example, at the request of the French government, the human rights workshop had to be held under the less challenging title of *État de droit et démocracie*. Although there is common agreement that human rights are inseparable from the rule of law and democracy, the avoidance of the term 'human rights' reflected the lack of political will to strengthen this issue on the agenda of Euro-Mediterranean relations. In addition, in Marseille human rights were dealt with only in one workshop among many others, rather than being the subject of a whole conference. This reduced the media attention given to human rights.[38]

A New Start for European Democratization Policy?

As a consequence of the corruption scandal involving the MED programmes, growing pressure from repressive MPCs and the ambivalent position of southern member states, the Commission has become increasingly careful, even restrictive, in its dealing with civil society. For example, it proposed to give preference to big projects of at least €500,000, instead of splintering the funds between many small grass-root projects. This step was severely criticized by civil society representatives during the EU human rights discussion forum in November 1999. They warned the Commission that this size of project was far beyond the capacity of most southern NGOs and would therefore favour larger European groups.[39] Such big projects in the Mediterranean have invariably attracted more government attention and interference, and are therefore a completely inadequate and inappropriate approach to strengthening genuinely *independent* sectors of civil society. It remains to be seen how the Europe Aid Co-operation Office, established in 2001, will deal with these problems. It is too early to assess the Office's performance comprehensively, but there have been some positive signals for civil society work: the proposal to delegate more competences to EU delegations in partner countries;[40] and the lowering of the minimum for projects to€300,000.

The Commission's communication on 'The European Union's role in promoting human rights and democratization in third countries' of May 2001 seems to indicate a new start for the EU's democratization policy, based on improved strategies and instruments.[41] According to this document, higher priority will be placed on human rights and democratization objectives in the EU's relations with third countries. So-called Country Strategy Papers, assessing the performance of each partner country in the sphere of human rights, democratization, the rule of law and good governance, are to become decisive instruments for the creation of more coherence in external relations and for the mainstreaming of human rights as a cross-cutting category. The document also emphasizes that the EIDHR is to be carried out primarily in partnership with NGOs and international organizations. The proposed guidelines acknowledge the importance of ensuring that civil society projects include micro-projects and are run independently of governmental consent.[42] Most civil society representatives are still sceptical, however, over the prospects for a reinvigoration of the bottom-up approach. Southern member states are likely to remain hesitant and administrative improvements cannot overcome their politically-motivated reservation against a reinforced EU democratization policy in the region.

The Special Role of Transnational NGOs: The Case of the Euro-Mediterranean Human Rights Network

European support for civil society in the framework of the EMP has led to various forms of transnational co-operation at the level of civil society, including among NGOs. These projects have not always been unproblematic, however. Southern NGOs complain that co-operation with European partner organizations often turns out to be to their own disadvantage, especially if the European partners are to a greater or lesser extent imposed on them. Being more experienced in co-operating with the Commission, some European NGOs have taken the bigger share of funds for themselves, actually undermining the aim of supporting civil society development in the MPCs rather than in Europe.

Transnational NGOs offer a means of mitigating such imbalance. Instead of working together in temporary projects with changing (and often unwanted) partners, transnational NGOs are able to pursue long-term, co-operative interests within the framework of stable institutional structures. Transnational NGOs can combine the capacities of all their member organizations, creating positive effects of synergy. They have more power in their struggle against repressive regimes than individual national NGOs could ever accumulate. Transnational NGOs could become the backbone of civil society co-operation in the EMP, a development that would reflect a general trend in international relations since the end of the cold war. Transnational NGOs are helped by the increasingly binding character of international norms and the increasing support offered to them by international organizations.

One of the most notable transnational NGO networks that has evolved in the context of the Barcelona Process is the Euro-Mediterranean Human Rights Network (EMHRN). This was set up in 1997 on the initiative of both northern and southern human rights organizations. Today it has more than 60 members representing human rights organizations and institutions, as well as individuals, from over 20 countries. The network's overall objectives are to support the development of democratic institutions and the promotion of the rule of law, human rights principles and human rights education in the Euro-Mediterranean region. It recognizes that the Barcelona Process has provided important instruments for the promotion and protection of human rights, but that its success is dependent on the active participation of civil society. The network defines itself as a constructive interface between the EMP institutions, human rights organizations in the region and other relevant agents involved in the Barcelona Process.[43]

The EMHRN is engaged in three interlinked and interrelated activities: the documentation and dissemination of information; dialogue, advocacy and campaigning; and capacity building and education. At its last general assembly in November 2000 in Marseille, the network adopted a plan of action that, apart from seeking to monitor the EMP and human rights developments, stressed the need to enhance human rights organizations' capacity to work on the ground through a synergistic process of exchange of experience and knowledge between different organizations.[44] Reports on human rights conditions in the Euro-Mediterranean region, the general activities of the EMHRN and the provisions of the EMP are disseminated to the MPCs, EU institutions, EU member states and the public on both sides of the Mediterranean. A computerized information service has been established, including a web site[45] and an electronic mailing list. The EMHRN is engaged in campaigns to raise human rights awareness, for example offering legal advice to immigrants and promoting seminars on gender equality. The network provides education and capacity-building programmes for human rights defenders, to strengthen the professionalism of the network itself. The EMHRN is also engaged in fund-raising and co-operates closely with major international human rights NGOs working in the region and with international organizations.

The EMHRN links its programme of activities to the official agenda of the EMP. It has set up an office in Brussels to follow and influence more effectively developments within the EMP. The office will help to maintain close contacts with the Commission, the EP,[46] the Council of Ministers, international human rights NGOs and international organizations based in Brussels. The EMHRN confronts authoritarian governments permanently with the discrepancies between their declared position on human rights, in particular as enshrined within the Barcelona Declaration, and their actual political performance. By doing so, it puts these governments under growing pressure to defend their repressive behaviour: the loss of control over political discourse is a severe setback for any authoritarian regime, forcing it gradually onto the defensive.

The EMHRN also presses the EU to stick to the commitments it made in the framework of the EMP. As the EU has linked its economic and financial co-operation to the precondition of democratic reform and respect for human rights, the EMHRN puts pressure on the Europeans to transform this principle into political practice. It recommends the use of positive conditionality, pressing the EU to offer stronger incentives for governments engaged in political reforms.[47] The EMHRN has focused on the Commission's 2000 document advocating a higher priority to be attached to the promotion of human rights and democratization, pressing the Council of Ministers to show the political will to act on this recommendation.[48]

In Brussels and EU member states the EMHRN has gained respect as an integrative, professional and politically credible consultant, and has benefited from stable financial EU support.[49] In contrast, the relationship between the network and repressive governments in the South is much more complicated. While dialogue and professional consultation has been a successful lobbying tool in the EU, southern NGOs are inevitably more cautious when addressing their governments. Southern human rights NGOs have to protect themselves against prosecution, but also against governmental co-option. The EMHRN is able to combat this problem, by taking on dialogue with Mediterranean governments as a transnational actor in a way that domestic NGOs would not be able to do on their own.[50]

As an umbrella organization, the EMHRN is open to any independent national or regional organization, or individual, that is active in the struggle for human rights in any of the 27 member countries of the EMP. Due to the politically sensitive issue of human rights, however, strict requirements have to be fulfilled to acquire membership. Application candidates need the support of two regular members and are carefully screened before being accepted. After having proved their active commitment to the struggle for democracy and human rights and their full independence from government authorities, they obtain membership if they gain the unanimous approval of the network's general assembly.[51] Such safety measures are necessary to protect the network from governmental infiltration.

The network tries to balance the interests of northern and southern NGOs, to avoid the dominance of single countries or (sub)-regions, and to reflect the functional diversity of human rights work. An effort is made to reach decisions on the basis of consensus, in order to strengthen confidence and mutual respect. The search for consensus is sometimes a difficult task owing to the extreme heterogeneity of the network. The spectrum extends from large, well-established NGOs through to micro-NGOs comprising only a handful of people. Some of the southern NGO activists have themselves been victims of human rights violations, while northern human rights activists lack this personal experience. Some NGOs are supported by their government, while others are repressed. Furthermore, cultural gaps within the network have to be bridged, not only between North and South but also within these two regions. It has often been difficult to reconcile the variety of interests and needs that exist under the common umbrella of the network. The biggest challenge arises from the fact that member NGOs are in competition with each other for resources. Moreover, all member NGOs are committed primarily to their work at home and have attached only a secondary importance to the interests and needs of the network.

An example of the tensions within the EMHRN was witnessed after the outbreak of the Al-Aqsa *intifada* in autumn 2000. Palestinian NGOs expected their partners in the network to support their fight against Israel's increasingly brutal oppression, not least since the right of self-determination is an essential human right and mentioned as such in the statutes of the network. The Palestinians did indeed gain overwhelming support for their cause. A fact-finding mission was sent to Palestine, reports and open letters were written, and the *intifada* was discussed intensely in meetings. However, the request for solidarity started to incur displeasure from some member NGOs as the ongoing debate on the Middle East conflict started to marginalize other tasks of the network. This internal conflict came to the surface during the Civil Forum in Marseille, when Palestinian NGOs called for a boycott of the Forum in protest against Israeli participation. While most Arab NGOs supported the boycott, members of several European NGOs complained that the Palestinians had exploited the Forum too much for their own interest, neglecting the equally important interests of other NGOs. The EMHRN solved the problem by putting the Palestinian issue at the top of the agenda of the *État de droit et démocracie* workshop. After firmly condemning Israeli human rights violations in the context of the *intifada* and Israel's ongoing neglect for the Palestinian right of self-determination, the workshop was able to give other NGOs room to present their reports on other subjects. This demonstrates how, despite the heterogeneity of its members, the network is held together by the strong commitment of all its members to defend human rights and by the many modest achievements the network has already made, especially as a consultant to the Commission. All members of the network are well aware that it needs the joint effort of a transnational organization to have any impact on the political development of the EMP.

Conclusion

In discussing the role of civil society in the EMP, this study has looked both at the EU's bottom-up approach to democratization and civil society's attempts to make use of this approach. The EU's bottom-up approach has not been implemented with great success. Problems related to the administering of grass-roots projects seem to have been mitigated by an institutional renewal within the Commission. A more serious problem is still unresolved, however: some member states, particularly France and

Spain, have political objections to a strengthening of the EU's democratization policy in the Mediterranean and would actually prefer to see it downgraded even further. Against this background, civil society activists in the region, among them the EMHRN, welcomed the Commission's 2001 communication on democracy and human rights, which indicated a desire to attach greater priority to democracy and human rights. According to the Commission, the promotion of democracy and human rights should no longer be neglected in favour of security and trade interests, but instead become a pivotal objective, cross-cutting all areas of EU foreign relations. It remains to be seen if the pressure of the Commission, the EP and some northern member states will be strong enough to persuade the Council of Ministers to follow suit, especially in the context of the EMP. If this support were forthcoming, this would improve the working conditions for transnational NGOs like the EMHRN and help them to carry out their difficult yet indispensable contribution to the promotion of democracy and human rights in the Euro-Mediterranean region.

NOTES

1. See the Barcelona Declaration adopted at the Euro-Mediterranean Conference (27–28 Nov. 1995), Final Version, *Agence Europe*, 6 Dec. 1996.
2. Ibid.
3. For an evaluation of the EU's asylum policy, see Wolfgang Genz, *Menschenrechte und internationaler Flüchtlingsschutz – Wohin geht die europäische Harmonisierung?*, Amnesty International, Sektion der Bundesrepublik Deutschland, Asylpolitik-Stellungnahme, 20 Jan. 2000. For a critical discussion of Europe's migration policy, see Annette Jünemann, 'Europas Migrationspolitik im Mittelmeerraum – Strategien im Spannungsfeld zwischen Festungsmentalität und neuem Partnerschaftsgeist', in Axel Schulte and Dieter Thränhardt (eds.), *International Migration and Liberal Democracies, Yearbook Migration 1999/2000* (Münster: Lit. Verlag, 1999), pp.185–211.
4. The Barcelona Conference that established the EMP in 1995 was accompanied by two conferences at the level of civil society, the Euromed Civil Forum, discussed later on, and the smaller Alternative Mediterranean Conference (AMC). The AMC was more critical of the EMP.
5. Annette Jünemann, 'Democratization – Reflections on the Political Dimension of the Euro-Mediterranean Partnership', in Peter G. Xuereb (ed.), *The Mediterranean's European Challenge* (Msida: European Documentation and Research Centre, University of Malta, 1998), p.92.
6. The strongest weapon of the EP is the assent procedure. Yet, this instrument is rather blunt and allows no gradual or modified response. Activities in the framework of the newly established Euro-Mediterranean Parliamentarian Forum have comparatively little influence. For details concerning the decision-making procedures in the EMP, see Annette Jünemann, 'Auswärtige Politikgestaltung im EU-Mehrebenensystem. Eine Analyse der strukturellen Probleme am Beispiel der Euro-Mediterranen Partnerschaft', in Gisela Müller-Brandeck-Bocquet and Klaus Schubert (eds.), *Die Europäische Union als Akteur der Weltpolitik* (Opladen: Leske und Budrich, 2000), pp.65–80.

7. For an in-depth reflection on civil society in European thought, see Charles Taylor, 'Die Beschwörung der Civil-Society', in Michalski von Krzysztof (ed.), *Europa und die Civil Society* (Stuttgart: Castelgandolfo-Gespräche, 1989), pp.52–81.
8. R. Mabro, 'Civil Society in the History of Ideas in European History', in Arab Thought Forum and Bruno Kreisky Forum (eds.), *The Role of NGOs in the Development of Civil Society – Europe and the Arab Countries* (Amman and Vienna: Arab Thought Forum, 1999), p.46.
9. For the problem of defining civil society, see Jean L. Cohen and Andrew Arato, *Civil Society and Political Theory* (Cambridge, MA: MIT, 1995).
10. This can be problematic: in the Mediterranean efficient NGO structures are needed to resist repression and persecution. The internal organization of NGOs therefore often reflects the authoritarian structures of the regime they oppose. European standards of internal democracy can thus not simply be transferred to the MPCs. On the sometimes problematic internal structure of civil society associations, see Wolfgang Merkel and Hans-Joachim Lauth, 'Systemwechsel und Zivilgesellschaft – Welche Zivilgesellschaft braucht die Demokratie?', *Aus Politik und Zeitgeschichte*, B No.6–7 (1998), pp.3–12.
11. For the contemporary discussion of civil society in the Arab world, see Ibrahim Ferhad and Heidi Wedel (eds.), *Probleme der Zivilgesellschaft im Vorderen Orient* (Opladen: Leske und Budrich, 1995).
12. Emmanuel Richter, 'Die europäische Zivilgesellschaft', in Klaus Dieter Wolf (ed.), *Projekt Europa im Übergang?* (Baden Baden: Nomos Verlag, 1997).
13. For the role of private business, see Jillan Schwedler, 'Introduction', in Jillan Schwedler (ed.), *Civil Society and the Study of Middle East Politics* (London, 1995), pp.1–32.
14. Mabro, op. cit., p.47.
15. Ibid., p.39.
16. Ibrahim Ferhad, 'Die arabische Debatte über Zivilgesellschaft', in Ferhad and Wedel, op. cit., p.39.
17. Ibid., p.28.
18. The need to integrate political Islam into Euro–Arab intercultural relations was one of the results of the Third German–Arab Media Dialogue. See Institut für Auslandskunde (ed.), *Deutsch-arabischer Mediendialog* (Stuttgart, dokumente No.3, 1999).
19. Radical groups are also often engaged in social welfare, so that charitable activities are not a sufficient criteria for choosing a partner organization.
20. Saad Eddin Ibrahim, 'Democratization in the Arab World', in Schwedler, op. cit., p.38.
21. See European Commission, DG I, *Manuel des Programmes MED. Votre Guide pour le Partenariat Euro-Méditerranéen* (Brussels: European Commission, 1996).
22. See Court of Auditors, *Special Report* (Brussels: Court of Auditors, 1996).
23. Author interviews, Directorates General (DG) IB, Brussels, Sept. 1996.
24. MEDA Democracy, Euro-Mediterranean Partnership, Information Note No.2, European Commission, Unit IB/A.1, Sept. 1997.
25. See MEDA Democracy Programme, Budget Line B7-705N, Criteria and Conditions of Eligibility, DG IB/A2, Brussels, 25 April 1996. MEDA Democracy was part of the European Initiative for Democracy and Human Rights, launched by the EP in 1994 to bring a series of budget headings specifically dealing with the promotion of democracy and human rights together in a single chapter (B7-70).
26. See Euro-Mediterranean Human Rights Network, *The MEDA Democracy Programme, Recommendations by the Euro-Mediterranean Human Rights Network (EMHRN) to the European Commission, the European Parliament and the EU Member States regarding the MEDA Democracy Programme* (Copenhagen: EMHRN, May 2000), p.4f.
27. Ibid., p.4. To avoid further political conflict between the governments of the MPCs and the EU in the context of MEDA Democracy, the Commission avoided co-operation with NGOs promoting the interests of ethnic minorities (for example, the Kurds in Turkey) and NGOs belonging to the Islamist spectrum.
28. See Khémais Chammari and Caroline Stainer, *Guide to Human Rights in the Barcelona Process* (Copenhagen: EMHRN, 2000), p.108.
29. See Council Regulation (EC) No.975/1999 and Council Regulation No.976/1999, which

came into effect on 11 May 1999.

30. For further information on the Euromed Heritage Programme, see 'The Euromed Heritage Programme – Cultural Heritage at the Heart of the Euro-Mediterranean Partnership', *Euromed Special Feature*, No.7, 29 Sept. 2000.
31. For more on Euromed Audiovisual, see http://europa.eu.int/comm/avpolicy/extern/coop_ de. htm.
32. For further information on the Euromed Youth Action Programme, see http://europa.eu.int/comm/education/youth/youthprogram.html.
33. For an analysis of the Euromed Civil Forum, see Annette Jünemann, 'The Forum Civil Euromed. Critical Watchdog and Intercultural Mediator', in Stefania Panebianco (ed.), *The Euro-Mediterranean Partnership in Social, Cultural and Human Affairs – The Human Dimension of Security as the Key to Stability and Prosperity* (London: Frank Cass, forthcoming).
34. For the results of the Forum in Barcelona 1995, see Institut Català Mediterrània, *Towards a New Scenario of Partnership in the Euro-Mediterranean Area, Forum Civil Euromed* (Barcelona: Institut Català Mediterrània, 1996). For the results of the Forum in Marseille 2000, see http://www.euromed_ong.org/decla_finales/decla_ong.htm. The Forum in Malta 1997 was comparatively small and restricted to a politically less challenging cultural dialogue. See Foundation for International Studies at the University of Malta (ed.), *Intercultural Dialogue in the Mediterranean. Civil Forum Euromed in Malta* (Valletta: Foundation, 1997).
35. Civil society's room for manoeuvre was wider in Stuttgart because Germany has no priority national interests in the region that could be challenged through a civil society conference. Furthermore, a new government had just come to power.
36. The Friedrich Ebert Stiftung functioned as host and co-ordinator, delegating the task of choosing the participants to two trustworthy partner organizations, the Euro-Mediterranean Human Rights Network and the Forum des Citoyens de la Méditerranée.
37. The human rights conference of Stuttgart is documented in Friedrich Ebert Foundation (ed.), *Human Rights and Civil Society in the Mediterranean, Stuttgart 15–16 Apr 1999* (Bonn: FES, 1999).
38. Marseille hosted one conference for the trade unions, a second one for local authorities and a third for NGOs.
39. These complaints are documented in Commission of the European Communities, *Report from the Commission on the implementation of measures intended to promote observance of human rights and democratic principles in external relations for 1996 – 1999* (Brussels: European Commission, 2000), p.86.
40. *Euromed Special Feature*, No.10, 10 April 2001.
41. See Communication of the Commission to the Council and the European Parliament, *The European Union's role in promoting human rights and democratisation in third countries*, Brussels, 8 May 2001, COM(2001) 252 final.
42. Ibid., p.13f.
43. According to its statutes, it is a 'non-partisan and non-profit membership organization dedicated to the welfare of the community'. Statutes of the Euro-Mediterranean Human Rights Network (EMHRN), approved by the Second General Assembly of the EMHRN at its meeting in Copenhagen, 12–13 Dec. 1997, p.1.
44. See Euro-Mediterranean Human Rights Network, 'Plan of Action', adopted at the Fourth General Assembly, Nov. 2000.
45. http://www.euromedrights.net.
46. The EMHRN advocates the establishment of a human rights committee within the framework of the Euro-Mediterranean Interparliamentary Forum, having the mandate to address human rights issues, including individual cases and country issues. See Euro-Mediterranean Human Rights Network, 'Plan of Action', p.7f.
47. See Euro-Mediterranean Human Rights Network, 'The Role of Human Rights in the EU's Mediterranean Policy. Setting Article 2 in Motion', European Parliament, Brussels, 9 Nov. 1999.
48. See Euro-Mediterranean Human Rights Network, 70th Information letter, Copenhagen, 7

June 2001. Another document of importance in this context is European Commission, 'Reinvigorating the Barcelona Process', *Agence Europe*, 14 Sept. 2000, a working document of the European Commission Services prepared for the 'think tank' meeting of Euro-Mediterranean Foreign Ministers, Lisbon, 25–26 May 2000. In this document the Commission proposes that preferential aid should be given to countries that engage in human rights and democratization reforms.

49. Funding an umbrella organization instead of single NGOs is in line with the Commission's new strategy to fund big rather than small projects. In June 1999, the EMHRN submitted a €2.5m project to the Commission covering the period 1 Jan. 2000 to 31 Dec. 2003. The project was finally approved at the end of 1999 and the contract was signed in late May 2000. See EMHRN Annual Report of Activities, http://www.euromedrights.net.
50. Regarding the dialogue conducted by members of the network with their respective governments, the EMHRN is in the process of designing a toolbox with good examples and methodologies, taking into consideration the different cultural and religious traditions and approaches to dialogues. See Euro-Mediterranean Human Rights Network, 'Plan of Action'.
51. The question of whether or not affiliation with political Islam is compatible with the statutes of the network has not been an issue of discussion until now, because no Islamist NGO or individual has ever shown interest in membership.

Dancing in the Dark: The European Union and the Algerian Drama

HUGH ROBERTS

> The European Union reconfirms its willingness to support a policy of democratic development and economic restructuring in Algeria. (Declaration by the European Union on Algeria, Brussels, 23 January 1995).[1]

> *Algeria*
> 76. The European Union stands ready to assist the political, economic and social reforms necessary for restoring peace, stability and prosperity. (Excerpt from the final communiqué of the Meeting of the European Council, Göteborg, Sweden, 15–16 June 2001).[2]

> Madam President, if we are absolutely honest with ourselves, we do not actually know what to do about Algeria. (Gary Titley [PES], in the debate on Algeria in the European Parliament, 17 September 1997).[3]

The concern to promote political stability, democratic principles and respect for human rights, as well as economic reform, has been a prominent element of the European Union's formal orientation to the states of the southern shore of the Mediterranean for some years. It assumed the status of an explicit commitment in the Barcelona Declaration, which launched the Euro-Mediterranean Partnership (EMP) in November 1995, but had already been a feature of European policy pronouncements for some time before this and, indeed, before the metamorphosis of the European Community (EC) into the European Union (EU) in 1993. How, then, are we to understand the Algerian experience as a case study in European policy? Algeria in 2001 – six years after the launching of the EMP, and eight years after the establishing of the EU and the inauguration of its Common Foreign and Security Policy (CFSP) – is neither stable nor a democracy nor a country where human rights, as a rule, are respected, nor is it a country generally reckoned to have satisfactorily completed the undertaking referred to as 'economic reform'.

Is Algeria a case of European policy failure? Two related difficulties in the way of answering this question concern the EU's political influence in the Algerian situation, and its responsibilities in respect of it.

Looked at from the vantage point of Brussels or Strasbourg, the EU's role may seem to bulk large. Looked at from the vantage point of Paris or Algiers, on the other hand, one suspects that it assumes more modest proportions. That the policy decisions on Algeria taken by or in a number of individual European states (notably, but not only, France) have been important is self-evident, but it is not self-evident that the EU's policy decisions have counted for much or that the EU has figured among the major *dramatis personae*; for much of the time, it has arguably been no more than one among several sources of 'noises off', or the provenance of minor players performing limited walk-on parts in Algiers itself – visiting Commissioners or Troika members or EP delegations – usually with few interesting lines to deliver and little impact on events.

If the true role of the EU has been secondary and modest, we should recognize that its responsibility in this matter has been limited. But we can properly enter this plea of diminished responsibility for the policy failure that has apparently occurred only if we also insist that the EU's own rhetoric has been seriously misleading in this connection. For, in committing itself to promote democratic principles – if not, indeed, to insist on their observance – elsewhere and in Algeria in particular, the EU has taken a lot on itself. The question is: *has it been in earnest*? Has official European rhetoric expressed a real – and enormous – ambition, or merely a vast pretension?

If the pertinence of these questions is admitted, the EU can evade responsibility for the failure of its Algerian policy only by pleading guilty to the (lesser?) charge of miscalculating the relationship between ends and means and overestimating its possibilities, or by admitting that either it has not really had a policy – as distinct from a line of patter – on Algeria or that its true policy has not been to promote stability, democracy or human rights in Algeria but has had other objectives.

In order to arbitrate between these hypotheses, we must first establish what Europe's positions on the Algerian drama have actually been.

Algeria's Partner

Retrospect often plays tricks. The grim knowledge which constitutes so much of our hindsight with respect to Algeria today makes it difficult to remember that the Euro-Mediterranean Partnership might well have appeared to at least some of its architects to have been initiated at a propitious moment. The conference in Barcelona which launched it on 27–28 November 1995 opened a mere 11 days after the presidential elections in Algeria. After nearly four years of dreadful violence, Algeria had returned to the electoral process at last and in a manner that had astonished most observers.

That the election had been held at all, let alone in an orderly manner, was remarkable, given the grounds for dismissing the prospect as fanciful when it was first mooted in 1994. Moreover, it was at least formally more democratic than almost all other presidential elections in the region as well as all previous presidential elections in Algeria. Three candidates had been allowed to run against the incumbent head of state, Liamine Zeroual – itself an unprecedented event, two of them had obtained respectable votes,[4] and Zeroual's victory had been of modest and credible proportions (61 per cent of the vote) by comparison with the tallies officially attributed to elected heads of states in Egypt or Tunisia. Finally, turnout had been spectacularly high; the official figure of 75.69 per cent, while perhaps inflated, was not seriously disputed, and few observers denied the electoral as well as constitutional legitimacy which Zeroual now enjoyed.

One might have expected this event to be warmly welcomed by the European Union. At the very moment that the EU was committing itself to promoting political stability and democratic principles among its prospective Mediterranean partners, one of these, whose crisis had been widely perceived as a threat to stability and democratic prospects throughout North Africa as a whole, seemed to be pulling itself together and resuming its 'transition to democracy'. What more encouraging development could there have been on the eve of the Barcelona Conference? Yet, far from expressing enthusiasm or congratulating the Algerian authorities, the European Union took a very different line. The official declaration published in Brussels on 20 November read as follows:

> The European Union takes note of the result of the Presidential Elections in Algeria and welcomes the fact that the elections were held in an atmosphere of calm. The observed level of participation reflects the firm will of the Algerian people to find solutions to their problems by peaceful means.
>
> The European Union hopes that these elections will be followed by rapid and effective progress towards the organization of legislative and local elections, with the aim of political normalization of the country by means of peaceful dialogue and free and incontestable elections.

> The European Union will pursue and, in line with developments in Algeria, intensify its co-operation in order to develop the potential for economic partnership, as well as sustain activities and programmes for economic adjustment and reform in Algeria, taking account of the relationship which exists between resolving political problems and the viability of such reforms.[5]

Modified rapture, one might think. The statement offered no recognition of the pluralist aspect of the election or any acknowledgement of the credibility of Zeroual's personal vote, nor that the election result, by enhancing his authority to broker a definitive settlement, might prove a turning point in the crisis. Instead, the EU merely took 'note of the result' in cool if not chilly tones and implied that the elections were, if anything, less than satisfactory in themselves by expressing the hope that they would be 'followed by rapid and effective progress towards the organization of legislative and local elections', and 'incontestable' ones at that.

Why did the EU take this line? Whether we regard it as grudging or merely cautious, it clearly offered not a word of support to the Algerian authorities. As for the European Parliament, which had already found time to debate and pass five resolutions on Algeria in the course of the year, it apparently attached no importance to the election, for no motions were tabled in respect of it and no debate took place.[6]

The EU's response to the 1995 presidential election provides grounds for the hypothesis that its true attitude was much less supportive of the Algerian authorities' attempts to resolve by political means the crisis they faced than EU rhetoric has generally suggested. And European policy towards Algeria over the previous three years corroborates this reading.

Making a Drama out of a Crisis: Europe and Algeria, 1991–94

Mohammed, Prend Ton Cercueil!

When the Algerian army deposed President Chadli Benjedid in January 1992 and aborted the election which had promised to give the Islamic Salvation Front (Front Islamique du Salut, or FIS) a large majority in the national assembly, the European Parliament responded by attaching political conditions to future EC financial aid to Algeria; henceforward, aid under the fourth financial protocol covering 1992–96 would be conditional on progress towards democracy.[7] This did not, however, apply to the Ecu 400m emergency loan to support Algeria's balance of payments which had been agreed the previous autumn, for the first instalment of this, worth Ecu 250m, was disbursed in January 1992.[8] But no new loans were forthcoming for a long time, and the second instalment of the 1991 loan was put on ice. And thereby hangs a tale.

The Council decision of 23 September 1991 to provide the loan had stipulated that the second and final instalment, worth Ecu 150m, was to be released 'after a period of at least two quarters' after the first instalment, subject to certain economic – but not political – conditions. The loan had been made 'with a view to ensuring a sustainable balance of payments situation, strengthening the reserve position, and facilitating the introduction of convertibility for the national currency', objectives premised on Algeria's exceptional balance of payments financing needs in 1991 and 1992, but also, more importantly, on the Algerian authorities' commitment to 'accelerate market-related reforms'. The Council made disbursement of the first instalment conditional on 'an arrangement between Algeria and its commercial bank creditors on improving the country's future debt servicing and repayment profile through new loans and/or new refinancing agreements' (a formula which, we may note, did not necessarily mean rescheduling), and stipulated that the second instalment would be released subject to verification by the Commission 'that the economic policy in Algeria is in accordance with the objectives of this loan and that its conditions are being fulfilled'.[9]

Despite this, the meeting of EC foreign ministers in Lisbon on 17 February 1992, while expressing its wish 'to provide help to Algeria', implicitly invoked the view expressed by the European Parliament on 15 January by linking this help to 'respect for human rights, tolerance and political pluralism'.[10]

Mélanie Morisse-Schilbach has suggested that the EC foreign ministers' position was more flexible than the Parliament's on the matter of human rights and so forth, since it only expressed the hope that these would be respected, rather than making this respect a condition of future aid, and she has argued that the substance of the conditionality introduced at this meeting regarding aid to Algeria was economic, not political, and concerned 'the necessary' – but notably unspecified – 'structural economic reforms which the Algerian authorities had to undertake'.[11] Moreover, it was not clear that the Parliament's position in January necessarily implied a freeze on the second instalment of the 1991 loan, still less that, if it did, it was impossible to persuade the Parliament to think again. That something could be done was clearly the view of a galaxy of leading French personalities, including former prime ministers Raymond Barre and Pierre Mauroy, who published an 'Appeal' in *Le Monde* on 18 March which declared 'At a moment when Algeria is traversing a grave economic and social crisis, we call on the French government and the European Community to furnish it with the support it needs'.[12]

However, this appeal was ignored by the French government and had no effect on the European position, which remained unchanged for the next three months. It was only after the meeting of the Council of Europe in Lisbon on 26–29 June that matters appeared to evolve, with the despatch to Algiers in July of a technical mission 'to study the conditions and modalities of the implementation of the fourth financial protocol and the unblocking of the second instalment of the balance of payments loan granted in 1991'.[13]

On 29 June, President Mohammed Boudiaf, one of the founders of the historic National Liberation Front (Front de Libération Nationale, FLN, in 1954)[14] who had returned from exile to head the High State Committee set up on 14 January to fill the vacant presidency for the remainder of Chadli's unfinished term, was assassinated. The intensity of public grief and disarray in Algeria at this event testified to the impression which Boudiaf had made on Algerian opinion and the extent of his success in winning the trust and respect of the Algerian people. Because his death deprived the regime of the only candidate it had who was capable of winning a popular mandate in a genuinely free presidential election, it destroyed all prospect of the progress towards democracy which the European Parliament had called for in January, and condemned Algeria to unconstitutional as well as undemocratic rule for the foreseeable future.[15] In addition, because his assassination was attributed by public opinion to one or another faction of the regime, it undid all that Boudiaf had done to restore the legitimacy of the state in the eyes of the people and gave fresh arguments to the Islamist rebellion.

From Lisbon, the Portuguese presidency of the European Community issued a statement expressing its consternation and the European Community's solidarity with Algeria.[16] This solidarity had not been worth a single Ecu between January and the end of June 1992, beyond the first instalment of the loan originally proposed in June 1991 and agreed in September 1991.

The Reason for Delay

Whatever achievements the technical mission dispatched to Algiers in July 1992 could claim, the unblocking of the second instalment of the 1991 loan was not among them. Eight months later, Claude Cheysson, leading a delegation of visiting MEPs, gave a press conference on 31 March 1993 in Algiers in which he reportedly expressed surprise at the obstructing of the second part of the loan provided by the protocol of agreement between Algeria and the EC.[17] Nine months later, the *Financial Times*, quoting EU officials, reported that until Algeria got 'into bed with the IMF' and produced 'a nice baby in the form of an economic reform programme', the second tranche of the 1991 loan would remain frozen.[18]

This prediction was accurate. On 16 May 1994, Jacques Delors proposed an EU aid package to Algeria which would include new loans worth at least $200m in addition to the blocked second tranche of the 1991 loan,[19] and a fortnight later the EU Troïka visiting Algiers reportedly confirmed the release of the second tranche.[20] Confirming its release fell short of actually releasing it, however. It was not until August that the *Middle East Economic Digest* was able, correctly, to report the EU's plans to release 'in the coming weeks' the Ecu 150m in question.[21]

Thus the second instalment of an emergency loan for balance of payments support during 1991 and 1992, which could have been released in July 1992, was delayed for over two years beyond that date. Of the other financial assistance agreed in principle by the EC during this period, a structural adjustment loan (SAL) worth Ecu 70m to fund housing projects was also subject to repeated delays,[22] as were smaller loans from the European Investment Bank (EIB) to help finance two dams.[23] As for the new loan proposed by Delors, this – now Ecu 200m – was finally granted in principle on 22 December 1994, to be disbursed in two instalments subject to the Algerian government's acceptance of 'economic policy conditions' to be negotiated subsequently.[24]

Why did Europe display this dilatoriness in the face of Algeria's deepening crisis? The answer is simple. The real policy of the EC and its successor the EU was to force the Algerian government to accept the rescheduling of Algeria's debt and all that this entailed, the obligation to undertake a structural adjustment programme dictated by the IMF. After January 1992, no funds were released until this objective had been attained, and the promise of funds was used as a lever to secure compliance. All other policy considerations – stability, democracy, respect for human rights – were sacrificed to this objective.

From War Economy to Terror Economics

Following Boudiaf's death, the High State Committee appointed Ali Kafi as its President and formal head of state, and Belaid Abdesselam to head a new government. These moves reflected a concern to mobilize historical and nationalist legitimacy to counter the Islamist rebellion, since neither democratic nor constitutional legitimacy were available to the regime and its claim to Islamic legitimacy was, of course, also contested. Kafi was the general secretary of the Organisation Nationale des Moudjahidine (the war veterans' association),[25] and was well known for his support for arabization, an important element of the Islamists' programme and appeal. Abdesselam also had strong nationalist credentials as a political activist before, during and after the war of liberation.[26] It was Abdesselam who had founded Sonatrach, the state hydrocarbons company, in 1963 and who, as minister for industry and energy from 1965 to 1977, had been the architect of Algeria's strategy for taking control of her oil and gas and using their revenues to finance an ambitious industrialization programme. In retirement since the 'de-Boumédiènization' of the early 1980s, he had preserved a reputation as a man of integrity with the courage of his convictions. As such, his appointment was also a response to the popular demand for firm and honest government which the FIS had exploited but which the better elements of the nationalist tradition could also hope to accommodate.

Because its nationalist credentials were vital to it, the regime could not agree to reschedule except at prohibitive political cost, since this meant surrendering Algeria's national sovereignty in the economic sphere and thus the regime's own nationalist legitimacy. And to accept rescheduling was to accept a structural adjustment programme which would aggravate the economic distress of the sectors of the Algerian population which the regime needed to win back from the Islamist rebellion.

Moreover, the Algerians argued, there was no need to reschedule. With its hydrocarbons and other mineral resources, Algeria was in principle a solvent country, and its repayments record was immaculate. These two factors alone – quite apart from the political crisis – entitled it to expect understanding and flexibility on the part of its creditors. Above all, its debt problem was primarily the result of mismanagement during the 1980s, which had saddled Algeria with an excessive amount of short-term debt. The EC itself had recognized, in the text of the Council decision granting the 1991 loan, that the 'heavy external debt servicing payments' which explained Algeria's 'exceptional balance of payments financing needs' were 'related to short-term borrowing and a bunching of repayments on medium-term debt'.[27]

Abdesselam's strategy, which he called 'war economy', was to reduce the payments problem to manageable proportions by persuading Algeria's creditors to agree to 're-profile' Algeria's debt (that is, convert short-term into medium- or long-term debt) so as to reduce the 'bunching of repayments' and thereby reduce the debt service ratio, while imposing an egalitarian austerity policy through strict control of the import programme to enable Algeria to maintain her repayments and obviate the recourse to rescheduling.[28] Since Algeria's national sovereignty was at stake and IMF-imposed structural adjustment would entail at least as much hardship as the austerity programme Abdesselam envisaged, he expected to be able to obtain domestic public acceptance of this policy, and thereby 'restore the authority of the state' in the eyes of public opinion. In addition to these arguments in its favour, his approach had the support of Algeria's second biggest creditor, Japan, which was flatly opposed to the rescheduling of Algeria's debt.[29]

None of this counted for anything with the EC policy-makers, who gave no support whatsoever to this strategy. Abdesselam's failure to secure the general consent of Algeria's creditors to his debt re-profiling proposal meant that his 'war economy' strategy was limping within a few months of his taking office, the regime's capacity to remobilize popular nationalist sentiment in support of it was undermined, and the self-confidence of and support for the Islamist rebellion grew, while debates within the regime increasingly pitted factions against one another and subverted its cohesion.

These were the circumstances that saw a dramatic escalation of the violence in the first half of 1993, with a wave of assassinations of prominent personalities and the onset of a climate of fear. Eventually the army commanders bowed to European pressure and replaced Abdesselam as prime minister on 21 August 1993 with Redha Malek, whose new government promptly signalled its willingness to reschedule,[30] although this decision was not finalized until 1994. Following Abdesselam's fall, the first of over a 100 lethal attacks on foreigners resident in Algeria occurred near Oran on 21 September, the world began to hear of an extremist faction within the Islamist rebellion called the Armed Islamic Group (Groupe Islamique Armée, GIA), and Malek, an admirer of the French Jacobins, entered history with his declaration that '*la peur doit changer de camp*' ('fear must change sides'), which confirmed the policy of state terror.

It was only after all this water had passed under the bridge that the European Parliament called, on 28 October, for the cancellation of Algeria's debts with her European creditors.[31] No one seems to have told the MEPs that the matter had already been decided, and no one paid any attention to their resolution.

The Politics of Dialogue

Following the expiry of the High State Committee's lease on life in December 1993, defence minister Liamine Zeroual was appointed to the position of 'President of the State' in January 1994. The regime's surrender of its nationalist pretensions in the economic sphere and the prospect of an aggravation of popular hardship as structural adjustment began to bite, combined with opposition within ruling circles to the terror policy, lent weight to the argument that there was nothing for it but to start talking to the rebels and negotiate an end to the crisis.[32] This was the policy explored by Zeroual, who immediately released two of the FIS leaders imprisoned since June 1991 with a view to sounding out the more flexible wing of the rebellion about a possible settlement.[33] But Zeroual's moves precipitated a vigorous conflict within the power structure, as factional divisions erupted in the dispute between so-called 'conciliators' and 'eradicators', the latter counting the army chief of staff, Major General Mohammed Lamari, among their number, not to mention Redha Malek, whom Zeroual had retained to finalize the agreement with the IMF and who publicly contradicted his president until Zeroual replaced him with Mokdad Sifi in April.[34]

Having had to drop his 'dialogue open to all' as a condition of getting his way over personnel changes in the regime,[35] Zeroual returned to this approach in August, inviting eight political parties for talks on how to secure a return to the electoral process. Five parties accepted – the FLN, ex-president Ahmed Ben Bella's Movement for Democracy in Algeria (MDA), Mahfoud Nahnah's HAMAS, Abdallah Djaballah's Movement of the Islamic Nahda (MNI) and Noureddine Boukrouh's Party of Algerian Renewal (PRA). The two secular 'eradicator' parties, Saïd Sadi's Rally for Culture and Democracy (RCD) and the ex-communist Ettahaddi, both rejected the invitation, as did Hocine Aït Ahmed's Socialist Forces Front (FFS), despite its 'conciliatory' profile.[36] It soon emerged that the parties participating in the talks favoured including the banned FIS in the dialogue process. Zeroual was accordingly able to hold talks with the senior imprisoned FIS leaders, Abassi Madani and Ali Ben Hadj, and these initially went so well that on 13 September he felt able to release three other FIS leaders completely as well as move Abassi and Ben Hadj from prison to house arrest to facilitate their consultations with the rest of the FIS leadership.

It was at this point that an abrupt escalation of the violence occurred such that it proved impossible for Abassi to consult, even indirectly, those leaders of the armed rebellion disposed to consider a settlement, and the whole process ground to a halt. This escalation began *immediately* on 13 September[37] and within a week it was clear that the deal which had seemed so close was in terrible trouble, with prominent 'eradicators' speaking out against it and previous supporters of the talks sliding off the 'dialogue' bandwagon. When Noureddine Boukrouh publicly opposed consultations with the rebel leaders on 24 September, the writing was on the wall. Although Zeroual did not announce the failure of his efforts for several weeks, everything from the last week of September onwards had been a kind of endgame, nothing more.

On 26 September the EU Presidency issued a declaration welcoming 'the renewed efforts to promote political dialogue in Algeria' and calling on 'all sides to cease all acts of violence immediately to allow a peaceful dialogue'.[38] The policy content of this was irreproachable. But an effective political declaration is not only a matter of content; it is also a matter of timing. Saying the right thing at the wrong time is worthless at best; at worst, it is the perfect way to let someone down while covering one's own flanks for the record. The EU Presidency's timing in this matter was exquisite. But we can only say that it was exquisitely bad if we assume that it had sincerely intended to give Zeroual's attempt to broker a settlement the external endorsement and reinforcement it needed. If this had truly been its purpose, why did it wait five weeks after the talks began on 21 August before 'supporting' them?

The Return to the Electoral Process, 1995–97

When Zeroual announced the failure of 'dialogue' on 31 October, he also announced his decision to cut short the three-year 'transition period' for which he had been appointed in January by holding presidential elections a year early. It was only after he had committed himself to this that the main opposition parties – the FLN, the FFS and the banned FIS – together with the MDA, the MNI, Louisa Hanoune's Workers' Party (Parti des Travailleurs, PT) and Abdennour Ali Yahia's Algerian League for the Defence of Human Rights (Ligue Algérienne pour la Défense des Droits de l'Homme, LADDH), met in Rome under the aegis of the Catholic Sant' Egidio Community in January 1995 and published on 13 January a *Platform for a Peaceful Political Solution of the Algerian Crisis*.[39]

This platform was mostly very reasonable and constructive, and elements of it could have complemented Zeroual's project. It should be remembered that the opposition parties had been demanding 'the return to the electoral process' since January 1992, that this return had to start with the presidency, given the constitutional vacuum at this level, and that this was what Zeroual had undertaken to organize. In practice, however, the Rome Platform developed into a rival to his project, and the political field was polarized by this rivalry for most of 1995.

Many have blamed the regime for this. On 18 January, an official statement in Algiers flatly rejected the Rome Platform. But this was not necessarily the end of the matter, for the vigorous statement of positions which are formally opposed is often only round one of a complex process of bargaining. Given the division in the army leadership, Zeroual could not afford to jeopardize his own project by appearing to defer to the opposition at the outset, but this did not mean that he had no interest in taking on board important elements of their platform as far as circumstances allowed, as subsequent developments suggested.[40] The very next day, however, the European Parliament passed a resolution which completely ignored Zeroual's commitment to hold presidential elections and invoked the Rome Platform in terms which implied that it furnished the *only* 'proposals aimed at breaking the deadlock obtaining in Algeria'; moreover, it both welcomed these proposals in themselves, 'in particular the renunciation of violence', and called 'on the Algerian Government to engage in a dialogue with the democratic opposition forces with the aim of establishing a democratic general election process'.[41]

This resolution misrepresented the Rome Platform in two respects. The platform did not include a total renunciation of violence, since the FIS signatories were not willing to cut themselves off from the Islamic guerrilla forces and insisted on a formula which tacitly endorsed the violence employed in a 'legitimate' rebellion, while renouncing violence in other contexts. Moreover, the resolution's call for 'a ... *general* election process' implied that it was legislative, not presidential, elections which should be held. But, whereas the Rome Platform had called for the holding of 'free and pluralist elections', it had *not* stipulated that these should be legislative or general elections; it had left this matter entirely open, and had therefore left its signatories with room to manoeuvre in respect of Zeroual's proposal to begin with presidential elections.

In this way the European Parliament couched its notional support for the Rome Platform in terms which misrepresented the Platform and pitted its signatories explicitly against Zeroual's project. Four days later, on 23 January, the Council issued a *Declaration on National Reconciliation* which made an imprecise reference to the Rome talks, but expressed its 'interest' in them and encouraged 'all participants in Algerian political life to agree on ways and means of developing the spirit of this dialogue and pursuing the concrete ideas that may arise from it'.[42] Insofar as these phrases amounted to anything, they tacitly echoed the Parliament's line; they certainly did not correct the damage done by the latter's reference to general elections and, like the EP's resolution, ignored Zeroual's commitment to hold presidential elections, and so reinforced the suggestion that the opposition's initiative was the only one in play.

Did the EU know what it was doing in January 1995?

A serious political intervention is one that calculates the likely reactions of other players. In tacitly endorsing the Rome Platform, the EU was tacitly supporting one of its central demands, namely the rehabilitation of the FIS. A case could certainly be made for this demand, even if, following the failure of dialogue the previous autumn, there was little prospect of Algiers accepting it in the short term, but for the EU to associate itself with this demand was enormously provocative, in view of Europe's previous positions. For not only had Europe failed to support the earlier dialogue effectively, it had said and done nothing when the FIS had originally been banned. Moreover, Zeroual had played no part in that decision, since he had been in retirement at the time; the situation he was trying to deal with in 1994–95 had been bequeathed to him by his predecessors in power as a *fait accompli*. He was not responsible for the banning of the FIS, and was facing an unmistakable veto on its re-legalization from his army chiefs, a veto which had enjoyed the vigorous support of French diplomacy throughout most of 1994.[43]

In these circumstances the EU had two coherent and defensible options. The first was to give democratic principles overriding priority over other (for example, economic) policy aims, perform a convincing *mea culpa* in respect of its earlier acquiescence in the banning of the FIS, give full support to the Rome Platform and its signatories, and brace itself for a protracted conflict with the regime. The alternative was to recognize the moral complexity of the situation and the existence of both proposals to break the deadlock, and take a position which maximized the possibility of a compromise of some kind between the signatories of the Rome Platform and President Zeroual.

Instead, the intervention of the EU at this delicate moment failed to give the Rome Platform *effective* support while tending, through the partisan tenor of its public positions, to make it harder than it otherwise might have been for a constructive dialogue between government and opposition to occur. Moreover, the same partisan attitude was even more evident in two further resolutions passed in quick succession by the Parliament on 16 March and 6 April, neither of which made any mention of Zeroual's project to hold a presidential election.[44] Whatever the reason for the EU's behaviour, it can be seen that the chilly tones of its declaration after the presidential election in November 1995 was consistent with its attitude before this event, namely one of unexplained hostility to it.

This attitude persisted thereafter. Despite its previous championing of dialogue, the EU issued not one declaration throughout 1996, whether supportive or critical, concerning the lengthy rounds of dialogue which President Zeroual held in April and July or the conference he organized with the parties in September, and made no comment whatever on the constitutional proposals which he submitted to all the partners in this dialogue process on 11 May and also made public. The European Parliament concentrated on the issue of press freedom, about which it passed two resolutions critical of the Algerian authorities in March and July,[45] and addressed the constitutional revision which had been the central issue throughout 1996 only on 12 December, that is after the matter had been decided in the referendum of 28 November. The resolution it voted contained a vehement criticism of the new constitution and supported *both* the re-legalization of the FIS *and* the idea of a secular state.[46] Meanwhile the Council and the Presidency maintained a studied silence throughout this crucial year.

On 6 February 1997, President Zeroual invited the United Nations, the Organization of African Unity and the Arab League (that is, international bodies to which Algeria herself belonged) to send observers for the legislative elections scheduled for 5 June. Despite the urgings of individual MEPs, the EU neither welcomed this initiative nor encouraged its own member states to contribute to the UN's mission; it said and did nothing.[47] France sent no observers at all, citing security concerns as its excuse.[48] The United Kingdom sent two observers;[49] most other EU member states sent a handful or none. Only Greece responded positively to Zeroual's invitation and sent 15.[50] On 5 June the elections were duly held, and produced a National Assembly in which 10 parties were represented including four of the signatories of the Rome Platform – the FLN (now under new and docile management) but also the still combative FFS and PT and Djaballah's MN.[51] Of the 380 deputies, 103 belonged to the Islamist parties (MSP and MN), 27 per cent of the total.

It was at this point that the EU's discourse underwent a peculiar change.

Accompanying Algeria

> [O]ur role is to accompany and encourage the different institutions to assume their proper role in this long process of peace. (George Wohlfart, president-in-office of the Council, replying to the debate on Algeria in the European Parliament on 17 September 1997).[52]

From 15 January 1992 to June 1997, the essence of the European discourse on Algeria had been a critique of the regime on democratic grounds. While the Parliament had been more uninhibited than the Council, resolutions and declarations alike clearly expressed a negative judgement on the Algerian authorities founded on the undemocratic character of their rule.

This critique had lacked any appreciation of the dynamics of the Algerian drama and had been combined, in the case of the Council and Commission, with support for a policy of forcing the Algerian state to surrender its sovereignty in the economic sphere and accept the imposition of a structural adjustment programme, a policy which, far from facilitating movement towards democracy, tended unquestionably to preclude this. But the critique in itself, abstracted from other considerations, was factually accurate. Algeria between 1992 and 1997 was certainly not a democracy.

However, having stigmatized the Boudiaf, Kafi-Abdesselam and Zeroual regimes for their shortcomings, the European discourse, and that of the Council in particular, began in mid-1997 to take a quite different line. Whereas Zeroual's various initiatives – the presidential election of 1995, the dialogues and constitutional revision of 1996, and so on – had been tacitly found wanting or loudly condemned as undemocratic, the outcome of the June 1997 legislative elections was endowed by the European Council with a degree of democratic potential that was in striking contrast to the Council's public assessment of every previous development.

The EU declaration on 10 June 1997 read as follows:

> The European Union expresses its satisfaction at the holding of the legislative elections on 5 June 1997, which enabled the Algerian electorate to vote in orderly and safe conditions.
>
> The European Union takes note of the declaration made by the joint group of international observers, confirming that polling took place under generally satisfactory conditions, although some notable imperfections were recorded.
>
> The holding of these elections marks a step forward in the process of political reform and bears witness to the Algerian people's wish to take charge of its future and to participate directly in the building of a democratic and non-violent society.
>
> The European Union hopes that the new Assembly will act as a driving force in the process of democratization and economic restructuring in Algeria.[53]

While the first two paragraphs of this were fair comment, the last two fundamentally misrepresented the significance of what had transpired on 5 June. The election had certainly been a further stage in the necessary process of political reconstruction and institutionalization, but the way this had been handled – the concoction of a new pro-regime party (the Democratic National Rally, RND), the rigging engaged in to secure its leading electoral score and especially the contriving of a multi-party (RND-FLN-MSP-MN) governing coalition which reduced the remaining opposition presence in the assembly to impotence – not only did not amount to a reform properly so called, it actively precluded the possibility of genuine political and economic reform for the foreseeable future,[54] and thereby fell far short of what the overall situation required, as the atrocious mayhem which erupted shortly afterwards in the massacres of July–September should have put beyond doubt.

Far from reconsidering its reading of the June elections in the light of the slaughter of civilians which followed them, the Council persisted in this misreading, recalling its June assessment in the declaration it issued on 12 September[55] and defending it to MEPs in the debate on 17 September.[56] In this way, the Council and the Commission headed off a proper reconsideration of the EU's Algeria policy when circumstances appeared to mandate this.

The practical upshot of this debate was the decision to establish an extraordinary *ad hoc* delegation of MEPs for the purpose of entering into dialogue with the Algerian parliament about the situation. This had been proposed by a French member, André Soulier, who chaired the Human Rights Sub-Committee of the Parliament's Foreign Affairs Committee. Despite objections from MEPs pointing out that it should be for the Parliament's standing Delegation on Relations with the Maghreb to go to Algiers, Soulier's proposal was approved, and a delegation under his chairmanship of nine MEPS – five of them French – visited Algiers on 8–12 February 1998.[57] Meanwhile, further terrible massacres had taken place over the New Year. Opening the debate on 'The British Presidency and the situation in Algeria' on 14 January, Foreign Secretary Robin Cook volunteered the remark, in respect of the massacres, that 'We have seen no evidence to support allegations of involvement by the Algerian security authorities'.[58] None the less, the demand that Algeria should allow an international commission of enquiry to investigate human rights violations was still being energetically canvassed in Europe and North America and, in deference to this pressure, the British Presidency of the Council dispatched a 'Troika' consisting of the junior foreign ministers of the UK, Austria and Luxembourg on what proved a conspicuously ineffectual visit to Algiers on 19 January. The troika failed to persuade the Algerian government to accept a visit from the UN's Special Rapporteurs on torture or extrajudicial executions, or to accept humanitarian aid, or to allow them to visit a massacre site. Having no other ends in view, they returned to Brussels to put the best possible face on this fiasco.[59]

No such misfortune befell Soulier's delegation, which pressed no embarrassing questions on its hosts and provoked no dusty answers. The result was a smooth and amicable dialogue[60] which enabled Soulier to report that 'a wind of change appeared to be blowing through Algeria'[61] and 'the Algerian Parliament is a reality – we have met it'.[62] As to the question '*qui tue qui?*', which articulated the widespread international suspicion provoked by the massacres (which, we may recall, had provided the delegation's formal *raison d'être*),

> Mr Soulier quoted the words of one of the religious representatives whom the delegation had met: 'Don't keep on asking who is killing who. We know and the victims know too.' Mr Soulier himself added, 'Nobody, when speaking to us, pointed the finger at the army.'[63]

The delegation went so far as to report sympathetically the Algerians' complaint 'that the embargo on anti-terrorist weapons was making the authorities' task harder'[64] and their regret over 'the lack of an overall partnership between the EU and Algeria'.

> There is indeed no such partnership, said Mr Soulier, and we must help devise a coherent overall policy between the two sides. In addition, the IMF and the other institutions should perhaps be asked to apply more flexible conditions to a country which is experiencing such problems.[65]

Thus the notion that the massacres were evidence of, at the very least, terrible failings on the part of the Algerian authorities, instead of prompting a judgemental European response and a dose of the once mandatory pressure, was completely dismissed; indeed, it was suggested that the position warranted a *more* rather than less co-operative attitude on Europe's part in respect of economic conditionality and even arms sales. In general, the message was that European concern over the issue of human rights ought not to impede the development of a Euro-Algerian partnership, since

> the Algerian MPs told us that their parliament was working on this matter within the framework of the separation of powers. We have no intention of interfering and we will not call for an international committee of inquiry.[66]

Why did Soulier add the last 11 words of this? Why go out of his way to help the regime off the hook? The only justification he provided of this was the assessment that 'the situation was no longer what it had been last May before the legislative elections'.[67] Indeed, notwithstanding the massacres, it could be inferred that the situation overall had distinctly improved, for

> [t]he delegation had been convinced by its visit, said Mr Soulier, that a democracy was emerging in Algeria and that it must be supported. Perhaps it had no chance but, if it had, it would be a serious mistake not to seize the opportunity ... Mr Soulier mentioned the setting up by the PNA [Popular National Assembly] of a committee of enquiry into fraud at the municipal elections.[68]

In this way, an *ad hoc* delegation set up by the European Parliament on the initiative of the chairman of its Sub-Committee on Human Rights functioned as an apologist – if not a lobbyist –for the Algerian authorities rather than as a representative of European concern for the human rights of ordinary Algerians, and as a cut-out rather than a bridge between Algerian reality and European democracy. Instead of enlightening the Parliament, Soulier's delegation undertook to tranquilize it.

With the end of the big massacres and the return to a routine level of violence from spring 1998 onwards, Strasbourg lost interest in the Algerian problem. On 8 July an EU declaration welcomed 'the establishment of a Panel of Eminent Persons by the UN Secretary General which will visit Algeria … at the invitation of the Algerian government', and praised the latter's 'spirit of openness' as 'an important step for Algerian democracy'.[69] Shortly after this important step had been taken, President Zeroual announced on 11 September his decision to resign in the wake of an unprecedentedly virulent and protracted press campaign against his security adviser Mohamed Betchine, a campaign in which the newspapers concerned had undoubtedly acted as the cat's paws of the army commanders.

On 22 September the UN panel's 'detailed report', which went down well with the Algerian government and explained approximately nothing of what had transpired the previous summer,[70] was in turn welcomed by the EU, which also declared that 'it is indispensable to strengthen democratic pluralism and to reinforce the civilian element in government, which is now feasible' (that is, feasible given Zeroual's departure, which was thus tacitly welcomed also); this being the case, the EU added that it 'remains supportive of the Algerian Government's efforts to consolidate democracy and protect its citizens from terrorism'.[71]

In short, the pressure was off. A perfunctory and comparatively mild resolution on press freedom in Algeria was passed on 19 November[72] but no parliamentary debates took place on Algeria throughout 1999 or 2000. While Parliament considered other matters, the 'political dialogue' – which in EU declarations now exclusively referred to dialogue between the Algerian government and 'the international community',[73] not dialogue between opposed points of view in Algeria – got off the ground and started going places. The troika's visit in January having formally inaugurated this, further rounds were held in Vienna on 21 October 1998, in Algiers on 3 November 1999 and in Lisbon on 12 May 2000.

Alongside this acceleration of friendly contacts at the top, moves to refresh EU–Algerian relations at other levels got under way. Although the negotiations over the association agreement had been suspended since June 1997, a MEDA Framework convention was initialled on 12 May 1998 and was signed by the Commission on 29 July and by the European Investment Bank on 15 September.[74] In the course of 1998, the EU finally disbursed the first instalment, worth €60m, of a €125m structural adjustment facility originally approved in principle on 2 December 1996.[75] In December 1998 it approved two MEDA programmes: the first, worth €38m, to support industrial restructuring and privatization; the second, worth €57m, to support the development of small- and medium-sized enterprises,[76] and

1998 also ended with the reopening of the Commission's delegation in Algiers, which had been closed since 1994.[77] A third MEDA programme, worth €23.2m, to modernize the financial sector was finally approved in 1999,[78] and at the end of the year €5m was committed to a project providing institutional support to some 50–60 Algerian NGOs and development associations, particularly those active in the fields of local development, the environment, and women's and youth issues.[79] It was also during 1999 that Algiers signalled that it intended to reopen negotiations for an association agreement.[80] In addition, the European Investment Bank (EIB) provided €10.7m worth of interest subsidies in support of industrial pollution abatement.[81]

As for the EU's MEDA Democracy Programme, a number of small-scale projects got under way as early as 1996; these focused on support for women and especially the Algerian press (reflecting regularly expressed concerns of the European Parliament) but also included a programme of human rights training for members of the Sûreté Nationale (the Algerian police force). The Algerian authorities had no problem with any of these projects, which a report evaluated as well managed for the most part, rating the impact of most of them as 'fairly positive'.[82]

Meanwhile, events began to demonstrate how ill-founded had been the suggestions that democracy in Algeria could be spoken of in the present tense, as something that was being 'consolidated' in a series of 'steps forward'.

On 14 April 1999, six of the seven candidates in the presidential election announced their 'withdrawal', leaving Abdelaziz Bouteflika to be 'elected' next day by default and thus lacking even the qualified legitimacy which Zeroual had obtained in 1995.

In a referendum on 16 September 1999 the Algerian people massively approved the unspecified 'approach' which Bouteflika was following to secure an end to the violence, but this meant little;[83] Bouteflika's conspicuous inability to form a new government until the eighth month of his presidency, and his audible resentment at the way the army commanders were queering his pitch, indicated that little had been resolved by his succession to the presidency.[84] The violence continued despite the regime's offer of a qualified amnesty to the rebels, foreign investors, vigorously wooed by Bouteflika, proved reticent, economic reform remained painfully slow and, faced with both a predominantly hostile press and a parliament in which he had little support, Bouteflika adopted a conspicuously authoritarian political style, which aggravated his difficulties with the parties and the media while yielding meagre dividends in his efforts to end the Islamist rebellion and attract foreign capital.[85]

Finally, a recrudescence of massacres in late 2000 and early 2001 at last prompted a debate in the European Parliament on 18 January,[86] while the international publicity given to eyewitness accounts of one of the worst massacres of 1997[87] and of the army's 'dirty war'[88] not only contradicted the bland assurances of Soulier's earlier report but also precipitated a fresh crisis within the regime. This finally exploded in the unprecedented violence in Kabylia from late April onwards, in which gendarmes deliberately provoked riots by outrageous behaviour toward the civilian population, and then fired live ammunition at the rioters with evident intent to kill, a scenario enacted dozens of times in over 40 different localities in Greater and Lesser Kabylia from 19 April to late June. At least 60 people, nearly all young men, were killed and hundreds wounded by gendarmes' bullets, and over 30 other people were killed in other ways in the course of these events, which vividly illustrated the true nature of the state–society relationship in Algeria.[89] A dreadfully misconceived reference to 'the Berber people' in the resolution voted by the European Parliament on 17 May[90] testified equally vividly to Europe's continuing and, by now, scandalous propensity to misread and misrepresent Algerian political reality.

Meanwhile, the negotiations for an association agreement eventually resumed in April 2000 and were concluded in 2001.[91]

Dancing in the Dark

> At the still point of the turning world. Neither flesh nor fleshless;
> Neither from nor towards; at the still point, there the dance is,
> But neither arrest nor movement. (T.S. Eliot, *Four Quartets*)

A frequently encountered line of criticism of contemporary western advocacy of political and economic reform, if applied to the EU's position on Algeria, would either credit Europe with good intentions but insufficient 'political will', or suggest that only the economic policy aims have been seriously pursued. An alternative view would posit a contradiction between Europe's political and economic objectives. Such criticisms do not quite grasp what has been going on.

The EU has not sought to promote economic reform capable of transforming Algeria into a prosperous capitalist economy, but to impose rescheduling and structural adjustment (imposed 1992–94, carried out 1994 to the present) and to secure Algeria's integration into a free trade area dominated by Europe (mooted since late 1995, pursued since June 1997). The EU's political discourse on Algeria has been neither irrelevant to this nor in contradiction with it, but *entirely functional* to it. It reiterated criticisms of a democratic nature when democracy was not a possibility of practical politics in Algeria, and then flattered the democratic pretensions of the pseudo-democracy that the Algerians eventually contrived. The criticisms had the functions of keeping the Algerian authorities *en mauvaise posture* by denying them any external legitimation to compensate for their internal legitimacy deficit, while simultaneously legitimating the EU's own refusal to provide financial assistance until they had capitulated to its economic demands (rescheduling and so on). The flattery had the functions of humouring the Algerian authorities, while drawing them into the EU's long-term economic scheme, and simultaneously legitimating the EU's own moves to secure an association agreement and sugar the pill with financial aid.

The source of this strategy has been Paris. In the positions it has adopted on the fringe of the Algerian drama since 1991, Europe has always been in step with France.[92] The withholding of assistance from Boudiaf, the opposition to Abdesselam's strategy, the reckless insistence on rescheduling, the failure to support Zeroual's dialogue in 1994, the sly manipulation of the Rome Platform, the negative reaction to Zeroual's election in 1995, the refusal to support the UN's mission to observe the June 1997 elections, the calculated patronizing of Algiers since 1998: the list is long and could be lengthened.

France's Algeria policy in itself is not the subject of this examination, but its influence on European policy is certainly relevant to it.

In her study of France's attitude to Europe's role in this affair, Morisse-Schilbach explains how, in the framework of the Common Foreign and Security Policy, France has expected her European partners to defer to her 'vital interests' in the Algerian situation, and how Paris has instrumentalized Europe while seeking to prevent it from acquiring an independent role or point of view. This analysis is shared by Baudoin Loos, who quotes an unnamed EU official as admitting, 'l'Algérie, c'est le domaine réservé de la France, point à la ligne'.[93]

Europe has been dancing to France's tune. This would have been an excellent thing to do if French policy had been other than what it has been, such that stability, peace and the onset of a genuine democratic development in Algeria had been the outcome. But, a decade on, with scores of thousands of Algerians dead and more killed every week, Algeria is still waiting for all these good things, and Europe is yet to emancipate itself from its dependence on Paris to tell it what to think and say and do.

Political realism dictates that the EU acknowledge France's interest in Algeria and accommodate it. But matters have gone *much* further than this. Paris has been allowed not only to defend France's interest, but also to define Europe's interest in this matter, and to do so not only in the Council and Commission, but also in the European Parliament as well, as the behaviour and composition of André Soulier's delegation graphically illustrated. As a result, a genuinely European interest has not been articulated and a genuinely European policy – which, while accommodating French concerns, takes other considerations properly into account – has been prevented from developing.

This is connected to the fact that Europe has allowed France to define the nature of the Algerian problem at every juncture. Claire Spencer has suggested that Europe's behaviour has been premised on 'the longest-standing European assumption about Algeria', that the French 'are the only outsiders to understand what goes on there and why',[94] an assumption which the evolution of the Algerian situation since 1991 has still not induced Europe to reconsider. The Commission and Parliament have never equipped themselves to develop an informed reading of Algerian politics that is independent of Paris's reading. But the far from disinterested reading that Paris has canvassed has not enlightened Europe, but misled it.

This perverse hegemony has not only been an affair of misleading theses, it has also been an affair of resounding silences. For the EU has never once called for

- the executive branch of the Algerian state to be accountable to the legislature;
- the army to withdraw from the political sphere and specifically for the legislature, instead of the army commanders, to be the source of ministerial mandates;[95]
- the judiciary to be independent of the executive;
- proper measures to be taken, to the satisfaction of all parties, to ensure genuinely fair elections to the national, regional and local assemblies.

And the EU has never commented on

- the regular renewal of the state of emergency, now in its tenth year;
- the fact that the upper house of Algeria's parliament has extraordinarily exaggerated powers to block legislation voted by the lower house;
- the fact that political parties are denied the right to develop formal links with trade unions and other voluntary associations.

These omissions are evidence that the EU has never been serious about promoting democracy in Algeria. The EU and the EC before it have not merely failed to promote democratic principles and respect for human rights in Algeria, they have even been accessories in the Algerian army's flouting of these things. And they have debased the very idea of democracy by pretending to promote it, and by affecting to recognize it in the 'pluralist' masquerade which the army commanders institutionalized in June 1997.

Because the executive–legislature relationship has not been properly reformed so as to empower the latter to hold the former to account, the factional conflict within the executive (army, police and administration) effortlessly dominates the elements of pluralism – parties, press and voluntary associations – which have developed since 1989, such that these have become the arenas and cats' paws of the factional conflict itself, which has expanded into this new terrain, manipulating and compromising everything it has found there.[96] And the failure to reform this relationship means that Algeria is as far, if not further, from being a state bound by law as it was in 1988.

In these circumstances, to insist on 'economic reform' has been largely fruitless. The imposition of structural adjustment and the pressure to privatize have sharpened and fuelled the factional conflict, but they have not created the conditions for the effective development of capitalist production in the non-hydrocarbons sector, on which Algeria's future really depends.[97] Only a state bound by law could provide the reliable framework that Algerian entrepreneurs require if they are to risk their capital in productive ventures in their own country. And for as long as Algerian capital, which exists in substantial quantities, is mostly invested abroad, there is little prospect of foreign capital being invested in Algeria's manufacturing sector.

The connection between political and economic reform properly conceived is actually very close. But only a caricature of this connection has been vehicled by the European discourse. There can be little doubt that EU officials and MEPs, preoccupied by other issues, have been largely unaware of this. At most, a handful have groped towards the truth, as when the Spanish MEP Jorge Hernández Mollar (European People's Party, EPP) told Robin Cook, 'Algeria is a very sick country, whose illness has not been diagnosed'.[98] Those who have knowingly participated in France's manipulation of Europe's Algeria policy are undoubtedly a small minority, and France's European partners have not necessarily acted in bad faith in deferring to her judgement.

Europe has been dancing in the dark. It is unrealistic to suppose that the Algerian authorities have been unaware of this, and that this has not robbed European pronouncements of moral authority in their eyes. Europe's injunctions have not arrested them in what they have been doing, or moved them to do what has needed to be done if they were not already doing this in any case. And Europe's decision-makers have not stopped to reconsider their position, and so no movement in the mind has occurred at their end either. Indeed, at the very moment that the European Commission has been admitting the limited achievements of the EMP to date and proposing to relaunch it, it has insisted that 'there is no alternative' to the approach it has been following up until now.[99]

Europe has not merely relayed France's positions, it has amplified them and legitimized them.[100] Whatever dissent from this orthodoxy has been voiced by independent-minded MEPs has led nowhere. Real debate requires the consideration of alternatives. The absence of real debate in Europe has helped to ensure sterile debate in Algeria. The mind-numbing quality of the European discourse has tended to inhibit those Algerians opposed to the political status quo in their country from conceiving how it might be transcended.

Until the fundamental problem – the inability of the Algerian parliament to hold government, administration and security forces to account – is resolved, other reforms will come to nothing. Europe's officials and parliamentarians do not need specialist insight into Algerian politics to know this. They take this knowledge for granted in the law-bound democratic states they call home. But it appears that they are induced to forget all about it in the peculiar environment of the European Union, which – neither flesh nor fleshless – has some of the organs of a state and a democracy without being one or the other.

For as long as there is no change in this respect, the development of law-bound and representative government in Algeria requires the Algerians to pay no attention to the EU's compulsive parroting of French discourse and, while reflecting on the constitutive principles of the European democracies, discover their own way through the wood to the lawful republic to which most of them certainly aspire.

NOTES

This article is based on research carried out at the London School of Economics (LSE) on 'The Political Economy of Contemporary Algeria' in 1997–99, and on further research on 'Globalization, Political Change and Political Violence in Algeria and Egypt' conducted within the 'Crisis States' research programme of the Development Research Centre at the LSE since October 2000. The author wishes to thank BP-Amoco for its support for this research in 1997–99 and the Development Studies Institute at the LSE for its support for both research projects.

1. European Union, Common Foreign and Security Policy (CFSP), *Algeria/National Reconciliation: Declaration by the European Union*, Brussels, 23 Jan. 1995.
2. *European Council, Presidency Conclusions*, Final Communiqué of the Meeting of the European Council, Göteborg, Sweden, 15–16 June 2001, p.16.
3. European Parliament (EP), *Situation in Algeria*, verbatim report of proceedings, 17 Sept. 1997, http://www.europarl.eu.int /plenary/default_en.htm. PES is the Party of European Socialists .

4. Mahfoud Nahnah, leader of the Movement for an Islamic Society (HAMAS), won 25.58 per cent of the vote; Saïd Sadi, leader of the Rally for Culture and Democracy (RCD), won 9.6 per cent with five times his party's vote in 1991; Noureddine Boukrouh, leader of the small Party of Algerian Renewal (PRA), won 3.81 per cent.
5. EU, CFSP, *Declaration by the European Union on the Presidential Elections in Algeria*, Brussels, 20 Nov. 1995.
6. The EU declaration was criticized during question time in the European Parliament by a Spanish MEP, Ms Maria Izquierdo Rojo (PES), who argued that the EU should recognize the elections as 'a decisive first step towards the establishment of peace and stability in Algeria', and that the EU 'should lend political support' and not 'restrict our support to co-operation in economic terms'; see *European Foreign Policy Bulletin*, Document 95/392, Question No. H-911/95, 12 Dec. 1995, http://www.iue.it/EFPB/lists/ list95.
7. Reuters, 16 Jan. 1992; *Africa Economic Digest*, 27 Jan. 1992.
8. Document 394D0938, 94/938/EC, *Council Decision of 22 December 1994 providing further macrofinancial assistance for Algeria*, Preamble, Official Journal L366, 31 Dec. 1994, pp.0028–0029, http://europa.eu.int/eur-lex/en/lif/dat/1994/en_391D0938.html.
9. Document 391D0510, 91/510/EEC, *Council Decision of 23 September 1991 providing a medium-term loan to Algeria*, Preamble and Articles 1–3, Official Journal L272, 28/09/91, pp.0090–0091, http://europa.en.int/eur-lex/en/lif/dat/1991/en_391D0510.html.
10. *Le Monde*, 19 Feb. 1992.
11. Mélanie Morisse-Schilbach, *L'Europe et la Question Algérienne* (Paris: Presses Universitaires de France, 1999), p.71 (my translation).
12. *Le Monde*, 18 March 1992 (my translation).
13. Morisse-Schilbach, op.cit., p.72 (my translation).
14. Boudiaf was second only to Mostefa Ben Boulaïd (d.1956) in the creation of the FLN.
15. On 8 June1992, Boudiaf announced the creation of a new party, the National Patriotic Rally (Rassemblement Patriotique Nationale, RPN) to mobilize support for his candidacy in the presidential election that was envisaged. This strategy offered the only possible way back to democracy in 1992. The RPN disintegrated after Boudiaf's death.
16. BBC news dispatch, Lisbon, 29 June 1992.
17. BBC External Services, Summary of World Broadcasts (SWB), 2 April 1993.
18. David Buchan, 'Out in the Cold', *Financial Times*, 21 Dec. 1993.
19. Jon Marks, 'Western fears propel refinancing package', *Middle East Economic Digest* (MEED), 27 May 1994.
20. *Le Monde*, 1 June 1994.
21. MEED, 12 Aug. 1994.
22. MEED, 13 March 1992, 18 Aug. 1992, 24 Sept. 1993.
23. MEED, 2 April 1993; funding for the Hammam Boughrara dam was approved in 1993, for the Taksebt dam not until 1998, according to Med Bank Watch Initiative. http://www.pangea.org/MEDForum/medbank.
24. *Council Decision of 22 December 1994*, see note 8.
25. Kafi had played a leading role in wilaya II (Nord-Constantinois) and commanded the *wilaya* from 1957 to 1959.
26. Abdesselam was a member of the central committee of the Parti du Peuple Algérien-Mouvement pour le Triomphe des Libertés Démocratiques (PPA-MTLD) before the war; having joined the FLN, he founded the Union Générale des Étudiants Musulmans Algériens (UGEMA) in 1955. He later served the FLN in Morocco.
27. *Council Decision of 23 September 1991*, see note 9.
28. For a critical but informative discussion of Abdesselam's policy, see Abed Charef, *Algérie, Le Grand Dérapage* (France: La Tour d'Aigues, Éditions de l'Aube, 1994), pp.369–72 and 434–46; see also 'L'avenir du régime est lié à la signature d'un accord sur la dette', *Le Monde*, 22 Feb. 1992.
29. *Africa Economic Digest*, 24 Feb. 1992; see also *Financial Times*, 9 July 1991.

30. The economy minister in Malek's government was Mourad Benachenhou, already known to favour rescheduling.
31. BBC, SWB 9 Nov. 1993; see also *Libération*, 10 Nov. 1993.
32. This outlook informed the resolutions of the Conference of National Dialogue held in Algiers in Jan. 1994.
33. Ali Djeddi and Abdelkader Boukhamkham, senior FIS officials imprisoned with Abassi Madani and Ali Ben Hadj in June 1991, were released on 22 February 1994.
34. See Hugh Roberts, 'Algeria between eradicators and conciliators', *Middle East Report 189*, Vol.24, No.4 (July–Aug. 1994), pp.24–7.
35. Following the new government announced on 15 April, a military reshuffle was announced on 5 May.
36. The FFS never convincingly explained its refusal to take part in these talks.
37. Five people were beheaded on the night of 8–9 September, the first reported beheadings since the violence began, but on the night of 13–14 September no fewer than 16 civilians were beheaded in eastern, central and western Algeria, certainly a co-ordinated affair and the most spectacular of several incidents which poisoned the atmosphere and sabotaged the dialogue.
38. EU, CFSP, *Statement on Algeria (on behalf of the European Union and Austria, Finland, Norway and Sweden)*, Brussels and Bonn, 26 Sept. 1994.
39. See Hugh Roberts, 'Algeria's ruinous impasse and the honourable way out', *International Affairs*, Vol.71, No.2 (1995), pp.247–67; an earlier round of the Rome talks was held on 21–22 November; all major parties plus the government were invited to these; HAMAS and the PRA attended but refused to sign the communiqué and were not invited to the second round in January.
40. Notably the statement by Foreign Minister Mohamed Salah Dembri on 26 February 1995 that the Rome Platform contained some positive ideas.
41. EP, *Resolution on the situation in Algeria*, 19 Jan. 1995, http://www3.europarl.en.int/plenary/default_en.htm.
42. EU, CFSP, *National reconciliation: declaration by the European Union on Algeria*, Brussels, 23 Jan. 1995.
43. Notably at the G7 summit in Naples in July 1994, where a proposed reference to the FIS in the summit's declaration on Algeria was dropped after France's vigorous objections; see Roberts, 'Algeria's ruinous impasse', p.262, n.24.
44. EP, *Human rights: resolution on the dangerous situation in Algeria*, 16 March 1995; EP, *Resolution on the situation in Algeria*, 6 April 1995.
45. EP, *Human rights: resolution on press freedom in Algeria*, texts adopted, 14 March 1996; EP, *Human rights: resolution on press freedom in Algeria*, texts adopted, 18 July 1996.
46. EP, *Resolution on the situation in Algeria*, 12 Dec. 1996; the re-legalization of the FIS was implicitly demanded in the call for the legislative elections 'to take place in circumstances which allow all political parties to take part'; since there was no question of legal parties being prevented from participating, this could only mean that the FIS should be re-legalized in time to contest the election. This reading was confirmed by a number of eminent French politicians who publicly called for the re-legalization of the FIS the following month.
47. In the debate in the European Parliament on 19 February 1997, support for participating in the UN election observers mission in June had been expressed by Armelle Guinebertière (Union for Europe, UFE), Dominique Souchet (Independents for a Europe of Nations), Jorge Salvador Hernández Mollar (European People's Party, EPP) and María Izquierdo Rojo (PES); the issue was ignored by the president-in-office of the Council in his reply to the debate, which produced no resolution.
48. Jean-Pierre Tuquoi, *Le Monde*, 10 May 1997, reported that France's refusal to participate was mainly motivated by a concern not to provide political endorsement for the elections.
49. The organization to which the Foreign Office sub-contracted the recruitment of election

observers was advised of the names of a number of suitable and potentially interested individuals; the decision to send only two observers was not based on a lack of recruits.

50. Athens News Agency, 4 June 1997.
51. The MNI became the MN in deference to the 1997 Law on Political Parties, which obliged it to drop the 'Islamic' element of its name; similarly, HAMAS (Harakat al-Mujtama' al-Islami, Movement for an Islamic Society) became HMS (Harakat Mujtamac as-Silm) or MSP (Movement of Society for Peace). Djaballah later lost control of the MN to its general secretary, Lahbib Adami, under whom it entered the coalition government.
52. EP, *Situation in Algeria*, verbatim report of proceedings, 17 Sept. 1997.
53. EU, CFSP, *Algeria/ Legislative elections*, Brussels, 10 June 1997.
54. See Hugh Roberts, 'Algeria's contested elections', *Middle East Report*, Vol.28, No.4 (1998), pp.21–4.
55. EU, CFSP, *Algeria/ Wave of killings*, Brussels, 12 Sept. 1997.
56. See the reply to the debate on the 'Situation in Algeria' by George Wohlfart, president-in-office of the Council, EP, *Situation in Algeria*, verbatim report of proceedings, 17 Sept. 1997.
57. The French delegates were: Soulier (EPP, chair), Hélène Carrère d'Encausse (UFE), Daniel Cohn-Bendit (Greens, Rapporteur), Mireille Elmalan (European United Left/Nordic Green Left) and André Scarbonchi (European Radical Alliance); the others were Anne André-Léonard (European Liberal Democratic and Reform Party, Belgian), Jorge Hernández Mollar (EPP, Spanish), Yiannis Roubatis (PES, Greek) and Hannes Swoboda (PES, Austrian, vice-chair).
58. EP, *The British Presidency and the situation in Algeria*, verbatim report of proceedings, 14 Jan. 1998.
59. Presidency Press Release, *EU/Troika Mission to Algeria: Statement by Mr Fatchett*, Tuesday 20 Jan. 1998, http://presid.fco.gov.uk/.
60. Enlivened only by a maverick declaration to the Algerian press by Cohn-Bendit, which the delegation disavowed, and by Soulier's refusal to accept a letter from the FIS delivered to him by Abdennour Ali Yahia.
61. EU *News Report*, 11 Feb. 1998.
62. EU *News Report*, 12 Feb. 1998.
63. Ibid.
64. Report of a press conference given by André Soulier on the delegation's return, EU *News Report*, 18 Feb. 1998.
65. Ibid.
66. EU *News Report*, 12 Feb. 1998.
67. Ibid.
68. EU *News Report*, 18 Feb. 1998; the report of this enquiry has never been published.
69. EU, CFSP, *Algeria: Panel of Eminent Persons / UN*, Brussels, 8 July 1998.
70. See Amnesty International, 'UN Panel Report a whitewash on human rights', News Release, 16 Sept. 1998; and Madjid Bencheikh, 'Le Rapport de la Mission de l'ONU: une analyse qui conforte le statu quo', on Algeria Watch, http://www.algeria-watch.org.
71. EU, CFSP, *Algeria: Report of the UN's Panel of Eminent Persons*, Brussels, 22 Sept. 1998.
72. EP, *Human rights: resolution on freedom of expression in Algeria*, 19 Nov. 1998.
73. From July 1998, the term 'dialogue' appeared in all EU official declarations with this meaning alone over the next three years; the notion of dialogue among Algerians reappeared in EU discourse only in the final communiqué of the European Council meeting at Göteborg in Sweden on 15–16 June 2001, following the violence in Kabylia.
74. *Annual Report of the MEDA Programme, 1998* (ARMP) (Brussels: European Commission, 1999), p.8.
75. *ARMP 1998*, pp.37–8; *North Africa Journal*, No.32 (13 June 1998); only €30m of this facility represented MEDA funding; the rest was left over from the financial protocols.
76. *ARMP 1998*, p.10.

77. *ARMP 1999* (Brussels: European Commission, 2000), p.23.
78. *ARMP 1999*, pp.24, 26.
79. *ARMP 1999*, p.25.
80. *ARMP 1999*, p.14.
81. *ARMP 1999*, p.26; Euro-Mediterranean Partnership, *The Barcelona Process, Five Years On 1995–2000* (Luxembourg: Office for Official Publications of the European Communities, 2000), p.30.
82. *MEDA Democracy Evaluation*, Part II: *Country Sections: Algeria*. For a further discussion of these issues, see Richard Youngs, *The European Union and the Promotion of Democracy: Europe's Mediterranean and Asian Policies* (Oxford: Oxford University Press, forthcoming 2002), ch.4.
83. Electors were asked whether or not they approved the president's *démarche*, which was not defined for their benefit in any way.
84. See Algeria_Interface, 'Le Président face à la désillusion algérienne', 7 Dec. 1999, and 'Le Président Bouteflika se soumet au système', 31 Dec. 1999, http://www.algeria-interface.com/.
85. The parties which formed the government's majority (RND, FLN, MSP and En-Nahda), while nominally supporting the president, were actually answerable to the army commanders, who used them to box Bouteflika in. In bypassing parliament in pursuit of his policy aims, Bouteflika exposed himself to criticism on democratic grounds but, while he exhibited unmistakably authoritarian traits, his critics greatly exaggerated the democratic credentials of the institutions he was bypassing.
86. EP, *Human rights: Situation in Algeria*, 18 Jan. 2001.
87. Nesroulah Yous, *Qui a tué à Bentalha? Chronique d'un massacre annoncé* (Paris: La Découverte, 2000).
88. Habib Souaïdia, *La Sale Guerre: Le témoignage d'un ancien officier des forces spéciales algériennes* (Paris: La Découverte, 2001).
89. See Hugh Roberts, 'Riots without end?', *Middle East International*, 1 June 2001; see also the unprecedentedly honest report of the inquiry chaired by Professor Mohand Issaad, *Rapport préliminaire de la commission nationale d'enquête sur les évenements en Kabylie*, Algeria_Interface, accessed 27 July 2001; an interesting report produced by Hélène Flautre MEP (Greens), who visited the region during the events, is available on Algeria Watch.
90. EP, *Situation in Algeria: resolution on the repression in Kabylia*, 17 May 2001. Berber speakers in Algeria are not, and do not consider themselves to be, a distinct people, but an integral element of the Algerian people. The resolution provoked an immediate written riposte from the Socialist Forces Front (FFS), the principal party in Kabylia.
91. *El Moudjahid*, 5 July 2001; European Commission, Euromed Special Feature, Issue N.27A, 15 Jan. 2002.
92. Morisse-Schilbach, op.cit., pp.71, 87–8, 112.
93. Baudouin Loos, 'L'Europe et l'Algérie', Algeria Watch, revised version, March 2000, http://www.algeria-watch.de/farticle/tribune/loos3.htm, p.2; see also Hans Köchler, 'US–European relations after the end of the East–West conflict: implications for Euro-Mediterranean co-operation', International Progress Organization (Vienna), Occasional Papers No.1, 1997, http://i-p-o.org/medit.htm, p.6; and Youngs, op. cit., ch.4.
94. Claire Spencer, 'Algeria: France's disarray and Europe's conundrum', in B.A. Roberson (ed.), *The Middle East and Europe: The Power Deficit* (London and New York: Routledge, 1998), pp.174–5; and Youngs, op.cit., ch.4.
95. I have explained the crucial importance of this point in Hugh Roberts, 'Algeria's ruinous impasse', and also in Hugh Roberts, 'The Struggle for Constitutional Rule in Algeria', *Journal of Algerian Studies*, Vol.3 (1998), pp.19–30.
96. I have explained how the character of 'pluralism' in Algeria has been vitiated by the factional conflict in Hugh Roberts, 'The International Gallery and the Extravasation of Factional Conflict in Algeria', *Cambridge Review of International Affairs*, Vol.12, No.1

(1998), pp.209–46.

97. Bradford Dillman, *State and Private Sector in Algeria* (Boulder, CO: Westview Press, 2000), pp.55–60.
98. EP, *The British Presidency and the situation in Algeria*, verbatim report of proceedings, 14 Jan. 1998.
99. Günter Verheugen, replying for the Commission to the debate on Algeria, EP, *Situation in Algeria*, verbatim report of proceedings, 17 May 2001.
100. Morisse-Schilbach notes that Paris's instrumentalization of the EU has had what she calls a 'multiplier' effect in France, in that external endorsement protects the government's policy against domestic French critics (Morisse-Schilbach, op.cit., pp.122–3); she overlooks the international multiplier or amplifier effect, which has forestalled any serious challenge to French policy within Europe.

France, Democratization and North Africa

JEAN-FRANÇOIS DAGUZAN

Breaking the Old Principles: France's New Focus on Democracy

Until the 1990s, France was one of the states that adhered most strictly to the principles of sovereignty and non-interference in the affairs of other states. General de Gaulle suggested that '*les États sont des monstres froids*' (states are cold monsters) in order to describe the implacable realism he perceived necessary to international relations. While the presidents that succeeded de Gaulle stuck firmly to these principles, the global context began to shift. In the United States, President Carter's focus on human rights raised questions of principle, and globalization offered to the French public immediate visions of people suffering around the world. At the same time, a new generation after 1968 sought to fight against violence and misery, progressively mobilizing a global conscience. Human rights abuses and poverty were brought home to French public opinion by non-governmental organization (NGO) activists, such as Medecins sans Frontières. Many of the latter had links with left-wing movements and through the French Socialist Party influenced the François Mitterrand presidency in the direction of a greater emphasis on democracy and human rights.

In a succession of speeches during the 1980s, French ministers referred to the need to intervene in international affairs to protect human rights, apparently creating a new doctrine beyond France's traditional realism.[1] This trend culminated in the Franco–African Summit at La Baule in June 1990, where Mitterrand introduced the concept of political conditionality, suggesting that henceforth 'France will tie its financial assistance to efforts made to progress towards more freedom'.[2] As a presidential candidate, Jacques Chirac laid out a similar doctrine: 'First, we must say loud and clear that democracy, freedom and human rights are not luxuries reserved for western societies, but values to be lived by all peoples and concretely realized. The requirement of democracy and the respect for human rights have to figure among the main criteria of our international action'.[3] In 1988, a Secretariat of State for Humanitarian Assistance was created – with Bernard Kouchner, the leading figure of the 'French doctors', as its first minister – and engendered some conflict of competence over human rights with the Quai d'Orsay.[4]

France and the Maghreb: A Slow Lifting of the Weight of the Past

Despite the sincerity of these commitments, French pressure on democratization and human rights was easier to apply in relation to more distant countries with which France did not have close historical ties. With some of its former colonies in sub-Saharan Africa, there were historical ties but France had the strength gradually to intervene more forcefully in domestic political processes. The Maghreb countries appeared to be something of an exception, with France having established such a special relationship with these states since their independence – and in the case of Algeria an extremely special and delicate relationship. The question of interference went to the heart of these special relationships and made any French action or declaration highly risky for bilateral links. This helps explain the paranoid behaviour exhibited by some EU member states during political discussions on the Maghreb countries and especially Algeria.[5] Looking at the three Maghreb countries, the French position regarding democratization and human rights was similar, but the situation was more complicated in Algeria owing to the unique nature of the colonial link, the liberation war and relations in the post-war period.

Morocco: Influence Through Public Opinion

France's relationship with Morocco has gone through different periods during the Fifth Republic. Under de Gaulle, the relationship was frozen owing to opposition leader Ben Barka's dramatic hijacking in Paris in 1964. Bilateral contacts remained poor under President Pompidou. During Giscard d'Estaing's presidency, however, the link between France and Morocco became stronger. Underlying the improving relationship was the conflict in Western Sahara, this creating a closer military assistance between the two countries. King Hassan praised Giscard as '*un bon copain*'.[6] Under Mitterrand the relationship became extremely complex. The feeling between Hassan II and Mitterrand was bad and many in the French Socialist Party had strong feelings against a widely-criticized monarchy. While official relations remained generally positive, the question of human rights and democratization in Morocco slowly but surely poisoned the relationship between the two countries.

Most of the pressure on democracy and human rights in fact came from the right wing of the Socialist Party, as well as from the foundation set up by President Mitterrand's wife (the Danielle Mitterrand Foundation) to promote human rights and democracy in developing countries. The Danielle Mitterrand Foundation and other organizations pressed increasingly strongly for the liberation of Abraham Serfaty, a political opponent of the regime jailed for 20 years (and eventually exiled in 1991) and other political prisoners. One of the most notable events was the publication in September 1990 of Gilles Perrault's pamphlet, *Notre ami le Roi*. This described the 'crimes' of the Moroccan monarchy and the suppression of human rights and democracy, and denounced French elites (politicians, academics, artists) for their accommodation with Hassan II and for 'selling' outside a brilliant image of what was in reality a corrupted and criminal kingdom.[7] Later in 1991, French public opinion was horrified by the uncovering of the conditions in the jail at Tazmamart, where young *cadets* implicated in the 1971 attempt of Kenitra against the king's villa had been held for 20 years.[8] In 1996, the expulsion of the Oufkir family provided a high profile demonstration of the king's lack of respect for human rights and of the power of the politicized police controlling the country.[9]

In this sense, it was the pressure from French public opinion that succeeded in producing many positive results. Through its campaigning, the French media succeeded in securing the release of Abraham Serfaty, the closure of Tazmamart and the exile of the Oufkir family to Paris. It is difficult to say if the French government played any direct role in these events. As with Algeria, the government, the administration and the political parties were all deeply divided between those who supported democracy and human rights as a principle for the new world order and the realists who wished to support weak governments struggling to cope with a growing Islamic risk. During this period, the Moroccan media portrayed the growing outside pressure as 'a French plot' and suggested that external criticisms were 'inventions' inspired by those who wanted to destabilize the kingdom.[10] In this context, the French government repeatedly protested its support to the Moroccan government and offered to Hassan II's state visit in May 1995 the highest status reserved for prestigious guests by Republic protocol.

It is clear that the 'friendly' pressure exercised by France through different means played a role in Morroco's partially positive political evolution. Hassan II was sufficiently clever to understand that the oriental despotic model had to be reformed in order to preserve international support for the monarchy. After the king's death, his young successor, Mohamed VI, followed the broad lines of his father's policy while adding his own personal touch. This has taken the country to the edge, trying both to modernize with respect to human rights and democracy, on the one hand, and to retain traditional authoritarian methods against the threat of Islam, on the other. Ultimately, the balance between these two trends will be conditioned by the success or failure of the economic development process.

Tunisia: The Tightening of Dictatorship

After Zine el Abidine Ben Ali's plot in 1987, the question of democracy and human rights in Tunisia was a non-subject in France. Ben Ali was perceived by the French government to be the wall against Islamism and the man capable of modernizing Habib Bourguiba's regime. French support for Ben Ali was seen as being made easier by the elimination of some of the most egregious corruption and repression of the Bourguiba family's final years in control of Tunisia. Progressively, however, Ben Ali's regime became more repressive than its predecessor. Despite the worsening conditions under Ben Ali, the French government continued to praise loudly the Tunisian president, in particular for his successes in the economic sphere. The increasing repression in Tunisia was discreetly covered over as the French political elite vaunted Ben Ali's merits – this strong support being particularly evident during President Chirac's visit to Tunisia in 1995 and President Ben Ali's trip to Paris in October 1997.

Since 1998, the Tunisian regime's suppression of democracy and human rights has started to gain more recognition amongst French public opinion. Ben Ali was elected for a third time with an improbable 99 per cent of the vote and is likely to be considering a fourth mandate officially forbidden by the Tunisian constitution. The security forces and the Interior Ministry have organized a systematic hunting down of political opponents and even the most discreet of human rights activists, proscribing every non-official association linked with democracy and human rights.[11] Moderate human rights defenders such as Moncef Marzouki, Nejib Hosni and Khemais Ksila have been either jailed or kept under close control and permanently humiliated of even physically abused by the regime's special police. A correspondent of the French newspaper *La Croix*, Taoufik Ben Brik, suffered incredible humiliation and in protest went on hunger strike in April 2000. The Ben Brik affair created a large-scale movement of indignation in France. One year prior to this, the success in France of a book called *Notre Ami Ben Ali*, replicating Gilles Perrault's criticism of France's indulgence of Hassan II in the context of Tunisia, created considerable tension between the two countries.[12]

French policy has begun to evolve slightly. The Tunisian dictatorship has become too harsh, too visible for the same degree of unconditional support to be given to Ben Ali. First, the Socialist Party spokesman issued a strong criticism of Ben Ali, and this was then followed by the minister of foreign affairs himself, Hubert Védrine, expressing his anger and disappointment over the deteriorating political conditions in Tunisia to the parliament in May 2001.[13] Immediately, the political links between France and Tunisia were frozen at a number of levels. Eventually a delayed visit of development minister Charles Josselin went ahead in June 2001. After extremely difficult negotiations, Josselin met Ben Ali and spoke directly about the question of human rights in Tunisia. This visit was presented as representing a clear change in French government behaviour towards Tunisia.[14] Now that France has begun to speak loudly and officially on the question of democracy and human rights in Tunisia, policy is only likely to develop further in this direction.

France and Algeria: A Schizophrenic Relationship

It is impossible to explain the special relationship between France and Algeria regarding democracy and human rights without an understanding of the history of relations between the two countries. These links are seen by observers and actors as constituting a 'privileged relationship', but what exactly does this mean?[15]

1962–95: An Ambiguous Example. The first 30 years of relations between France and independent Algeria were marked by pronounced symbolism on both sides. On the French side, de Gaulle wanted to create a symbol of a new form of exemplary post-colonial co-operation in the eyes of the world. Except during the time of Giscard d'Estaing, it was, for French governments, to some extent a question of transforming the political defeat of France in Algeria into a victory on the ground of the principles and practice of new North–South relations. This was why the French government accepted without a murmur the non-execution of the Evian accords by the Algerians, as well as a long series of diplomatic snubs of which it was the object. The apogee of this policy was the signature of the exorbitant gas agreement of 1982, which also represented the swansong of this unusual period. On the Algerian side, behind public utterances bitterly denouncing the former colonizer, and resentment at the slightest suspicion of interference or attacks on national sovereignty, co-operation developed in all economic, social and education sectors, reaching a volume as large as it was discreet.

To some extent it can be said that in its post-colonial relationship France demonstrated a blindness which caused it piously to overlook the defects of the authoritarian and oligarchic regime which was installed under Houari Boumédiène and which reached its peak under Chadli Benjedid. During the same period France's progressive intelligentsia, lost in its theoretical designs, vaunted the Algerian industrial revolution. What is more, the fascination which the Algerian president held for Mitterrand clinched the French position. It took the crisis and the riots of 1988, when the Algerian army fired into a crowd, to produce a salutary galvanizing shock. Economic ruin and political chaos combined in violence and opened the way to the Islamists, the only alternative political force after 30 years of totalitarianism. Paralysed by all these years of self-absorption, France could only note with alarm that its preferred model of development had unravelled.

Against this background, it is clear that nothing is simple in Franco–Algerian relations. For the new Algeria, France represented an ambiguous fascination. Critical or openly anti-French public statements structured the Algerian public debate, while at the same time multi-faceted co-operation linked the two countries, and the interpenetration of the two societies became a reality. These two countries intimately linked by a historical, political, social and financial imbroglio had to manage an unprecedented crisis following the sudden halt to the democratic process in 1992.

Following the catastrophic first round of legislative elections, which would ineluctably have brought the FIS to power, the senior military hierarchy and the Haut Comité d'Etat (High Committee of State) halted the democratic process, creating the first divisions between the various elements of administration and power in France, as well as in public opinion. Although Mitterrand adopted a crafty prudence in his declarations, an element of public opinion protested against the 'official' intrusion of the military into public life. Within the administration voices were heard declaring that the process should have run its course with the Algerians taking the consequences. From 1992, two schools of thought faced each other: the pragmatists, or realists, who considered that the military coup was a lesser evil than the worldwide and growing Islamist threat; and the moralists, or idealists, who felt that principles come first, and that the coup was a blow against democracy and human rights in general. A little later, when Islamist violence was devastating the country with a crescendo of massacres, the first category divided into two camps: those who considered that the Islamists were likely to take power and that it would be best to anticipate their victory by adopting a reserved attitude to the existing regime, and those who believed on the contrary that despite the violence of the counter-insurrection, good sense and geo-strategic rationality favoured discreet support (moral and economic) for the current regime while promoting a return to the interrupted democratic process[16] – a process which was to be re-established by General Liamine Zeroual after the presidential election by universal suffrage in 1995. French prevarications and concerns were aggravated by the assassination, after 100 days in power, of Mohammed Boudiaf, the historic leader urgently recalled from 30 years in exile in Morocco to take over the presidency of the High Committee of State.

Whatever the circumstances, the Algerians keenly felt this turbulence within the French leadership whilst the violence became radicalized, the Islamists occupied whole regions of the country and the assassinations of intellectuals, journalists and senior officials multiplied. Each French move was over-interpreted by an Algerian leadership that was on the defensive. The situation became critical when the Armed Islamic Group (GIA) attacked the French community in Algeria. The French government was obliged to steer an extremely difficult course at that time. Most of the attacks represented direct pressure by the Islamists to force France to abandon its support, even though distanced, for the Algerian government. On the other hand, some cynics saw, in some of these dreadful acts, the hand of factions of the Algerian security services aiming at dragging France into the war in support of the regime. However, foreign minister Roland Dumas gradually imposed a tone and firmness on French policy that was not repudiated during the second phase of cohabitation by the government formed by Prime Minister Edouard Balladur in March 1993, and was not exploited politically within domestic debate.[17]

French Procrastination: Between Support, Incomprehension and Discord. The Balladur government, while keeping to the line established by Roland Dumas, was characterized by a scattering of the power of decision. This vagueness in the discussions with Algiers contrasted with official support, and contributed to a gradual breaking down of the links with the government that it was supposed to support. *De facto*, President Mitterrand retained a powerful influence on foreign policy. The prime minister and the foreign minister, Alain Juppé, defined a harder line implying, and this was a new departure, 'help for the Algerian government in its struggle against terrorism'.[18] Minister of the interior Charles Pasqua, having his own contacts and networks, maintained his own links with some members of the senior military hierarchy known as 'eradicators', while minister of defence François Léotard wondered about the need for a real dialogue with the Islamists.[19] 'It is interesting to note', Mélanie Morisse-Schilbach commented, 'that the divergence of views was not the result of cohabitation but of differences within the French Right'.[20] French public opinion was torn between horror and indignation at Islamist violence, and protestation against the disregard for human rights manifested by the Algerian government. By this time, Franco–Algerian relations, inspired by emotion, had become schizophrenic.[21]

It thus became difficult to find one's bearings amid the chorus of discordant voices coming from the French capital. The Islamists took advantage of this period of indecision to take the war on to French soil. From this time the inhuman violence of the Islamists gradually turned French and international public opinion against them. The attacks in France and, above all, the rural massacres in conditions beyond the imagination swung opinion towards the supporters of eradication. The Algerian government recovered its legitimacy and gradually re-established its control over practically the whole of the country. Some critical analysts have pondered about the willingness of the leaders of the GIA to provide such decisive arguments to the Algerian state.[22]

France, the European Union and Algeria: From Private Property to Careful Opening. The care with which France maintained its exemplary relations with Algeria transformed them into an exclusive relationship. This led the French authorities to keep the European Union at arm's length from any political intervention in the country. The first years of the civil war were accompanied by 'trench warfare' in Brussels, during which France was keen to avoid any involvement by European organizations, except in the collective dimension of the Euro-Mediterranean Partnership after this was created in 1995. As Mitterrand stated at the end of the extraordinary meeting of the European Council of 27 October 1993, 'We have not spoken of it at the European Council ... I do not think that the current drama in Algeria is currently in the domain of the European Union. As far as that is concerned, France is acting as she must in respect of this neighbouring country'.[23] In the same vein in 1995 Alain Juppé, as president of the Foreign Affairs Council, made no mention of the conference at Sant' Egidio, which had proposed a new political platform for Algeria, developed by the non-governmental parties, Islamists and FIS included, but referred instead only to 'recent developments'.[24]

Meanwhile, as the violence perpetrated by the Islamists was met with pitiless and dark repression, public opinion, the media and governments, notably northern European, showed growing vocal disapproval. The Algerian government, already essentially suspect for having abruptly interrupted the democratic process, found itself warned about its repressive practices which combined torture, arbitrary arrest, disappearances and exile to the Sahara (the figure of 10,000 disappearances being generally admitted). It therefore became more and more difficult, as time went by, for France to maintain a position of tacit 'veto', blocking any European involvement, other than financial, in Algeria.

The opening to more engagement by the EU was progressive. It corresponded, certainly, to a growing demand for more involvement on the part of European public opinion but was also linked to the blocking of the Franco–Algerian bilateral relationship, which became increasingly intractable after the affair of the Air France Airbus hijacking and the beginning of the attacks on French territory. The rationalization and Europeanization of French policy with respect to Algeria took off with the arrival of Jacques Chirac as President in 1995. The Balladur years had been marked by a cacophony of discordant voices amongst the main French players. The Juppé government defined a clear political line which the minister of foreign affairs translated into action, while President Chirac did not himself intervene in the debate. This line was: firm support for the Algerian government and for President Zeroual but pressure for the acceleration of democratic processes; and facilitation of relations with Algeria in the setting of negotiations within the Barcelona Conference, the Mediterranean Forum and other international negotiations. France thus redefined its role as a bridge, or mediator, in relations between Algeria and the EU, as when she successfully pressed Algeria to accept a visit by EU representatives (the Troika and the European Parliament) without the habitual outcry against meddling and attacks on sovereignty.

So the visit of Commissioner Marín to Algiers in December 1996 represented an alignment of the EU with French themes. Marín expressed his pleasure at the progress of the democratic process and announced a new aid package of €125m, along with a qualitative upgrading of the EU's diplomacy, through which the EU would become a full participant in the Algerian scene. The Union knew how to manage the pressure of European idealists cleverly. The visit of the Troika in January 1998, even if it led to few concrete results, marked the solidarity of the EU with the Algerian people, and the visit by members of the European Parliament in February of the same year, although agreed with difficulty and in spite of the constraints imposed by the Algerian authorities, eventually led to a partial opening by the Algerian authorities towards greater transparency. Besides, while the Algerian government was successfully pursuing its struggle against the Islamist guerrillas,[25] the EU recognized the necessity of the struggle against terrorism in the framework of the Euro-Mediterranean Partnership. Thus, two Euro-Mediterranean conferences took place on this theme between 1995 and 2000 as well as a number of seminars, and this theme of co-operation has been discussed in the Euro-Mediterranean 'charter for peace and stability' framework under negotiation.

Morisse-Schilbach saw three explanations for France's new Algerian policy via the European Union.[26] First, France sought a re-balancing in regard to other member states and critical European opinion, these increasingly rejecting the notion of there being certain issues that constituted 'diplomatic private property': one cannot be a paragon of the EU and at the same time act in a totally exclusive way in specific circumstances. Second, the French government was eager to conceal the immobility, or rather the blockage, which characterized the Balladur years for reasons as much French as Algerian. Third, there was a search for a multiplying effect for French diplomacy, the effectiveness of national action increasingly undermined in a globalized world, and of which the Barcelona Process was a practical illustration.

In this evolution, France's jealous protection of the Maghreb – and of Algeria, in particular – as a field of purely national French action slowly gave way to a recognition of the role to be played by the EU in backing up concerns over human rights and democracy. Foreign minister Védrine spoke, prior to the Euro-Mediterranean conference at Marseilles, of the EMP as a 'complementary means for improving in a concrete fashion the respect of human rights'.

Indirect Action for Democracy and Human Rights: The French Strategy for North Africa

The foregoing account shows clearly that France's room for manoeuvre in North Africa is narrow. The elements of a French strategy for democracy and human rights have, however, been developed. Various democracy and human rights initiatives are directly sponsored by the French government, but this type of work is channelled mostly through independent organizations.

At the governmental level, the Ministry of Foreign Affairs manages the *Fonds de solidarité prioritaire* (priority solidarity funds) devoted to supporting actions in the *Zone de solidarité prioritaire* (priority solidarity zone), which encompasses a number of developing countries around the world and which includes North Africa. The first objective of this zone of solidarity is to support actions in order to 'consolidate the rule of law and the reinforcement of democracy'. Moreover, support for democracy and human rights is also included within the framework of technical co-operation and development assistance. The main guidelines of this programme focus on the strengthening of the rule of law and democratic institutions, in order to give political freedom more effective content; they also emphasize the role of constitutional courts, and include a remit to support parliaments, other judicial institutions and human rights commissions.

A notable example of this approach has been the French programme of judicial co-operation with Morocco. Launched in 1996, this programme has included support for the creation of commercial courts, co-operation between the French Cour de Cassation and the Moroccan Supreme Court, and the funding of educational and training links between the Bordeaux magistrates school and the national institute for legal studies in Rabat. Nearly FF 1.5m was allocated for this programme in 2001. The Ministry of Foreign Affairs has also supported NGO projects. For example, in 2001 FF 159,000 was given to the organization Juristes solidarité in Morocco to support a project on legal and developmental training.

While these new programmes are significant, French democracy and human rights assistance to North Africa has remained modest. In 1998, the Maghreb took only 0.32 per cent of France's global budget for supporting NGOs. In North Africa, French support for democracy and human rights is still limited compared to the scale of traditional development projects in the region. Although on a relatively small scale up to now, democracy and human rights assistance in North Africa is set to increase. Still, most significant French action on democracy and human rights is carried out by NGOs or political party foundations. This sometimes benefits from indirect, secretive support from the French government, but often takes place specifically in conflict with the government's aims and wishes.

In the Maghreb, many French civil society organizations have played a substantial role in denouncing democratic and human rights abuses: the Danielle Mitterrand Foundation, the René Seydoux Foundation for the Mediterranean World, the Human Rights League, the International Federation for Human Rights (FIDH), the World Organization against Torture (OMTC), the League against Racism and Anti-Semitism (LICRA), university researchers from the House of the Mediterranean (Maison de la Méditerranée) at Aix-en-Provence, the review *Confluences Meditérannée*,[27] the editorial team of *Le Monde diplomatique*, and many smaller organizations, including some led by North African residents in France. This network of organizations represents an increasingly powerful civil society lobby acting in support of individual citizens and associations in North Africa and pressuring the French government to this end.

During the preparation of the Marseilles EMP conference, the Ministry of Foreign Affairs gave FF 1m for the holding of the Euro-Mediterranean Civil Forum, which organized informal civil society debate, dealing especially with democracy and human rights. As with its broader diplomatic relations, so too in the field of democracy and human rights assistance France evolved from the concept of a North Africa *pré carré* (with exclusive relations) toward a more Europeanized policy. Now the Euromed programme is seen as the most positive and neutral way to develop actions and indirect pressures on democracy and human rights. At the Gothenburg European Council, in June 2001, member states advocated greater EU co-operation in Algeria 'to assist the political, economic and social reforms necessary for restoring peace, stability and prosperity'.[28]

Conclusion

French policy in North Africa has become more Europeanized. There may be some resistance to any shift further in this direction, but this will need to be read as a relic of the past. Where there are still discrepancies with European partners, it is over the right kind of democracy strategy, in particular the choice between crude or softer pressure over North African countries. The French position was clearly expressed by Védrine during the Warsaw conference on the promotion of democracy in June 2000, when France refused to sign the declaration proposed by the US advocating direct pressure upon non-democratic leaders. The French ministry commented that many western countries have a tendency to see democracy too much as a religion that has to be adopted in absolute terms. In practice, nobody has a magic formula and the concept of democracy is more evolutionary than revolutionary.[29] This illustrates the continuing tension in French elite thinking between the will to act against human rights abuses and the fear of destabilization in weak countries. For this reason France has supported discreet, indirect action through NGOs or political parties, helping these organizations even when they contradict official policy. The discrepancies between the Socialist Party and Jospin's government on Tunisia do not point to a schizophrenic but to a rationalized strategy. In sum, the progressive transfer of democracy and human rights policy pressure to both the EU and NGOs aims to transcend France's paranoid relationship with North Africa and especially with Algeria, and will remain a dominant trend in French foreign policy towards the Maghreb for the foreseeable future.

NOTES

1. François Mitterrand, *Réflexions sur la politique extérieure de la France – Introduction à 25 discours (1981–1985)* (Paris: Fayard, 1986), p.425.
2. *Le Figaro*, 9 Jan. 1996, p.46.
3. Speech of 16 March 1995, p.3.
4. See Mario Bettati, *Le droit d'ingérence: mutation de l'ordre international* (Paris: Odile Jacob), pp.96–9.
5. See for instance Claire Spencer, 'Algeria: France's Disarray and Europe Conundrum', in B.A. Roberson (ed.), *The Middle East and Europe* (London: Routledge, 1998), pp.170–84.
6. Nicole Grimaud, 'L'introuvable équilibre Maghrébin', in Samy Cohen and Marie-Claude Smouts (eds.), *La politique extérieure de Valéry Giscard d'Estaing* (Paris: Presses de la FNSP, 1985), pp.323–48.
7. Gilles Perrault, *Notre ami le Roi* (Paris: Gallimard, 1990).
8. See Christine Daure-Serfati, *Tazmamart, une prison de la mort au Maroc* (Paris: Stock, 1992).
9. General Oufkir was the number two of the regime. In 1971 he was the leader of the plot. After its failure he was 'suicided' by the king's men. His family was immediately isolated for 19 years until Hassan's pardon in 1991. Always under tight police control, the family fled to France in 1996. See Malika Oufkir, *La prisonnière* (Paris: Grasset, 1999).
10. See *La gazette du Maroc*, No.436, 11 March 1999.
11. See *L'état du Monde 2000* (Paris: La Découverte, 2000), ch. on the Maghreb, pp.124–5; Florence Beaugé, 'La ligue tunisienne des droits de l'Homme continuera d'exister, affirme son président', *Le Monde*, 3–4 June 2001.
12. Nicolas Beau and Jean-Pierre Tuquoi, *Notre ami Ben Ali* (Paris: La Découverte, 1999).
13. *Le Monde*, 17 April 2001.
14. Press conference, 1 June 2001, Tunis.
15. For more on this subject, see Hubert Védrine, *Les Mondes de François Mitterrand: A l'Elysée 1981–1995* (Paris: Fayard, 1996); J.F. Daguzan, 'Les rapports franco-algériens, 1962–1992, réconciliation ou conciliation permanente?', *Politique étrangère*, No.3 (1993–94), pp.885–96.
16. Daguzan, op. cit., pp.893–4; Mélanie Morisse-Schilbach, *L'Europe et la question algérienne* (Paris: Perspectives internationales, 1999), pp.62–9; Paul-Marie de la Gorce, 'La France et le Maghreb', *Politique étrangère*, No.4 (1995–96), pp.936–7; and Védrine, op.cit., p.687, which records, 'With Roland Dumas, he (the president) refused moreover to reduce economic aid to Algeria, in opposition to those who demanded that it should be subordinated to a compromise with the Islamists, since such a reduction could only aggravate the situation of the Algerian people and feed their revolt'.
17. 'Cohabitation' refers to phases in the history of the Fifth Republic during which rival parties have controlled the presidency and the government.
18. Cited by de la Gorce, op. cit., p.933.
19. See François Léotard, 'Comment aider les Algériens?', *Le Figaro*, 1 Feb. 1995, quoted by de la Gorce, op. cit., p.937.
20. Morisse-Schilbach, op. cit., p.121.
21. See, in this context, the very interesting book by Lucille Provost, an official of the Quai d'Orsay specializing in Algeria and writing under a pseudonym, which describes very well the politico-social crisis and crisis of conscience of the time, L. Provost, *La seconde guerre algérienne: le quiproquo franco-algérien* (Paris: Flammarion, 1996).
22. 'The GIA ... contributed greatly to French support for the Algerian regime ... and its claiming of attacks perpetrated in France in 1995 made it the enemy of the Algerian authorities and France, as well as the FIS. Also, many doubts remain about the "emirs" of the armed gangs of the GIA, who have done so much to weaken the cause which they were supposed to serve', Khartala, *La guerre civile en Algérie* (Paris: Recherches internationales, 1998), p.349.
23. Quoted by Morisse-Schilbach, op. cit., p.79.
24. Ibid., p.85.
25. For an analysis of the civil war and civil–military relations in general in Algeria, see J.F.

Daguzan, *Le dernier rempart? Forces armées et politiques de défense au Maghreb* (Paris: Publisud/FMES, 1998).

26. Morisse-Schilbach, op.cit., pp.122–3.
27. See Driss El Yazami, 'Les droits de l'Homme: critère central du PEM?', *Confluences Méditerranée*, No.35 (2000), pp.119–29; and Monique Prim's interview, 'Faire émerger un espace de citoyenneté', ibid., pp.137–45. Monique Prim is president of the Forum des citoyens and of the French group of the Euromed Civil Forum.
28. http://ue.eu.int/Newsroom/load.cfm.
29. *New York Times*, 27 June 2000.

Two Cheers for Whom? The European Union and Democratization in Morocco

SAID HADDADI

During the 1980s, economic liberalization was advanced as the magical potion that would cure the economic, political and social ills befalling the developing world. The argument was that economic liberalization was conducive to political change and social equality. Though the argument did not prove completely unfounded, efforts to test it have shown that different countries have had different experiences with liberalization. In some, economic liberalization bore political fruit. In most, it did not: it simply exacerbated social inequality, reinforced political sclerosis and ultimately exposed the inability of the state to deliver on its promises as well as the deep political malaise from which it suffered. Fading into the background without really being abandoned, liberalization in the 1990s became consolidated by the need to develop good governance and democratic reforms for it to achieve its goals. The rule of law, civil society and non-governmental organizations (NGOs) started to be perceived as vectors for political change and democracy promotion. In this way, foreign aid and financial assistance have become contingent on respect for human rights and a declared will to support democratic institutions and principles. In line with the democratic peace argument, human rights and democracy have turned into a sort of *leitmotif*; building democracy has been introduced as both condition and objective in most, if not all, co-operation agreements contracted with developing countries. International pressure following the fall of the Berlin Wall and the subsequent changes that swept eastern Europe have obliged the authoritarian regimes of the southern Mediterranean to declare their commitment to political liberalization and democratic reforms, at least at the discursive level.

At a time when the democratic experience in neighbouring Algeria has proved tragically bogus and Tunisia has witnessed marked political inertia sprinkled with intermittent bouts of human rights violations, the political situation in Morocco seems to offer varying and rather different features.

Some see Morocco as making unprecedented political moves towards democracy – albeit under the shadow of the monarch. Others deem the very involvement of the king as the initiator of these moves to be disruptive of any democratic development, arguing that these moves do not actually translate into signs of genuine democracy. At the domestic level, the release of political prisoners in 1991, 1994 and 1998, the constitutional reforms of 1992 and 1996, the establishment of *alternance* with the arrival in government of the socialist opposition in 1998, the return of historical political dissidents (Abraham Serfaty and the family of Ben Barka) after the death of Hassan II, the spectacular sacking of interior minister Driss Basri, the release from house arrest of the Islamist leader Abdessalam Yassine and the 'desecuritization' of the Western Sahara have all given positive signals that the political system in Morocco is 'breaking' with the practices of the past. At the regional level, the country is seeking ever-closer relations with the EU, as witnessed by the signing of the Euro-Mediterranean Association Agreement (EMAA) within the framework of the Euro-Mediterranean Partnership (EMP) established by the Barcelona Declaration of 1995. At the international level, Morocco has ratified a number of conventions committing it to respect human rights and democratic principles. In the course of these openings, a young civil society started to develop with the emergence of a number of NGOs focusing on democracy and development. On the other hand, the role of external actors (the EU, international non-governmental organizations, and so on) in the development and promotion of democracy has often been stressed, sometimes exaggeratedly, as facilitating democratic transitions. Changes or improvements in the political situation of some countries have been trumpeted as a success story and sometimes unduly accredited to pressures exerted by these international actors, often undervaluing the role played by the interaction (complementary or distortive) between international programmes/activities and domestic dynamics.

Within this framework, Morocco's relationship with the EU deserves particular consideration because of the North African country's declared commitment to democracy and its interest in developing stronger relations with the European Union, and the EU's declared will and desire to promote democracy as an integral part of its foreign and security policy. It is in order at this stage, after a decade of 'political co-operation', to reflect on the relationship between Morocco and the EU, focusing in particular on democracy promotion activities and examining the forces at work behind the ongoing changes in the country. This study examines the EU's democracy promotion activity in Morocco. First, it looks at the development of EU–Moroccan political relations during the 1990s together with the Moroccan political reforms of the period. Then it considers the EU's initiatives to promote democracy in Morocco with particular reference to the MEDA Democracy Programme (MDP) elaborated within the framework of the EMP.

EU–Moroccan Relations in the 1990s

The EMAA establishing an economic, political and socio-cultural partnership between Morocco and the EU was signed in February 1996 and entered into force only in March 2000. Yet relations between Morocco and the Community date back to the late 1960s. Just over 12 months after its independence on 2 March 1956, Morocco had witnessed how, through article 238 of the Treaty of Rome, the European Community had established a provision that seemed to express a readiness to negotiate a form of economic association with countries that remained part of an independent area based on the Franc. A bilateral association agreement was signed in July 1969 for a period of five years, only to be superseded in 1976 by a co-operation agreement within the framework of the more ambitious EEC Global Mediterranean Policy (GMP) initiated in 1972. Co-operation under the GMP was limited to economic and financial aid in the form of bilateral financial protocols.[1] The EEC's Mediterranean enlargement to include Greece (1981) and later Spain and Portugal (1986) paradoxically contributed to an intensification of relations with Morocco. The third generation financial protocol (1987–91) represented an increase in aid of 62 per cent, but remained focused on classical developmental and technical assistance. Despite increased financial aid, Hassan II decided, to the surprise of the Europeans, to file a formal application to join the EEC. He did this in July 1987 after an informal approach had been rebuffed in 1984. Not surprisingly, the Moroccan application was rejected with an expected European jibe, not least on the grounds that Morocco was not a European country. The rejection was based on article 237 of the Treaty of Rome envisaging membership of other European countries without, however, excluding applications from non-European members. It is interesting to note that Hassan II's letter to the Danish president of the Council of Ministers requesting EEC membership contained three arguments: Morocco's commitment to develop a liberal economy; its close economic ties with the European Community; and, most important, the *democratization* of domestic political life. Though this shows Morocco's use of a discourse on democratization, it should be stressed that the latter was presented merely in terms of the development and consolidation of a multiparty system and the circulation of a local and international press, featuring a variety of opinions. Issues of human rights, for example, remained absent. Though the Moroccan application failed, it was a successful strategic manoeuvre that brought Morocco more conspicuously onto the European agenda. Indeed, the visit by Jacques Delors, the then President of the Commission, from 7 to 11 October 1987, confirmed the Commission's intention to strengthen the special relations it had with Morocco.

The failure (or stalling) of the Arab Maghreb Union (AMU) – partly owing to the outbreak of violence in Algeria and the international sanctions imposed on Libya – prompted a sense of urgency in Morocco regarding its relations with the EU during the 1990s. Between a poor Mauritania to the south and a bellicose Algeria to the east, Morocco could not but look to the EU, seeking to develop special relations with it. Some analysts and officials involved in European external relations with the Mediterranean have accredited to Morocco the idea of creating a free trade zone as early as 1990.[2] For the EU, Morocco's 1980s political and socio-economic difficulties, engendered by a dramatic fall in the prices of oil (causing a loss of financial assistance from the Gulf monarchies) and phosphates (the country's main export at the time), were major incentives to enhance its relationship with the kingdom. Conscious of the difficulties facing Mediterranean countries, EU members devised the Renovated Mediterranean Policy (RMP), increasing the aid package associated with the fourth generation of financial protocols. What was new about the RMP was that, although it continued with the policy of development assistance, it also emphasized the importance of human rights, with a new provision enabling the European Parliament to freeze the budget of a financial protocol when faced with serious human rights violations.

The content of this provision affected Morocco and Syria first. By virtue of the Single European Act of 1986, the signing of the fourth generation of financial protocols required the support of an absolute majority in the European Parliament. By June 1991, the European Council of Luxembourg had adopted the Declaration on Human Rights as part of the Community's external relations policy, as an essential component of its co-operation and development initiatives. Against the background of this new *acquis*, in January 1992 the European Parliament decided to freeze Morocco's fourth financial protocol (1991–96) on the grounds of human rights abuses (citing as the reason for its action UN Resolution 660 on the Western Sahara) and the shocking conditions of political prisoners (some of them just released). The rejection was also a culmination of a number of complaints that were voiced during European parliamentary discussions regarding human rights violations in Morocco since the mid-1980s.[3] Morocco's riposte was swift and strong: it cut off negotiations with the Commission concerning the renewal of the EC–Moroccan fisheries agreement and renounced the principle of assistance in the form of the fourth financial protocol.[4] The ill-timed rejection by the European Parliament reflected a lack of political dialogue between the two parties, especially given that Morocco was then starting to introduce a number of democratic elements into its political system (on which more below). Paradoxically once more, the tension between the EU and Morocco triggered some high-gear diplomacy, culminating in a significant upgrading of their co-operation. On 17 February 1992, the idea of developing a comprehensive partnership with Morocco was discussed in the Council within the framework of European Political Co-operation (EPC), without however reaching a final decision. As a result of this and because of the political situation in Algeria, the Spanish government put forward the idea of developing even closer relations with all the countries of the Maghreb. This was the aim of the Commission policy document of 2 March 1992 entitled 'The Future of Relations between the European Community and the Maghreb', issued just 46 days after the Parliament's rejection of the fourth protocol. The Lisbon summit of 26–27 June 1992 endorsed proposals for a Euro–Maghreb Partnership, thus shifting the emphasis from development co-operation to partnership.

This partnership put a premium on a common commitment to: (i) respect for international law, the principles of the UN Charter and the Resolutions of the UN Security Council; (ii) respect for human rights and fundamental freedoms in civil, political, economic, social and cultural matters and for democratic values exemplified by free and regular elections; (iii) the establishment of democratic institutional systems guaranteeing pluralism, effective participation by citizens in the lives of their states and respect for the rights of minorities; and (iv) tolerance and coexistence between cultures and religions. In comparison to the RMP, the Euro–Maghreb Partnership's political dialogue became more explicit with more reference made to democracy and respect for human rights. None the less, it was limited to a 'regular exchange of information and greater mutual consultation on political and security matters'.[5] Though the Euro–Maghreb Partnership quickly lost momentum, its spirit lived on in the principles of the Barcelona Declaration (1995).

The Barcelona Declaration reiterated more forcefully the tone of the political dialogue initiated with the Euro–Maghreb Partnership. Promoting democracy and developing civil society are listed as objectives in baskets one and three respectively. To sustain these objectives, the EU developed, within the framework of the European Initiative for Democracy and Human Rights of 1994, the MEDA Democracy Programme (MDP) as a component of the EMP, granting financial support to civil society members and public bodies that engage in the promotion of democracy and democratic institutions. In May 1995, the EU injected a clause on respect for human rights and democracy as a major foundation and condition for its bilateral relations with third countries.[6] Thus, the continuity of co-operation between the EU and Morocco has become contingent on acceptance and respect of the principles of democratic reform as embedded in the political dialogue of the EMP. EU–Moroccan bilateral co-operation within the EMP was enhanced by the signing of the EMAA whereby the provisions of the political dialogue became legally binding. With this agreement, relations between the EU and Morocco entered a new, and perhaps more structured, phase. Morocco's signing of the agreement as early as 1996 shows the national government's will to endorse the principles of the Barcelona Declaration. No doubt economic ties and stakes played a decisive role in the signing of the agreement. It is not surprising that the first countries to sign the EMAAs were those with the more substantial economic interests tied up with the EU, namely Tunisia and Morocco. Even the signing of the Barcelona Declaration took place with the prior knowledge that funds would be made available through the MEDA I programme (1996–99) to support the implementation of the objectives set for the EMP. None the less, article 3 of the MEDA Regulation governing the EMP stipulates that 'this Regulation is based on respect for democratic principles and the rule of law and also for human rights and fundamental freedoms, which constitute an essential element thereof, the violation of which element will justify the adoption of appropriate measures', thus clearly adding a suspension clause to the EU's co-operation with Mediterranean partners. Economic matters aside, the EMP's emphasis on security and stability made some southern regimes perceive the partnership as a means of confirming their legitimacy and guaranteeing their continuity. This highlights the need to look at the domestic political reforms in Morocco prior to and since the launch of the EMP.

Political Reforms in Morocco

By the time of the signing of the EMAA, Morocco had already embarked on a number of changes introducing democratic elements to its political system. The succession of Hassan II had prompted much speculation about future scenarios and was awaited with a great deal of apprehension considering the country's fragile socio-economic and political situation. Yet it passed calmly amidst promising signs for the future. King Mohamed VI's determination to continue with the political opening initiated by his father in the early 1990s and the speed with which he introduced new changes fascinated domestic and international public opinion alike. During the early 1990s Morocco had faced a lot of pressure from different sides. The international community and international NGOs had exposed the reality of human rights violations and arbitrary arrests – as witnessed by the publication of Gilles Perrault's *Notre Ami le Roi* (1990), the rejection of the fourth financial protocol by the European Parliament and the reports of Amnesty International, for instance. At the regional level, the outbreak of violence in Algeria had encouraged Morocco to rethink its domestic political life. Thoughts of reform were complicated, however, by the widespread urban strikes in Fez, Casablanca and Rabat particularly at the time of the 1991 Gulf War.[7] Nevertheless, Morocco now entered a new period of political reforms, aimed at initiating more democratic openings and respect for human rights.

Already in December 1988, King Hassan had approved the holding of meetings by the Organisation Marocaine des Droits de l'Homme (OMDH), these having been banned following its creation a few months earlier.[8] In May 1990, the king announced the creation of a Conseil Consultatif des Droits de l'Homme (CCDH) to examine cases of human rights violations and assist their victims. In June 1991, 300 political prisoners were released. Reinforcing the significance of these changes, the 1992 constitution had made reference in its preamble to Moroccan respect for human rights and had created a Conseil Constitutionel to look into the constitutionality of laws. Notwithstanding this preamble, the 1992 constitutional reforms had changed very little, however: they remained largely in line with the tradition of the previous constitutional amendments of 1970 and 1972, that is, changes in the number of seats subject to direct suffrage rather than in the conventional power of the monarchy.[9] The 1993 elections, the first since 1984,[10] did not yield the expected results. Despite the palace's promises of 'free and fair' elections and the use of the US-based International Foundation for Electoral Systems to monitor them, these elections were fraudulent – especially during the second round, which resulted in a surprising victory for the centre-right. As a result, the opposition refused to participate in the government despite the king's offer of 31 out of 35 ministries. On the other hand, the king refused to respond to their demands to cancel the elections and instead appointed a technocratic government headed by Mohamed Karim Lamrani, thus announcing the failure of the first attempt at political *alternance* and the beginning of a long *bras de fer* between the palace and the Koutla opposition.

Despite their apparent failure to bring about political *alternance*, the 1993 elections did, nevertheless, bring on stage taboo issues that until then had been absent from electoral programmes. Political parties started to call for more attention to be given to human rights. To circumvent international criticism and silence national human rights militants, Hassan II, in characteristic fashion, created a cabinet-level Ministry of Human Rights in the newly formed government, invited Amnesty International to visit the country (which resulted in the setting up of a Committee for Dialogue with Amnesty International in order to improve the human rights situation), promoted the efforts of the CCDH, ratified the international conventions against torture and discrimination against women in 1993, and granted an amnesty to more political prisoners in 1994.[11] While being positive moves towards democratization, these initiatives actually undermined the role of other political actors and highlighted the central role of the king. Furthermore, the 1993 elections showed a bipolarization of political parties into two blocs: the democratic Koutla and the national Wifak,[12] a bipolarization which Hassan II welcomed, comparing it to that of the US and the UK.

On another level, debate over the participation of the opposition laid the ground for further constitutional and political reforms emphasizing the need for more democratic openings and a transition to a less overbearing constitutional monarchy. In fact, six months before the September 1996 constitutional referendum, the opposition addressed a memorandum to the palace calling for (among other things) a wider commitment to human rights, reform of the electoral law and an explicit and clear definition of constitutional parliamentary monarchy. This shows that constitutional reforms were no longer seen solely as a royal prerogative. Indeed, political parties collaborated with the electoral reforms preceding the 1997 elections, though the nature of these reforms was monitored by the Ministry of the Interior. Negotiations to reach a compromise between the palace and the opposition were accelerated by the health problems Hassan II suffered during his visit to the US in November 1996. Unlike in 1992, the opposition campaigned for a 'yes' vote in favour of the 1996 constitutional reforms. Also, before the campaign for the 1997 elections, 11 political parties, including the opposition, signed with interior minister Driss Basri a 'national pact' aimed at the consolidation of a democratic regime founded on the monarchy. The 'national pact' committed all the signatories to respect the electoral law, and the administration to remain impartial and to punish fraudulent practices. By March the National Commission for the Control of Elections had finished cleaning up the electoral lists. In the same vein, the OMHD, the Ligue Marocaine pour la Défence des Droits de l'Homme (LMDDH) and the Association Marocaine des Droits de l'Homme (AMDH) signed a national charter of human rights on 12 December of the same year. 1996–97 seemed a period of mobilization for all political actors to push forward the democratic experience, which culminated in the opposition winning the elections and forming a coalition government headed by Abderrahmane Youssoufi, a veteran opposition leader. Thus, the 1997 elections ultimately led to the long-negotiated and much applauded transition to a system of political *alternance*. This event was seen as a precedent for Morocco and southern Mediterranean Arab countries. Nevertheless, some criticized the opposition for accepting what it had refused to accept in 1992 (that is, the king keeping control over the four 'ministries of sovereignty').[13] Others considered *alternance* itself to be a manoeuvre contrived by the king and the opposition to 'neutralize' any challenge by the Islamists.

In fact, the Democratic openings of 1996 also created an opportunity for the main Islamist groups, Al Islah wa Attawhid and Jamaâ Al Adl wal Ihssan, to become integrated into the legal political life of the country and put forward their ideas and values. This was particularly true of Al Islah, which won nine seats in the lower house in the 1997 elections. This happened only when it fielded its candidates under the banner of the Mouvement Populaire Constitutionel Démocratique (MPCD), with which it allied first in 1992 and then in 1996. After the elections, the MPCD became the Parti de la Justice et du Développement (PJD) to reflect its Islamist component. In this way, Al Islah came to participate in the government and to voice its 'conditional or critical support' of the government.[14] In addition to political *alternance*, the presence of Islamists in parliament has also been deemed a positive sign of democratic openness. However, for many, including members of Al Adl, Al Islah did not win: it was co-opted. The PJD was criticized as a political card that Youssoufi used according to circumstances. The special stance of the party as the main protester against the National Plan for the Integration of Women in Development has been considered a tactic to counter more radical reactions from Al Adl. Unlike Al Islah, the more radical Al Adl decided to stay away from the political game until the conditions were ripe for its participation. For Al Adl, the 1997 elections added more complications instead of solving them,[15] and the *alternance* was nothing but a gentleman's agreement.[16] If the co-opting of Al Islah together with Al Adl's refusal to follow suit and participate in parliamentary politics by becoming a political party isolated the latter, at the same time Al Adl reinforced its role as the only real opposition on the political stage at present. Al Adl can also use its acquired 'opposition status' as an electoral card if ever it is officially recognized and decides to organize itself for the forthcoming elections of 2002, considering the weak nature of the incumbent government and its relative failure to deliver on promises. In a memorandum to Mohamed VI, Yassine declared that 'if we accept the democratic procedure, we adamantly reject anything that drifts us away from our *raison d'être*: Islam'.[17] Notwithstanding the ambiguity of this declaration, it still shows a major shift in Yassine's thinking through him accepting democratic procedures within the confines of Islam; this sets him apart from Islamist leaders in other countries.

'Mort le Roi, Vive le Roi': Political Power in Morocco

To what extent do the constitutional reforms, the opposition's access to government and the participation of the Islamists in parliament constitute the start of a genuine political pluralism and democratization in Morocco? Answers to this question entail first and foremost an understanding of the meaning and workings of opposition in Morocco. With the success of the 'Green March' in November 1975, the final element of the rules of the political game was put in place. These rules are succinctly translated in the Moroccan national motto: 'God, the Country, the King'. As such, the motto sets the rules, draws the boundaries and determines the actions of political actors.[18] Opposition is defined in relation to any refusal or questioning of the foundations of the national motto. The religious status of the king as *Amir Al Mouminin* (Commander of the Faithful), which was emphasized even more after the Iranian revolution of 1979 and the creation of a council of *ulama* in January 1980, limits the legitimacy of the Islamists and restricts their politico-religious claims.[19] Thus, the king emerges as the '*pièce maîtresse*' of the political system in Morocco. Therefore, apart from any international pressure, the democratic openings in Morocco should also be read in the light of the perennial struggle for control over the political system between the monarch and the political parties. The striking feature of this struggle is the fluctuating role of the king between acting as an absolute monarch, a flexible authoritarian, a cunning manipulator and an active arbitrator. Paradoxically, the participation of the opposition and of Islamists in the government has now further reinforced the role of the king as arbiter *vis-à-vis* political actors of all stripes.

In this context, a distinction is necessary between political transition and transition of power. In western democracies, political transition can generally be used interchangeably with the transition of power. A transition in government is a transition of power from one majority to another, or from government to opposition. Political transition in Morocco does not transfer power from government to opposition because *real* political power lies outside the realm of political party competition. It lies in the palace, with the monarch who sets himself up above and beyond any power equation.[20] Though the king does not interfere directly in politics, preferring to remain invisible, his actions are carried out indirectly via the omnipresent *makhzen*, a network of patronage, grants, arbitration and distribution of rewards that is controlled from above and centres around his person.[21] As such, the opposition government and the integrated Islamists are usually seen as (and often criticized for) being 'makhzenized'. The shadow of the *makhzen* also extends to the economic field, where political allegiances are guaranteed through the distribution of economic favours and protection. None the less, anchoring Morocco to Europe and the commitment to an open market economy are bound to change these allegiances, especially with the emergence of new groups of independent entrepreneurs denouncing corruption together with the illegal practices of the *makhzen* and calling for more administrative transparency.[22] The anti-corruption campaign of autumn 1995, which was a response to a World Bank report of the same year, is equally seen as an attempt to control and establish new allegiances.[23]

The preponderant weight of both the *makhzen* and personalized power has been felt significantly with the death of Hassan II and the sacking of Driss Basri. Upon his arrival in power, Mohamed VI showed a vehement will to change the socio-economic and administrative situation of the country, calling for the establishment of a state of law and more respect for human rights. But the sacking of Basri on 9 November 1999 was seen as and still remains the sign *par excellence* of a new era, even though his dismissal was not followed by major institutional changes at ministry level.[24] Indeed, for the media, political parities and the population at large, the succession started only with the dismissal of Basri as minister of the interior. This reaction is telling not only of the concentrated and personalized nature of power in Morocco but also, and most importantly, of the relationship between citizens and the state – a relationship characterized by fear and mistrust: fear of the arbitrariness of authority (which is mainly embodied in the Ministry of the Interior); and mistrust of political life and politicians (which is manifest in low turnouts at elections).[25] In a speech to Moroccan regional and local administrative bodies, Mohamed VI introduced a 'new concept of authority' based on respect for individual liberties, the rule of law and the preservation of social stability.[26] The new definition of authority is a step towards reconciling citizens with the state, a reconciliation that is best embodied in the state acknowledging its responsibility for a number of disappearances, cases of torture and arbitrary arrests, and its commitment to compensate the victims of such practices. The start of state–citizen reconciliation is, in fact, the fruit of continuous efforts by a number of NGOs and civil society members.

The political and economic omnipresence of the state in the 1980s triggered a spring in associational life,[27] initially in socio-cultural spheres. With the relative retreat of the state, the challenge of civil society in Morocco has been to broaden the political agenda to include human rights, democracy and social and economic justice. Associational life in its modern form started during the mid-1980s with cultural regional associations such as Ribat Al Fath, Fes-Saiss, Bou Regrag and Souss-Casablanca. Most of these associations were created and headed by individuals close to the palace. Their objectives and activities were limited to socio-cultural development, the environment, arts and sports. Progressive political liberalization in the 1990s has led to a burgeoning of associations with a more active spirit in the spheres of human rights and democratic development. The map of civil society spans a variety of areas such as human rights, women and children, development and civic education, as well as Islamic associations. This surge in civil society has been positively perceived and encouraged by the EU as a 'democracy promoter' in its partnership co-operation with Morocco as an 'emerging democracy'.

The EU and Democracy in Morocco

With the Declaration on Human Rights adopted at the Luxembourg European Council on 28–29 June 1991, the EU emphasized the importance of democracy as a cornerstone of its foreign and development policy. It also put a premium on the indivisible character of human rights and highlighted the catalytic role civil society and NGOs can play in promoting democratic principles, good governance and the rule of law. For this reason, it has based its actions and programmes in third countries mainly on a partnership with civil society and NGOs. This enthusiasm is reflected in the EU's spending in terms of building and reinforcing a pluralist civil society.[28] In its efforts to promote democracy, the EU places special emphasis on themes such as democratization and the rule of law, the development of a pluralist civil society and confidence-building measures to restore peace, while its target groups range from those requiring special protection (such as women, children, minorities, prisoners, victims of torture and so on) to those that can promote democratic principles (especially journalists, magistrates and police forces). This focus is clearly present in the MDP, a programme specially designed to foster democracy in EMP countries.[29]

Morocco was one of the first southern Mediterranean countries to be affected by the new dimension of the EU co-operation strategy and its emphasis on democracy and human rights. The strong reaction of both Morocco and certain EU governments to the European Parliament's refusal to give assent to the fourth financial protocol showed the adverse effect that strictly applying 'negative' conditionality could have on relations with third partners as well as on EU governments that have special ties with them. These reactions informed the tuning down of the tone in which human rights and democracy objectives were to be formulated subsequently. The formulation of the Barcelona Declaration remains quite vague and cautious as to the kind of democracy to be developed, 'recognising … the right of each of [the partners] to choose and freely develop its own political, socio-cultural, economic and judicial systems'. With the signing of the Barcelona Declaration, Morocco and the EU committed themselves to closer co-operation at the political level, with special reference to respect for human rights and democratic principles. Within the MDP framework, Moroccan governmental and non-governmental bodies can apply to the EU to fund projects intended to promote human rights and democratic principles. In the period 1996–2000, the EU financed a total of 46 projects in Morocco: 32 centred directly on Morocco, while 14 others involved Morocco indirectly at a regional level.[30] Morocco emerged as one of the principal beneficiaries of MDP funds with 12 operations in 1997 alone, taking 19 per cent of the €8m allocated to the MDP for that year. Also, of the 13 projects approved for 2000, Morocco had two direct projects funded, and was a partner in five regional projects. Excluding regional programmes, however, for Morocco the MDP represents only a minute amount, just 0.3 per cent of the total amount it received from the MEDA I programme for 1996–99.[31]

Of all the direct (as opposed to regional) operations financed within the framework of the MDP in Morocco in 1996–2000, only nine were focused directly on national civil society, representing 19 per cent of the funds allocated to non-governmental bodies. Some 17 projects were managed by international NGOs and represented 73 per cent of the total funds. Only two projects were co-managed by Moroccan and international civil society actors, representing just eight per cent of the funds. It is interesting to note that 18 per cent of the MDP funds went to four projects designed by the ministries of human rights and education (that is, governmental bodies). At the regional level, Morocco benefited from a total of 13 horizontal projects during 1996–2000, worth €7,119,357. Indeed, regional projects absorb a large amount of money, though their impact is sometimes compromised when they are not organized in Morocco or when their proposed activities do not involve rotation among the countries involved. In terms of the distribution of funds, national civil society actors seem less successful (or less skilful?) in filing applications.[32] In comparison, international NGOs with programmes directed to Morocco seem to do well both in the number of projects successfully filed as well as in the amount of funds allocated to their implementation. If anything, this reflects the immature nature of civil society in Morocco – not least in its lack of experience with foreign sponsors – and the need for the EU to 'vulgarize' the application procedures for MDP funds.[33] Also, the sheer size of ministries compared to national civil society makes them potential fund competitors, especially given that they enjoy an already existing institutional structure.[34] Among the projects designed by governmental organizations, there is, for instance, the introduction of human rights education in school curricula put into place by the ministries of human rights and education. Within the framework of this project, a number of actions were taken, for example the publication of a collection of the human rights conventions ratified by Morocco. The other projects undertaken by the Ministry of Human Rights centre on the rights of prisoners and awareness-raising operations.

In addition, a number of projects supporting the development of associational life in Morocco were funded from the MEDA programme, such as a project for an 'integrated programme for the support of developmental associations', which was financed for an amount of €4m and supervised by the Ministry of Social Development, Solidarity, Employment and Professional Training. This project aimed at strengthening the institutional and organizational structure of Moroccan associations, focusing mainly on 'intermediary' associations working in the fields of the environment, development and the protection of women, children and youth. With such an operation, Morocco has been the first country to integrate the development of civil society, as an essential recommendation of the Barcelona Declaration, in its National Indicative Programme (NIP). The interaction between the MEDA programme and the objectives of the MDP can also be found in projects such as 'support for basic education', aiming at the education of young girls, and 'support for the Ministry of Social Development', seeking to contribute to the integration of women in development.[35]

The democracy promotion policy of the EU focuses on action-themes such as democratization and the rule of law, the development of pluralist civil society and initiatives for target groups. A look at all the projects financed reveals the orientation of the EU's democratization efforts in Morocco. In terms of the volume of funding, the building of a pluralist civil society appears at the top of the list with 46 per cent, which merely confirms the general orientation of the EU worldwide. Another 37 per cent goes on democratization and the rule of law and only 17 per cent on target groups. Support for 'pluralist civil society' in the case of Morocco is granted mainly to human rights education and public awareness (12 per cent), both through seminars and the dissemination of information via radio programmes and information centres. Indeed, eight projects are sponsored in this intervention area. These include a programme proposed by the Ministry of Human Rights in collaboration with the Ministry of Education, a radio programme supported by the Moroccan NGO, *Afak*, a number of seminars on democracy and development organized by Association Alternative, and an Arab documentation and information network set up by the Arab Institute of Human Rights (AIHR). It should be noted that though the area of equal opportunities and non-discrimination receives 13 per cent of the funds, it includes only one regional project financed for 2000 comprising the Maghreb area. Although funds allocated to assisting NGOs are the highest (19 per cent), they cover only five projects in total. Within this area of action, freedom of expression and the media receives only two per cent of funds.

In the area of 'democratization and the rule of law', defence of human rights comes top with 22 per cent. None the less, the largest chunk here comes as part of perhaps the biggest regional programme so far with an amount of €1,660,838 for 2000 covering Algeria, Egypt, Jordan, Lebanon and Morocco, and with Tunisia as the applicant country. Elections, which are vital to any democratic development, benefit from only four per cent of the funds with three projects, including training seminars for electoral observers organized by the OMDH and the Hellenic Foundation for European and Foreign Policy (ELIAMEP). The area of 'initiatives for target groups' suffers from a scarcity of projects, especially for children and judicial personnel. Out of the 17 per cent that this area absorbed, only one per cent each went to children and judicial staff. On the other hand, eight projects have been introduced and financed in relation to the empowerment of women. Women's rights also figure as part of wider human rights and development projects, which contributes to putting women's issues forcefully on the national agenda. Some attention has been paid recently to the condition of prisoners and immigrants under the 2000 projects. The only project designed to promote immigrants' rights in Morocco so far is one set up by the International Organization for Migration to create a migrant resource centre in co-operation with the Ministry of Human Rights and national NGOs with similar interests. The centre will promote campaigns targeting potential and seasonal immigrants as well as those that might fall victim to human trafficking networks.

The mapping of projects financed within the framework of the MDP[36] thus reveals areas of concentrated action, areas that remain underrepresented and others that are completely neglected. There is a concentration of intervention mainly in the area of human rights education and women's rights. The human rights scene is overshadowed by the issue of forced disappearances, torture and deaths in prisons. Indeed, the main task of the CCDH is to deal with a total of 5,879 applications for compensation for victims of human rights abuses.[37] Women's projects are not top of the list in terms of funds (especially those allocated to the empowerment of women), but the fact that they are numerous and small in nature makes women's rights an omnipresent issue. None the less, there is still a wide gap between *de jure* and *de facto* rights for Moroccan women.[38] The situation of women still needs to be upgraded, especially in relation to political rights and participation, domestic violence and the civil code. With the relative exception of women, other target groups remain clearly underrepresented. For example, only one project has been financed for the protection of children. Although the textile and shoemaking sectors managed to banish child labour in order to improve their image *vis-à-vis* European consumers, child labour is still on the rise in the informal sector. A number of children below the age of 12 still work as apprentices in the carpet industry or to mechanics, or as domestic servants in the case of girls.[39] Similarly, the rights of prisoners remain underrepresented and have only recently received a relative boost with a 2000 regional project by Penal Reform International aimed at supporting and promoting national reforms in the fields of penal and penitentiary matters.

Even if the other two intervention areas (that is, pluralist civil society and democratization and the rule of law) absorbed higher percentages of MDP funds, they still suffer from a lack of support in some intervention sub-areas. For instance, despite the restrictive nature of the directives regulating the press, only two per cent of the funding is invested in promoting more freedom in this area. Though the government tolerates sporadic criticism from the press, there have been, in parallel, a number of bans, the most recent being that of *Le Journal* for publishing a letter explicitly implicating Prime Minister Youssoufi in the coup attempt of 1972. Newspapers, like political parties (and most newspapers *have* party affiliations), still have to operate within the confines of the political rules discussed above and, as such, exercise a sort of self-censorship. Further, support for election-related issues remains generally weak. Other intervention areas such as the rights of minorities and freedom of association for Islamist non-violent associations are still absent from the efforts of national *and* international civil society. Though the Berber issue is not as pronounced in Morocco as in neighbouring Algeria, demands for any official status to be given to the Berber language face state rigidity, as witnessed by the number of arrests in the province of Errachidia in 1994. The sticky issue *par excellence*, however, remains that of non-secular pacific groups that wish to set up associations. A number of religious associations are still denied the right to establish an organization or are not officially recognized and therefore are not entitled to MDP funds. This raises the question of whether the EU can, or is willing to, sponsor civil society members and NGOs that are not officially recognized by the Moroccan government. This in turn brings to the fore the kind of civil society the EU wants to develop in Morocco.

Granted, MDP projects for Morocco are financed because they have been put forward by members of civil society, and thus, arguably, they simply reflect areas where this civil society is active. This, however, should not lead us to ignore the influence of the EU as a donor, which allows it to favour applications for funds that correspond most closely to its priorities. In this sense, these projects mirror the EU's interests as well. Therefore, MDP projects should be looked upon as the fruits of a combination of EU interests and civil society activism. And so should responsibility for the lack of interest in some areas be a shared one between the EU, civil society and the local government.

Conclusion

Considering its worldwide funds for the promotion of democracy, EU policy in this regard hinges on the promising role of civil society as representative of grass roots. For this reason, projects financed by the EU are comfortably seen as good examples of the bottom-up approach that the EU cherishes. But as seen above, the majority of projects for Morocco are put forward by international civil society, which dilutes any claim for them being a reflection of a bottom-up democratization process. Such a claim is sometimes equally difficult to make even by national civil society. Moroccan civil society (at least the one dealing with the EU) remains elitist and therefore is not representative enough for one to speak of it as contributing to the development of a grass-roots democracy. True, it does contribute to the promotion of democracy, but some of its worries seem to be '*un règlement de compte*' rooted in the post-independence period, especially in relation to human rights.[40]

Since this is the case, the question is whether applying a top-down approach to democracy – that is, proposing programmes for the promotion of democracy precisely in areas where there is a shortage or total absence of projects – would help complement those projects that international and national actors put forward. For it to be fruitful, however, such an exercise would entail *a priori* extensive scrutiny of national civil society in order to spotlight the needs and preoccupations of associations that are absent or underrepresented by the civil society known to the EU. As a matter of fact, there are a number of local and rural associations that do not benefit from the MDP, either out of ignorance of such a programme or a lack of knowledge of the technicalities involved in drafting a successful proposal and setting up a project. If the principal objective of the EU is to promote democratic socialization more than anything else, then targeting such small associations could prove even more rewarding than pursuing big projects whose impact remains confined to urban areas or to a limited number of actors. Indeed, small *and* multiple projects are likely to diffuse democratic principles more effectively and to help encourage the build-up of a bottom-up democracy by engaging more actors. Smaller projects are also less likely to create tensions between the EU and the Moroccan government.

Moreover, in accordance with EMP principles, the EU is inclined to support horizontal projects. Horizontal projects may have the potential to support a wave of democratization across more than one country, but their effectiveness is sometimes compromised owing mainly to differing degrees of political (un)openness in the southern Mediterranean, which tends to create a sort of *décalage* (disruption) in the stages of the project and causes it to suffer inconsistency and/or lack of follow-up. Therefore, the task for the EU remains, on the one hand, to find a mid-way between bottom-up and top-down approaches through involving new and small civil society groups, which will generate a larger base for democracy promotion. On the other hand, intervention areas for regional projects need to be focused on issues where participating countries have similar degrees of openness and tolerance, because the failure of regional projects means a greater financial loss as they absorb more money than non-regional ones. Areas where there is less tolerance can be the focus of local, more targeted projects.

To support and complement EU efforts, the task for civil society and the government in Morocco is to find the right dose of political opening needed to carry out the process of democratization and deliver its promises without too much pain. Civil society seems still unable to find a way between the two extremes: it is either too close to the official discourse (which makes it less independent and less credible), or too aggressive (which leads to its being banned). Democratization should be understood as a process that is usually practised on shifting grounds between political openness and a stark lack of political rights. It is a process involving various attempts to set the right tune for all the different voices to be heard, which explains the ambivalent attitudes and signals governments undergoing democratization usually transmit. Therefore, both parties have to find a constructive balance in their relationship in order to make the transition a success. In this relationship, one cannot overlook the key role of the monarchy. The presence of the monarch on the Moroccan political scene has often been considered with mixed feelings of acceptance and rejection. Like civil society, the king faces a dilemma over the degree of political opening needed to carry the country to the safe shores of democracy. Some criticized Hassan II for being omnipresent, too manipulative, too domineering. Some now tend to think the new king is a little too self-effacing and distant (despite his spectacular beginnings). This is owing to the fact that, unlike in other monarchies, in Morocco the people have great expectations of *their* king.[41] The different initiatives undertaken by the monarchy seem to have ushered in some democratic principles to the extent that talk of a democratizing monarch and comparison with other constitutional monarchies (especially the Spanish one) are now being heard. Whether the monarch's attempts to democratize emerge from an individual will is hard to tell. None the less, the pressure of political parties and their struggle for political power, as well as the opening towards Europe, have certainly played a role in triggering the need for democratization. The role of the king now hinges on his willingness to withdraw progressively from the political stage, as well as from the economic scene.

The other question is how ready Morocco is for a retreat of the monarch from political life. The answer to this question will become clear after the forthcoming elections in 2002. Changes to the electoral code are being discussed, even unexpectedly by Driss Basri himself.[42] What will these changes consist of? Which political coalitions will be able to survive or be constructed for the next elections? These are the questions that will determine, to a great extent, the direction Morocco will take on its path towards democracy. At this juncture, our two cheers seem to be evenly distributed between the EU and Moroccan actors; the result of the elections will, however, determine whether they will grow louder or fade into a sigh of disappointment over yet another delay of the train toward democracy.

NOTES

1. Financial protocols included grants and European Investment Bank (EIB) loans with the following amounts: first financial protocol (1978–81) €130m; second financial protocol (1982–86) €199m; third financial protocol (1987–91) €324m.
2. Eberhardt Rhein, cited in Richard Gillespie, 'Spanish Protagonismo and the Euro-Med Partnership Initiative', *Mediterranean Politics*, Vol.2, No.1 (1997), p.37. In this respect, some people refer to Hassan II's metaphor of Morocco as a tree whose roots are in Africa with branches stretching over to Europe.
3. For example, see European Parliament resolution on human rights in Morocco, 29 Oct. 1987, OJ No.C 318 of 30 Nov. 1987, p.112.
4. Michael Sutton, 'Euro–Maghreb Partnership: A New Form of Association?', *Economist Intelligence Unit: European Trends*, No.3 (1992), pp.62–3.
5. Conlusion of the Lisbon European Council, 26–27 June 1992.
6. Commission Communication COM (95) 216 of 23 May 1995 on the inclusion of respect for democratic principles and human rights in agreements between the Community and third countries.
7. International issues such as the 1991 Gulf War and the plight of the Palestinians in Israeli-occupied lands have often been used as a pretext to protest against the domestic situation.
8. The first human rights organizations were the Ligue Marocaine pour la Defence des Droits de l'Homme (1972) and the Association Marocaine des Droits de L'Homme (1979).
9. The 1992 constitution strengthened the parliament somewhat: it stipulated that the prime minister be drawn from the majority party, required the parliament to debate and vote on the agenda prepared by the majority, and allowed the prime minister rather than the king to distribute portfolios, though final approval rested with the monarch.
10. In 1989, Hassan II proposed that the elections be delayed due to the Western Sahara situation, a proposal that was approved by referendum.
11. The most famous cases of this wave of releases were the Oufkir family (General Oufkir was allegedly behind the 1972 coup d'état and, according to official records, committed suicide) and Abraham Serfaty. In both cases, the families were forced to leave the country.
12. For a detailed analysis of the political parties and the *alternance*, see Abdelkebir Khatibi, *L'alternance et les partis politiques au Maroc* (Casablanca: Eddif, 1999).
13. The four ministries, still controlled by the palace, are interior, foreign affairs, Islamic affairs and justice.
14. See 'Le Cheikh Yassine nage à contre courant', *La Nouvelle Tribune*, March 2000.
15. Fathalla Arsalane, 'Religion-Morocco: Banned Moroccan Islamists Refuse to Take the Algerian Path, Inter Press Service, 16 Jan. 1998, http://www.oneworld.org/ips2/jan98/religion.html.
16. See Abdessalam Yassine, 'A qui de droit', Feb. 2000, http://www.yassine.net.
17. Ibid.
18. See, Bernard Cubertafond, 'L'opposition au Maroc', *Pouvoirs*, No.89 (1999).
19. For a detailed analysis of the relation between the king and the Islamists, see Mohamed Tozy, *Monarchie et islam politique au Maroc* (Paris: Presses Sciences Po., 1999).
20. The power of the monarch is constitutional and reinforced by arts.19, 35 and 72.
21. Rémy Leveau, *Le sabre et le turban* (Paris: François Bourin, 1993), pp.84–91.
22. Beatrice Hibou, *Les enjeux de l'ouverture au Maroc. Dissidence économique et contrôle politique*, CERI, No.15 (1996), p.35.
23. Rémy Leveau, 'Morocco at the Crossroads', *Mediterranean Politics*, Vol.2, No.2 (1997), pp.98–100.
24. The only changes were the creation of the position of secretary of sate to the interior, given to Fouad Ali El Himma, a close friend of the king, and the nomination of a number of new staff (both at the central bureau of the Ministry of the Interior and in the regions).
25. The turnout for the 1997 elections remained outstandingly low (58.3 per cent of eligible voters) despite promises that these elections would be transparent and the generally positive atmosphere that preceded the elections.
26. '*Nous voudrions à cette occasion expliciter un nouveau concept de l'autorité et de ce qui s'y*

rapporte, un concept fondé sur la protection des services publics, des affaires locales, des libertés individuelles et collectives, sur la préservation de la sécurité et de la stabilité, la gestion du fait local et le maintien de la paix sociale. Cette responsabilité ne saurait être assumée à l'intérieur des bureaux administratifs qui doivent, au demeurant, rester ouverts aux citoyens, mais exige un contact direct avec eux et un traitement sur le terrain de leurs problèmes, en les associant à la recherche des solutions appropriées', speech by King Mohamed VI, Casablanca, 12 Oct. 1999.

27. Associational life in Morocco is regulated by the *dahir* (decree) 1-58-376 of November 1958. Few amendments were introduced to this law in the *dahir* 1-73-283 of 10 April 1973. On the contrary, it acquired a restrictive interpretation.
28. More than one-third of the EU's spending in relation to the promotion of democracy and human rights in 1996–99 went to reinforcing a pluralist civil society; see Report from the Commission, 'On The Implementation of Measures Intended to Promote Observance of Human Rights and Democratic Principles in External Relations for 1996–1999', COM (2000) 726 final, p.7.
29. Commission document, 'MEDA Democracy Programme, Budget Line B7-705 – Criteria and Conditions for Eligibility', DG 1B.A.1.1, 17 July 1996.
30. The number of projects is calculated from material published by the Delegation of the European Commission in Morocco (for 1996–99 projects) as well as documents received from the Commission's Human Rights and Democratization Directorate (for projects approved in 2000).
31. These figures refer to funds actually disbursed in 1996–98 and to allocated funds for 2000.
32. Unfortunately, data concerning unsuccessful applications remains inaccessible because it is said to be confidential!
33. After the Commission's report, COM (2000) 726 final, the procedure for applications for funding changed and application forms are now made available on the Internet.
34. Note that institutional issues such as bank account availability are sometimes a major problem facing applications for funds.
35. See projects number 19, 15, and 20 respectively, 'MEDA au Maroc', *Bulletin of the European Commission Delegation in Morocco*, No.165 (1999).
36. There is a difficulty in classifying projects financed within the MDP in accordance with the intervention areas of the EU's democracy promotion policy (as presented above) because most projects extend over more than one area of action, which might be seen as the result of a lack of focus.
37. *La Vie Economique*, 12 July 2000, p.5.
38. See 'Parallel Report of Moroccan NGOs on the Application of the Convention on Eliminating all Forms of Discrimination Against Women', Association Démocratique des Femmes du Maroc, December 1996, http://magnet.undp.org/docs/gov/arab/Engcedaw.htm.
39. See *Le Journal*, 4–10 Nov. 2000, pp.20–1.
40. For example, the LMDH and the AMDH are associated with the political parties of Istiqlal and the Union Socialiste des Forces Populaires (USFP) respectively, which often blurs the demarcation line between civil and political society. Also, the Comité pour la Défense des Droits de l'Homme was formed by a former member of the AMDH in 1993.
41. 'Le "retrait" du roi', *L'Express*, 7 June 2001.
42. Driss Basri, 'Code électoral: Il faut changer le mode de scrutin', *L'Economiste*, 12 June 2001.

Spain and North Africa: Towards a 'Dynamic Stability'

BERNABÉ LÓPEZ GARCÍA and
MIGUEL HERNANDO DE LARRAMENDI

After Algeria's independence in 1962, Spain was the only European country that still had a territorial presence in North Africa. This difference from its European neighbours was the origin of a territorial dispute between Spain and Morocco that has caused a cyclical situation of conflict in relations between Spain and the Maghreb. After Spain abandoned the Western Sahara in 1976, inertia maintained the remnants of a policy that had been formulated during the previous decade, in which the defence of territorial interests was the priority for Spain's external activities in the region. A divided Maghreb undermined by regional conflict was seen as the best guarantee for the defence of Spanish territorial interests. In this context, the Treaty of Oujda, signed by Morocco and Libya in 1984 to form the Arab–African Union, caused concern in Spanish political circles and among the public.

Spain's policies in the Maghreb had started to change during the years of the transition to democracy. In a difficult balancing act in Spain's bilateral relations with Morocco and Algeria, themselves in conflict over the Western Sahara, the governments of Adolfo Suárez (1976–81) initiated a move towards a more 'global' policy in the region that would no longer be hampered by an obsessive preoccupation with having to compensate each country with an equivalent gesture for every initiative taken towards the other. The Maghreb began to become a clearer concept and to be taken into account as a region in Spain's foreign policy – within the context of European Community membership from 1986 – while also benefiting from the détente between Morocco and Algeria that led to the constitution of the Union of the Arab Maghreb (UMA) in 1989.

The stability of the region as a whole became a priority objective of Spanish policy towards the Maghreb, with Morocco as the more privileged partner. The objective of regional stability would contribute to its economic, social and political development as well as to its integration, and it coincided with the objectives of the European Community. At a bilateral level, Spain's diplomacy designed a policy that sought to inject normality into relations between Spain and the Maghreb by increasing co-operation in all sectors and developing economic and financial relations. This was referred to in the jargon of the Ministry of Foreign Affairs as 'the creation of a cushion of shared interests'. In the political field, Spanish diplomacy sought the institutionalization of political dialogue with the different countries of the Maghreb, in order to keep open constant channels of contact in the hope of preventing or limiting the scope of the cyclical crises that used regularly to afflict bilateral relations.

In 1994 during a speech in parliament, the then secretary general for foreign policy, Francisco Villar, expressed himself along the following lines when he defined the government's policy in the Maghreb as a policy centred on the 'creation and consolidation of a shared space of stability and prosperity in which both the just aspirations of the people of the Maghreb and Spanish interests could be accommodated'.[1] These objectives could be achieved through institutionalized political dialogue and co-operative activity of diverse kinds. The Maghreb was described as 'one of the priority regions' for Spanish foreign policy, which was going through an 'historical stage of searching for economic and political models' as well as a 'struggle to find or reassert its identity'. Villar maintained that the Spanish government was 'not trying to defend the "status quo", a kind of stability viewed as static, but rather a dynamic kind of stability', in order to contribute to 'a gradual evolution, from a political point of view, towards more participatory and democratic political formulae that would ensure a greater representativeness of Maghrebian citizens within the context of the preservation of human rights'.[2] The different governments of José María Aznar since 1996 have continued this policy, defined under a socialist government – maybe out of inertia. As one of the people currently in charge of Spanish policy towards the Maghreb has said, however, this political approach has since been broadened by adding the social dynamics of change in the region as a new dimension, thus moving on from a preoccupation with short-term developments to a long-term strategic approach, to be pursued in conjunction with the European Union.

The concept of 'dynamic stability' defended by those in charge of Spain's foreign policy is a sign of their timid willingness to support gradual democratizing changes in the political processes of North African countries, providing that these do not interfere with Spain's strategic and economic interests. It must not be forgotten that there is still a dispute between Spain and Morocco, one of the key countries of the Maghreb. This dispute is partly territorial but also relates to other issues that have become important, such as immigration, and in fact limits the possibility of applying a principled policy in relation to the active defence of human rights and democratization. An indication of this is that, in spite of the official rhetoric, development co-operation with North African countries and the aid allocated to support them are very modest and are not even openly presented as being directed towards promoting democracy. In the case of the central and eastern European countries, this goal is clearly stated. If the concept of dynamic stability emerged as a cautious formula designed to accommodate interests as well as principles, it has since become merely a rhetorical expression of 'wishful thinking'.

The priority given to relations with Morocco among the Maghreb countries led to this country becoming the first with which an institutionalized political dialogue was attempted. This was then tried later with other countries of the region. With Morocco it led to the Treaty of Friendship, Good Neighbourliness and Co-operation, signed in Rabat in July 1991,[3] which later served as a model for a treaty signed with Tunisia in October 1995.[4] The instability suffered by Algeria since 1992 has prevented a similar treaty being concluded with that country thus far. However, during a visit by Algerian foreign minister Abdelaziz Belkhadem in May 2001, his Spanish counterpart Josep Piqué expressed a wish to sign a treaty similar to those signed with Morocco and Tunisia on the occasion of a future visit to Spain by President Abdelaziz Bouteflika. These treaties provide for the institutionalization of annual high level meetings that take place alternately in the capitals of the signatory countries, at which the different issues relating to the treaty are reviewed. In fact, ups and downs in bilateral relations have prevented these meetings being held as regularly as was decided initially.

During the 1990s, Spanish diplomacy took advantage of the friendship treaties signed with Morocco and Tunisia to introduce references to human and political rights into the texts. In the case of Mauritania a reference was also introduced in a political statement published in May 1994 on the occasion of a visit of the king and queen of Spain to that country. Concerning Algeria it was necessary to wait until the visit of Prime Minister Aznar in July 2000 for this issue to be mentioned in a joint declaration made by the secretaries of state for foreign policy of the two countries.

These merely rhetorical declarations were accompanied in diplomatic practice by a cautious approach, avoiding the raising of specific questions in the bilateral forums for political dialogue. During the high level meetings held in Morocco and Tunisia, economic and commercial issues are usually dealt with, but political subjects are skirted around and are merely mentioned in very general official statements. Spanish diplomacy prefers to reserve human rights issues for meetings of the association councils that are held periodically by the European Union with those countries with which an association agreement has been signed: Morocco and Tunisia. The European Union framework is effectively used as a place where these issues can be diluted in order to avoid direct friction in the bilateral relations between Spain and the countries of the Maghreb. Spanish diplomacy, without dissociating itself from EU positions, acts as a mediator *vis-à-vis* the Maghrebian regimes in order not to lose the position it has achieved with them. It therefore tries to neutralize the positions of other EU countries that are geographically remote from the Maghreb, have less direct interests in the region and thus place the issue of human rights before economic and security relations.

Official Relations with Morocco

As the nearest country within the region and the one most involved in all aspects of Spain's relations with the Maghreb, Morocco receives priority attention from Madrid. Its 'anchorage' to the European Union has been sought above all others. This is the idea that informs the Moroccan association agreement with the European Union. The word 'anchorage' has been present in the declarations of foreign ministers of different political stripes, including Javier Solana of the Socialist Party and Abel Matutes of the People's Party. It represents a firm desire to intensify contacts in order to achieve greater interdependence and harmony. Economic aspects have always been prevalent in the effort to anchor Morocco to Europe, as suggested by references to the 'importance and beneficial effects of Spanish investments in Morocco',[5] but there is also a degree of concern for the state of human rights, as expressed in the friendship treaty of 1991 – at least, this is what is maintained in ministerial answers to parliamentary questions. The general principles outlined in the treaty include respect for human rights and basic civil liberties, and there is also a commitment to promote and encourage the effective exercise of civil, political, economic, social and cultural rights and liberties, inherent to all human beings and essential for their free and complete development. However, these references have been accompanied by a conditionality clause affecting the development of relations in other areas.

In response to a question from a senator from the Coalición Canaria (Canary Islands Coalition), the government has claimed that the inclusion of these principles in the friendship treaties indicates progress in relation to its human rights concerns.[6] In the case of Morocco, such progress has gained recognition in reports by Amnesty International, it is maintained. This support for human rights, cautiously and timidly expressed in the early 1990s, became more concrete in 1996, following the last high-level meeting held under the socialist government of Felipe González, held in Rabat in February of that year. Initiatives taken then, such as the creation of the Averroes Committee, to promote knowledge and mutual understanding between the two peoples with the aim of removing prejudices and suspicions, and the decision to create a Spanish–Moroccan Parliamentary Friendship Group, have been continued by the governments formed by the People's Party. During the opening session of Congress in October 1998, talking about the personality of Averroes, former foreign minister Matutes said, 'today foreign policy is no longer the monopoly of governments' and belongs to civil society as well.

The Averroes Committee, constituted under the joint presidency of the Spanish and Moroccan foreign ministers and composed in principle of a civil servant and four civil society representatives from each country, took time to be formed because of differences between the conception that the Partido Socialista Obrero Español (Spanish Socialist Workers' Party) had of it and the new approach of the People's Party. Between its creation in Rabat and its effective constitution some months later in Granada, Spain, a change of government took place following the victory in the elections of March 1996 of José María Aznar. The new officials in charge of Spanish foreign policy showed the first signs of wanting to control the committee through the appointment of people closer to the ruling party, thus making the new institution a mere appendix of the official activity of the foreign ministry instead of being an autonomous reflection group drawn from civil society. In the years since its creation, the few meetings that have been held have demonstrated the ineffectiveness of this committee, buffeted by tensions between the two countries and failing to take autonomous initiatives as a result of members from each side being submissive to their respective diplomatic services.

In spite of the many disputes between Spain and Morocco over the past five years, support for governmental 'alternation', the political formula referring to the incorporation of the Moroccan opposition into government under the direction of the socialist Abderrahmane Youssoufi, has been perhaps the main feature of the Aznar governments in their relations with Morocco since 1996.

Even before the constitution of the government of alternation, the support of the Spanish government was expressed during the electoral process that led to this political change. In November 1996, within the framework of a scientific and technical co-operation agreement, the Spanish government approved an agreement between the interior ministries of the two countries. Under this, the Moroccan ministry received aid worth Ptas.300m from the Spanish Agency for International Co-operation (AECI) to 'finance technical assistance and the use of computer equipment and other materials for the purpose of the electoral process between June and November 1997'. This co-operation in electoral matters permitted some degree of transparency in the process and also led to a seminar being held in Morocco on technical aspects of the elections. Also envisaged was the creation of an Institute of Electoral Studies, but this failed to materialize.

In October 1998, in response to a question from José Navas, a deputy from the United Left (Izquierda Unida), about the justification for this AECI subsidy for the Moroccan government, the Spanish government replied that 'Spain has made co-operation one of the main axes of its relations with Morocco, and electoral co-operation could not be kept out of this domain ... This way our country has contributed to the aspirations of the Moroccan authorities and political forces to give credibility, clarity and transparency to the last elections'.[7]

After Morocco's elections were held on 14 November 1997, the Diplomatic Information Office of the Spanish Ministry of Foreign Affairs issued an official statement in which it described the elections as 'one more step, probably the most important, in the process undertaken by Morocco and promoted by King Hassan II, towards the consolidation of a state of law in this country, and the achievement of higher levels of participation of the Moroccan population in its political life'.[8] This bold statement hides the fact that only technical support was provided while no political evaluation was made of the real extent of democratic transparency in the electoral process. This reveals the limits within which the Spanish administration develops its activity in relation to democracy promotion.

A few months later on 13 October 1998, during a round table in Madrid organized by the Averroes Committee entitled 'Morocco at the Threshold of the 21st Century', in which five ministers of the new cabinet participated, Matutes, in a toast to his counterpart Abdellatif Filali, said:

> the new stage initiated by Morocco with the Government of Mr Abderrahmane Youssoufi, having received the confidence of HM Hassan II, has aroused great expectations in Europe and especially in Spain. It has also shown the capacity of innovation of Moroccan institutions to face the transformations of all kinds that have occurred in its society, as well as in its Maghrebian and Euro-Mediterranean

> surroundings … with the conviction that Morocco will continue to find in Spain a loyal partner and a faithful interpreter of its aspirations.[9]

After the death of Hassan II, during a session of the Spanish Senate the government made it known through an intervention by Matutes, that 'it has followed with special interest the political evolution of Morocco, confirming with satisfaction how the reforms initiated by the late King Hassan II have set new constitutional foundations for the transition of the neighbouring country … A year and a half later, following the death of the king, the government considers the hope with which it has contemplated the future of Morocco to be confirmed'.[10]

The audience given to Prime Minister Aznar by Mohamed VI during the official period of mourning for his father's death was interpreted by the Spanish foreign ministry representative, at a meeting of the parliamentary Committee on Foreign Affairs in September 1999, as a sign of 'the privileged and preferential character of our bilateral relations'. He stressed that Aznar was the first European and western head of government to have met the new monarch. At the same meeting it was said that:

> the fundamental objective of the visit was to communicate to the new monarch, and also to the new government, the solidarity of Spain and its government in this new stage, and to stress our will to support, and co-operate and collaborate in, the transformations and priorities announced by the king in his 'speech from the throne'. In sum, to offer Spain's political and economic support for the consolidation of a democratic and developed Morocco.[11]

The government has insisted in successive declarations that there is continuity with the process initiated under the previous king, and thus it is not appropriate to talk of there being 'new political relations' with the Kingdom of Morocco, as the foreign minister said when addressing the Senate Committee on Foreign Affairs in November 1999.[12] He echoed the same sentiments in an appearance in Parliament when, answering a question from a Basque deputy, he expressed his pleasure at the 'determined pledge of the crown in favour of openness' and over the transparency of an instrument such as the Treaty of Friendship, Good Neighbourliness and Co-operation which had enabled the two countries to strengthen and enrich their bonds.[13]

There is one issue over which Moroccan diplomats and the various political forces of the country have been particularly vigilant: that is, any Spanish position affecting the present status of the Western Sahara and Moroccan activities in this territory. For many years, Morocco reacted negatively each time Spain voted at the United Nations in favour of resolutions proposed by Algeria calling for negotiations between 'the two sides', Morocco and the Polisario Front. Since the peace plan was drawn up and Morocco agreed to meet representatives of the Saharawi movement, tensions have arisen on several occasions: after humanitarian aid was granted by Spain to the Saharawi refugees in Tinduf; after meetings of Spanish officials with the Polisario leader Mohamed Abdelazizi; following the support given to the Saharan Arab Democratic Republic (RASD) by some regional parliaments; and after the creation in 2001 of an association called 'Peace for the Saharawi People', created by all the parliamentary groups except that of the People's Party after they had participated in celebrations marking the 25th anniversary of the proclamation of the Saharawi Republic. This last measure provoked a very angry reaction from the mouthpiece of one of the main political parties in the current Moroccan government. An editorial published on the front page of *Al Alam*, an Arabic language newspaper belonging to the Istiqlal party,[14] went as far as to urge support by the Moroccan government for the Basque terrorist group ETA in retaliation against the solidarity shown by Spanish political parties with the Saharawi movement. This reaction was considered disproportionate in many Moroccan circles and the prime minister and his government hurriedly rejected it, at the request of Spanish foreign minister Piqué.

The attitude of Istiqlal was not an isolated one. A few months earlier, the then communications minister Mohamed Larbi Messari, a member of the same party, stated in the French language Istiqlal newspaper that 'Moroccans will never accept, under any pretext, that Spain has any role in the Sahara issue'.[15]

In spite of this, when a model is sought for a 'third way' on the Sahara question, Spain is always a point of reference. In 1987, during the first visit to Morocco by the president of an autonomous region, the Canarian Jerónimo Saavedra, Hassan II asked him for a translation of the autonomy statute of the Canary Islands as a possible inspiration for his plan to leave to his son a 'Morocco of the *länder*', of which he spoke in an interview with *Le Monde* on 3 August 1988. Autonomy for the Sahara seems to have been the reason for the regionalization plan approved by the Moroccan parliament in 1997. Paradoxically, it was the Istiqlal newspaper that suggested in January 2001 that the autonomy system of a Spanish region – Catalonia – be chosen as a model for the autonomy of the Saharawi region.[16]

Official Perceptions of the Algerian Crisis

Over Algeria, the tendency of Spanish policy has been to recognize political reality while trying to safeguard as much as possible the energy supplies that this country provides to Spain. When the electoral process was interrupted in January 1992, the construction of a gas pipeline between Algeria and Spain passing through Morocco was already under way. In the months prior to this event, consultations took place between high-ranking officials of the Spanish Ministry of Foreign Affairs – including the director general for Africa Jorge Dezcallar – and Abbasi Madani, leader of the Front Islamique du Salut (FIS), aimed at ensuring that Spanish interests would not be affected in the event of an Islamist government being formed. However, the interruption of the electoral process and the outbreak of violence plunged bilateral relations at all levels into a period of uncertainty.

Cautiousness has always been the main characteristic of Spanish diplomacy concerning the evolution of events in Algeria. Francisco Villar, replying to a question from a People's Party deputy about the influence of events in Algeria on the pipeline project, described the political crisis as a 'systemic crisis, a general crisis'. On the appointment of General Liamine Zeroual as president, he added that 'cautiousness demands that we do not prejudge how successful the new head of state will be', explaining that 'the Spanish position is to encourage a true process of democratic transition in Algeria, with the consensus of all the national political forces' that accept democracy.[17] However, this cautiousness did not prevent Spanish diplomacy from encouraging a negotiated solution that would include the FIS, a position which the US administration was prepared to consider, but not France. In this context a Spanish–American seminar on the Maghreb was held in El Paular in May 1995. During its opening session, the then director general for Africa and the Middle East, Miguel Angel Moratinos, remarked that Spanish and American political thinking had been drawing closer over the previous years and that now one could talk about 'a common analysis of Maghrebian reality'.[18]

In spite of these postures, Spanish policy in Algeria was developed mainly in agreement with that of the European Union, which it has used as a shield to protect its bilateral interests. European Union policy towards Algeria is summed up in a declaration made public by the EU in Brussels on 14 September 1994, expressing satisfaction with the measures adopted by the Algerian government to 'bring into dialogue the political leaders of the Islamist movement', and insisting on the need for peaceful co-operation 'between all sides' as the only way to reach 'political reconciliation and the restoration of stability'.[19] A few months later, after the celebration in Rome of the meeting organized by the Community of Sant' Egidio, the EU in its declaration of 23 January 1995 exhorted 'all participants in Algerian political life to reach an agreement on the way to develop a spirit of dialogue'.[20]

While the parliamentary opposition in Spain pushed for stronger measures to protect some 650 Spanish residents in Algeria and Spanish gas interests, the socialist government in its final months awaited the outcome of the presidential elections of November 1995, trusting in a declaration issued on 17 November that they 'would be followed by progress in the democratization of the country, by way of dialogue with the main political forces, bringing an end to violence, [the holding of] free and indisputable general and local elections, and the establishment of a stable model of political coexistence and economic and social development in Algeria'.[21] During these years, the Spanish diplomatic service was one of the most active in Algeria because it took on the representation of other states during the worst moments of violence against foreigners.

After the People's Party took over the government in Spain in 1996, cautiousness was again the characteristic of its Algerian policy. In September, a few months after his appointment, foreign minister Matutes travelled to Algiers at a time of relative pessimism that would continue for months to come. In May 1997, in an intervention in the Cortés about the Algerian crisis, Ramón de Miguel, secretary of state for foreign policy, confessed that 'one does not see a clear perspective of improvement'. He expressed his fears about the 'particularly worrying' prospect of events in Algeria exerting an influence on Morocco and about 'the very negative effect in the sphere of human rights'. His conclusion was that the solution to problems could only be found 'through dialogue of the [Algerian] government with representative political forces'.[22] The same situation and his impression of it remained unchanged a few months later, after an upsurge of violence in the country during the summer of that year. The same Ramón de Miguel, speaking in Parliament in November, referred to 'a wave of massive crimes combined with large-scale operations by the army, that have upset all the political calculations that had been made about the possibility of understanding and dialogue between the Islamists and the government'.[23]

The idea that violence in Algeria had become a generalized phenomenon, going beyond that carried out by terrorist groups, and that anti-terrorist action had to be complemented by dialogue and a widening of the political spectrum, began to emerge. This can be inferred from the answer by the Spanish government to a Galician nationalist deputy in

February 1998, in which it said that, 'in addition to the anti-terrorist action, the future of Algeria requires a widening of the political field, in order to include all the political forces that reject violence'.[24]

A month earlier, an EU Troika visit was made to Algiers, causing tension with the Algerian government, which saw it as interference. Although Spain approved of the visit, it was very cautious and said that it was not questioning the Algerian government's actions. Matutes affirmed this in an appearance in Parliament in February of the same year, saying that 'from a cautious, constructive position, the government has maintained a scrupulous respect for Algeria's independence and sovereignty. It has avoided, and encouraged others to avoid, positions that could be interpreted as a denial of the authorities' legitimacy in the fulfilment of their duties'.[25]

Another crucial episode concerning Algeria took place in June 1998, during the 54th period of sessions of the UN Human Rights Commission, at which a Spanish delegation of observers was present 'as part of the EU delegation'.[26] There was pressure on the Algerian delegation for the government in Algiers to make a public commitment with respect to the defence of human rights, and the EU complained about the lack of co-operation from the Algerians in this basic aspect of their relations. The 15 concluded nevertheless that, both for 'tactical reasons' and for 'political reasons',[27] they did not think it was appropriate to appoint a special rapporteur for this question, although they issued veiled threats about raising the issue of human rights in Algeria at the UN General Assembly or during the next period of sessions of the Commission.

EU pressure on the Algerian government in support of demands for transparency concerning public information on human rights was reflected in the sending of a UN information mission headed by Mario Soares. The sending of this mission was greeted 'very positively' by the Spanish government, which welcomed the choice of Soares and the scope of the mission mandate, as well as the attitude of the Algerian government when they heard of it.[28]

In August 1998, minority groups in the Spanish parliament, such as the Galician National Bloc and the New Left Party, accused the Spanish government and the EU of having an 'accommodating and complicit' attitude and asked them to adopt a clear position concerning the accusations that the Algerian government had tolerated disappearances and mass slaughter. The response to this was that the responsibility of the Algerian government in these matters could not be proven.

More recently, following the elections in April 1999 which gave the presidency to Bouteflika and the referendum on the Civil Concord in

September of the same year, the Spanish attitude has been generally positive regarding the Algerian situation, hoping that these developments represented a means of ending the cycle of violence. Prime Minister Aznar encouraged the process during his visit to Algiers in July 2000, where he spoke in favour of the new approach to overcoming the crisis; he offered Spanish co-operation with the civil authorities in security matters and pledged support for the building of a state of law.

Tunisia, Mauritania and the Libyan Exception

Although the official discourse always refers to 'Maghrebian' policies, the primacy of the two countries just discussed is in fact almost total. Tunisia, Mauritania and Libya have always been in the background of the political and diplomatic scene, although the cyclical crises that arise mainly with Morocco sometimes lead to a re-examination of the role of some of these Maghrebian countries in matters such as fishing.

High-level official relations with Zine el Abidine Ben Ali's Tunisia started with a state visit of the Tunisian president to Madrid in 1991, subsequently reciprocated by the king and queen of Spain in November 1994. Spanish–Tunisian co-operation has centred more on the economy than on the development of civil society links because the Tunisian authorities reject anything they consider to be acts of interference in their internal affairs. Tunisians are willing to accept mediation by Spain and Italy when tensions arise with the EU, when they are faced with demands by Germany and other northern European countries wishing to make the MEDA programme's aid conditional on the protection of human rights, and also in relation to France, whose positions they accuse of being duplicitous.

Official Spanish declarations are carefully worded to avoid Tunisian suspicions. The response to a question in Parliament from Socialist MP Rafael Estrella about the human rights situation in Tunisia[29] was an abuse of evaluative language that spoke of the 'undeniable successes' in fields such as education, workers' rights and the situation of women in the last 40 years, to the point of presenting Tunisia as 'one of the most advanced countries in the African and Maghrebian regional contexts', although it was acknowledged that successes were 'not always accompanied by a fully satisfactory respect for and protection of civil and political rights' and that 'some obstacles to the liberty of expression, press freedom, freedom of movement and the development of political pluralism still exist'.

This double-talk was even more obvious in the declarations made during Matutes's visit to Tunisia in June 1997, when the Spanish minister went so far as to maintain that 'Tunisia is becoming a land of freedom and tolerance.

Its high level of stability is the result of a policy that combines economic openness towards the great challenges of globalization with an important social dimension, which, in turn, will require a context of strengthening of liberties and respect for human rights'.[30]

Mauritania only features in Spanish foreign policy as a recipient of humanitarian aid in times of drought or natural disaster or as the beneficiary of development projects or preferential credit, with very few civil exchanges apart from communications in the sphere of commercial tourism in the Canary Islands. Official visits, such as that of the king and queen of Spain to the Islamic Republic in May 1994, are purely formal. However, it should be added that Spanish diplomacy did mediate in relations between Mauritania and Israel, leading to a first official meeting in Madrid on 12 June 1995 between foreign ministers Mohamed Slem Ould Lakhel and Shimon Peres.

As regards Libya, although Spanish diplomacy defended – unsuccessfully – the participation of this country in the Barcelona Process, there has not been any departure from EU policy towards Libyan leader Muammar Qadhafi. During the first Spanish presidency of the EU in September 1995, the European Union expressed its 'deep concern' about the Libyan leader's declarations concerning the expulsion of Palestinian citizens, and called on Libya to reconsider its attitude.[31]

According to Ramón de Miguel, speaking in Congress in October 1998, Spain was the only country at the US–EU summit on extra-territorial laws that maintained that 'the waivers that are being negotiated with Iran should also apply to Libya', which caused friction with the UK. Nevertheless the EU position defended against the Americans was the Spanish one, and Libya was included as a country that might be exempted from the application of the d'Amato and King-Kennedy laws. In official declarations, Libya is always presented by Spanish diplomats as 'an important state in the Mediterranean and Maghrebian context', as Matutes put it when addressing parliament to explain the government's support for an official visit to Libya in 1998 by one of the founders of the People's Party, the current president of the Galician Autonomous Community, Manuel Fraga.[32]

The EU Framework

Relations with the Maghreb acquired a new dimension after Spain entered the European Community in 1986. Until then those relations had been bilateral, but now a new, multilateral dimension was provided by the framework of EC–Maghreb relations and began to be used by Spanish diplomacy.

The Mediterranean region ceased being a focus of the more passive aspects of Spanish exterior projection and became one of the privileged areas where the capacity of a medium power like Spain to exert international influence in international affairs now materialized within the EU framework. After the fall of the Berlin Wall in 1989, fears that the centre of gravity of the European Union might shift eastwards, leaving Spain once more on the periphery, provoked an active response through Spain's Mediterranean policies. Together with Italy, Spain in 1990 proposed a Conference on Security and Co-operation in the Mediterranean (CSCM). The 1991 Gulf War also contributed to making the Maghreb a priority region for being 'an area of risk for Spain's global security', the latter in the socio-political sense of the word and not in the traditional military one.[33]

Since the 1990s Spain has reactivated its presence in the region, seeking an area of influence in an area vital for its security. On occasions Madrid has acted as an intermediary between Maghreb countries and Brussels. This was the case in 1992, when Spanish diplomats actively supported the need to find a new framework for EU relations with Morocco after the European Parliament had refused to endorse the financial protocol between Morocco and the EC because of the 'violation of human rights in Morocco and the obstacles that Rabat placed in the way of holding a referendum to permit self-determination in Western Sahara'.[34]

The proposal to hold a Euro-Mediterranean Conference and its organization in Barcelona in November 1995, as well as the active role of Spain during the European Council at Cannes in June of the same year in helping to secure a more equal balance between EU aid for the former eastern bloc and the Mediterranean, reinforced Spain's image as a champion of Maghreb and Mediterranean interests.[35] From 1996, the annual reports of the Spanish Agency for International Co-operation underlined the active role of Spanish diplomats in the MED Committee responsible for assigning the €4,685m of the MEDA I financial package for the period 1995–99. The building of the Euro-Mediterranean Partnership is a very slow process, and thus far only the creation of a free trade area has been started, somewhat timidly. This raises the question of Spain's and other Mediterranean European countries' capacity to exert influence by promoting Mediterranean policy and relations with the Maghreb countries. The insufficient use of the MEDA I financial package, of which only 28 per cent was disbursed, fuels the dissatisfaction felt by the countries of the southern Mediterranean.

Spanish diplomacy is very cautious when it raises questions at the bilateral level relating to political processes and human rights in the various countries of the Maghreb. It prefers to deal with these aspects within institutions dealing with Euro–Maghreb relations, where criticism is diluted because all members of the EU are identified with it. In the association councils, a distribution of roles often occurs with the northern countries of the EU defending more active positions on the promotion of human rights while southern European countries such as Spain present themselves as mediators, sometimes supporting the Maghreb's interests *vis-à-vis* Community representatives. Regimes such as Ben Ali's in Tunisia, always defensive over human rights issues, have sought Spanish mediation for fear that the MEDA funds might be denied them because of the democratic conditions set out in their association agreement. This mediating role is also played by Spanish diplomacy in the monthly meetings of the Maghreb–Mashreq group for the Common Foreign and Security Policy (CFSP). Spanish diplomats sought to achieve a consensus on the agenda for the dialogue with Algeria, launched by the EU following the bloodshed of 1997.

The Role of Spanish Co-operation in Promoting Democracy

There are two levels at which the official Spanish aid programme seeks to promote democracy in the Maghreb countries. First, the Ministry of Foreign Affairs, through the Institute for Co-operation with the Arab World, the Mediterranean and the Developing Countries (ICMAMPD),[36] which forms part of AECI, devotes part of its non-refundable aid to specific projects which it carries out either alone or in collaboration with other public administration bodies. Second, non-governmental organizations (NGOs) carry out co-operation projects that are largely financed by AECI, or by autonomous communities and local entities. In both cases, the NGOs present projects in response to public announcements and adapt them to the nature and geographical priorities of the funding body.

Spanish co-operation policy was characterized by the absence of a legal framework to regulate it until the Law for International Development Co-operation was approved in 1998.[37] The government's approval of an initial International Co-operation Plan covering the period 2001–04 was postponed until November 2000 and is still awaiting parliamentary ratification. Article 2.b of the 1998 law establishes 'the defence and promotion of human rights and fundamental liberties, peace, democracy and civil participation in conditions of equality' as one of its governing principles. Article 3.d defines one objective of the law as being 'to promote the establishment and consolidation of democratic regimes and respect for human rights and fundamental liberties'. The specific priorities set out in Article 7 include 'the protection and respect of human rights, equal opportunities, participation and the social integration of women and defence of the most vulnerable groups of the population' as well as the 'strengthening of democratic and civil society structures and support for institutions, especially those nearest to the citizen'.[38]

The Management Plan for Spanish Co-operation for 2001–04 establishes 'social participation, institutional development and good governance' as applications of these directives and as one of six sectoral priorities. Among the objectives pursued are the defence of human rights and support for a state of law, the promotion of social participation and institutional development. According to the plan, the practice of good governance must include the establishment of an adequate regulatory economic and financial framework and a struggle against corruption in the field of public policy.[39]

Until 1998, the annual AECI reports included the strengthening of institutions as one of their priorities. That is, 'support for public institutions with the aim of consolidating democratic states, which are quite new in some countries'.[40] In practice, this support consisted of technical assistance to ministries to improve the management and functioning of public services. This priority – and here there is no mention of strengthening the fabric of civil society – has consisted in fact, in the case of the Maghreb, of financing a limited number of projects based in those countries where a formal commitment to a political opening exists, as is the case of Morocco. Although they also exist elsewhere, they are less common in other countries, such as Algeria or Tunisia, where, because of political crises or a regime shift in an authoritarian direction, there is less receptiveness to this type of aid. The financial commitment made to this kind of institutional support is very small in comparison to that invested in areas such as medical co-operation, drinking water, education and infrastructure. None the less, Spanish aid has financed various projects of this type in Morocco. On top of the logistical and technical support given at the time of the 1997 elections, some other programmes have been launched, their aim being the consolidation of a state of law through an exchange of experiences during visits by members of the Supreme Court of Morocco and General Council of the Judiciary in Spain. Spanish aid has also supported the training of the Moroccan security forces and programmes to fight corruption. In 1999, the budget granted by ICMAMPD for the strengthening of institutions in Morocco was very limited, only Ptas.77m (approximately $430,000), shared between support to the Agency for the Development of Northern Morocco (Ptas.38m) and two projects carried out by NGOs to support associations in eastern Morocco (Ptas.21m) and the training of Moroccan NGO personnel (Ptas.18m).[41]

The 'delicate political situation' is the reason put forward in AECI reports to justify the low level of co-operation with Algeria. In the field of institutional reinforcement, some programmes for the training of local administration staff have been financed. Although in 2001, for the first time, Algeria was considered a priority for Spanish co-operation, it was allocated an overall budget of only Ptas.240m, well below the Ptas.2bn for Morocco, the Ptas.600m for Mauritania and the Ptas.450m for Tunisia. Aid for institutional reinforcement in Tunisia has been limited to support for its energy development agency and a training course in international commerce for Tunisian public servants.

Although the projects aiming at institutional and democratic reinforcement and the consolidation and strengthening of states of law were among the sectoral priorities announced in AECI calls for bids for funding from NGOs, there has not been a significant number of projects of this type in the Maghreb. Spanish NGOs, which have extensive experience of working in Latin America, started to become interested in the Maghreb in the 1990s after new guidelines published by AECI called for a more balanced approach to the main geographical areas benefiting from Spanish co-operation. The weak presence of Spanish NGOs in the region was – and still is – a reflection on the frailty of the bonds at the level of civil society, weakened by the distorting influence of the Western Sahara conflict, which since the 1970s has been an obstacle to the development of relations between trade unions, political parties and non-governmental actors. The activity of Spanish NGOs in this region has not been centred around the promotion of human rights but rather upon other areas of co-operation.

This feeble support allocated to the strengthening of institutions, both in the type of projects and in the financial resources assigned to them, contrasts sharply with the financial effort made since 1998 by ICMAMPD on these issues in central and eastern Europe.

In conjunction with the Ministry of Foreign Affairs, some autonomous communities, especially those bordering the Mediterranean, carry out complementary actions of institutional co-operation. In the mid-1990s, the Junta (regional government) of Andalusia, in collaboration with ICMAMPD, promoted a training programme for local communities in northern Morocco. In September 1995, the Institut Català de la Mediterrània, a cultural organization linked to the Generalitat de Catalunya, organized the first Euro-Mediterranean Civil Forum at the time of the Euro-Mediterranean Conference of foreign ministers in Barcelona. Since then, this research institute, which is an instrument serving the external relations of Catalonia, has funded studies and organized seminars on civil society in the Maghreb. Among other things, it has sponsored a study on 'The Emergence of Civil Society in Morocco' and periodic meetings between journalists, intellectuals and businessmen from Catalonia and the Maghreb, especially from Morocco and Tunisia.

The growth of Spanish interests in the Maghreb since the early 1990s has led some companies with important interests in the region to promote opportunities to meet and debate, such as the Foro Formentor promoted by Repsol-YPF, the main Spanish oil company with interests in Algeria and Libya. This forum exists to promote an institutional dialogue as an instrument serving the interests of business in the region.

The promotion of democracy and of civil participation in the political life of the Maghreb countries has been subordinated to a policy in which economic interests and the development of trade are given precedence. This is demonstrated in the Amnesty International report for the year 2000, in references to Spanish foreign policy. It describes Spanish actions in this sphere as 'minimal', characterized by passivity, a lack of initiative, non-fulfilment of commitments and a lack of specific objectives for the defence of human rights.[42]

The weakness of action in this field is anomalous given that the Spanish transition is often presented as a model for political change in the region. The success of the Spanish process and the economic growth that accompanied it, make this a point of constant reference for various political and social actors in the Maghreb. The Spanish Ministry of Foreign Affairs and organizations such as the Association of Spanish Journalists have promoted meetings and debates on the Spanish transition, funded by AECI. At the non-governmental level, Spanish activities in the field are limited, and have none of the dynamism developed by the foundations linked to the main German political parties. In Spain, there are no equivalents of the Friedrich Ebert and Konrad Adenauer foundations, which participate actively in the promotion and strengthening of civil society through financing political associations such as *Alternatives* in Morocco and groups that promote democratic and political debate such as GRET (the Research Group on Region and Territory), or that finance the publishing of books or the organization of seminars.

As for the Spanish political forces, they have maintained hardly any contacts with North African parties. The PSOE may be the only party that has kept continuous links with a party of the same ideological denomination, its Moroccan counterpart the Socialist Union of Popular Forces (USFP); it has secured from this party reassurances that it does not identify with the anti-Spanish phobia of other parties such as Istiqlal or the

Party of Progress and Socialism (PPS). During the governments of Felipe González (1982–96), some institutions related to the PSOE established links with foundations and institutions associated with Moroccan socialists, such as the Bouabid Foundation, and also with party leaders through meetings and university forums in the second half of the 1980s. Some of them, like the *Seminarios de Gredos*, promoted from the university world by the economist Alejandro Lorca and from the Ministry of Foreign Affairs by diplomats such as Miguel Angel Moratinos, succeeded in creating something approaching a lobby. Some Moroccan socialists, including Fatallah Oualalou and Habib el-Malki, or intellectuals from other left-wing forces such as Abdallah Saaf, even shared what was then called the 'Gredos spirit'. All of them were later to become ministers in the government of 'alternance' after the PSOE had already been voted out of office in Spain. Although some Tunisians and Algerians also participated in these meetings, permanent bonds were not established with them, as they did not belong to parties or civic institutions because of the non-development of their civil societies at that moment.

Conclusion

There is no doubt that relations between Spain and Morocco have been passing through one of their worst moments, after fishing negotiations between Morocco and the EU broke down in the spring of 2001. This situation is partly a consequence of the fears of the People's Party concerning Morocco, a country it has always regarded in terms of so-called 'negative mutual dependencies' (security obsessions and a negative vision of migration from the South). The PP lacks stable links with parties or pressure groups in Morocco and in the other countries of the Maghreb. The PSOE has taken advantage of these circumstances to try to undermine the government's credibility, by attributing the failure of the fishing negotiations and the general impoverishment of relations between Spain and Morocco to a loss of Spanish influence in the EU. In a parliamentary debate in April 2001, the Socialists demanded that the prime minister should travel to Morocco in order to overcome the impasse that had arisen in various spheres of bilateral relations.

The recent crisis with Morocco has prompted a resurgence of old tendencies that were believed to be a thing of the past, with government policy reverting to a triangular game with Algeria included. Proof of this is the reactivation of political relations with Algeria, in which Spain has gone as far as praising the 'efforts' of that country in favour of human rights during a visit to Madrid by the Algerian foreign minister in May 2001. In another domain, the search for new fishing opportunities in Tunisia and Mauritania is part of the same strategy.

The earlier attempt to create a 'cushion of interests', which would make it easier to control any crisis, thus avoiding contagion to other domains and permitting a normalization of relations, appeared positive and appropriate. However, in spite of some positive results on various occasions, its fragility has become apparent in relation to Morocco, the country that is still the central pivot of Spanish relations with the Maghreb. This fragility was made evident during the fishing crisis of 1995 and has emerged very clearly once more in the more general crisis of 2000–01.

The context of this crisis must not be forgotten. On the Moroccan side, there exists a power vacuum owing to the withdrawal of the king from the public scene and a lack of decision in government policy, paralysed by the contradictory action of seven different parties that have found great difficulty in working together. This is making it easier for the military to gain access to the political scene. The deterioration of the crisis with Spain is a consequence of this power vacuum. On the Spanish side, meanwhile, the context is defined by a factor that profoundly affects Spain's foreign policy: the absolute majority of the People's Party in parliament. This enables policy making to proceed without the agreement of other parties, the main objective being commercial and linked to short-term economic interests. In this context, the Maghreb, given its various difficulties and the insecurity of its legal systems (which deters investment), is being left behind; diluted within the Mediterranean framework, it is losing its status as a priority region for Spanish foreign policy. The recent reorganization of Spanish co-operation structures is significant: the Institute for Co-operation with the Arab World (ICMA), an old institution that formed part of AECI, was transformed into the ICMAMPD, its scope extended to include co-operation with Mediterranean and other developing countries, while it has lost its identity in a new general directorate for Africa, Asia and eastern Europe. The creation in June 2001 of the Fundación Carolina for the diffusion of Spanish culture has been achieved to the financial detriment of the student grants policy that existed for Maghreb countries, among others. The threats issued by prime minister Aznar, talking about economic reprisals against Morocco in response to the refusal of that country to renew the fishing treaty with the EU, are in line with a strictly 'utilitarian' vision, based on economic interests, which leaves in the shade the promotion of civil society and Spanish efforts to promote a state of law in the countries on the other side of the Mediterranean.

NOTES

1. *Boletín Oficial de las Cortes Generales* (BOCG), Congreso de los Diputados, 21 Dec. 1994.
2. Ibid.
3. *Boletín Oficial del Estado*, 26 Feb. 1993.
4. *Boletín Oficial del Estado*, 9 Jan. 1996.
5. Government reply to People's Party senator Carlos Ramírez, BOCG, 25 Oct. 1994.
6. Government reply to Canary Islands senator José María Galindo, BOCG, 25 March 1995.
7. BOCG, 16 Oct. 1998.
8. 'Comunicado de la OID sobre las elecciones legislativas en Marruecos', in *Actividades, Textos y Documentos de la Política Exterior Española* (ATDPEE) 1997 (Madrid: Ministerio de Asuntos Exteriores), p.801.
9. 'Brindis del Ministro de Asuntos Exteriores Abel Matutes en el almuerzo ofrecido a su homólogo marroquí Sr. Filali', ATDPEE 1998, p.221.
10. BOCG, 15 Sept. 1999.
11. Abel Matutes at a meeting of the Comisión de Asuntos Exteriores del Congreso de Diputados, BOCG, 29 Sept. 1999.
12. Abel Matutes at a meeting of the Comisión de Asuntos Exteriores del Senado, BOCG, 25 Nov. 1999.
13. Government reply to Basque deputy Begoña Lasagabaster, BOCG, 29 Oct. 1999.
14. 'Spain and the passive neutrality in the Sahara issue', *Al Alam* (Rabat), 13 March 2001.
15. 'Il est inacceptable que l'Espagne joue un rôle au sujet du Sahara', *L'Opinion*, 25 Sept. 2000.
16. Mohamed Lemine Habib, 'Le modèle d'autonomie interne de type catalan est-il transposable au Sahara?', *L'Opinion*, 2 Jan. 2001. A few months later, in the weekly *Le Journal Hebdomadaire*, 10 March 2001, a series of articles was published on the subject 'Quel fédéralisme marocain pour un royaume uni,?', in which the model of the Spanish autonomous regions was appraised in an interview with the scholar Ali Sedjari entitled 'L'autonomie comme source d'unité'.
17. BOCG, 9 Feb. 1994.
18. Personal notes taken by Bernabé López García.
19. 'Declaración de la UE sobre Argelia', ATDPEE 1994, p.828.
20. 'Declaración de la UE sobre Argelia', ATDPEE 1995, p.998.
21. 'Declaración del Gobierno español sobre las elecciones presidenciales en Argelia', ATDPEE 1995, p.1035.
22. BOCG, 8 May 1997.
23. BOCG, 5 Nov. 1997.
24. Government reply to BNG deputy Francisco Rodríguez Sánchez, BOCG, 18 Feb. 1998.
25. BOCG, 18 Feb. 1998.
26. Government reply to New Left deputy Manuel Francisco Alcaraz, BOCG, 19 June 1998.
27. Ibid.
28. BOCG, 13 Aug. 1998.
29. BOCG, 15 Oct. 1996.
30. 'Discurso del Ministro de Asuntos Exteriores Abel Matutes durante su visita oficial a Túnez', ATDPEE 1997, pp.144–5.
31. 'Respuesta al diputado del PSOE Rafael Estrella', BOCG, 28 Oct. 1998.
32. BOCG, 10 June 1998.
33. See Esther Barbé, 'La cooperación política europea: la revalorización de la política exterior española', in Richard Gillespie, Fernando Rodrigo and Jonathan Story (eds.), *Las relaciones exteriores de la España democrática* (Madrid: Alianza Universidad, 1995), p.166–9.
34. See Miguel Hernando de Larramendi, *La política exterior de Marruecos* (Madrid: Editorial MAPFRE, 1997).
35. See the statements to the Joint Commission of the Congress and the Senate in November 1995 by the secretary of state for the European Community, Carlos Westendorp.
36. At the end of the year 2000, the name of ICMAMPD changed to Dirección General de Cooperación con Africa, Asia, y Europa del Este.
37. *Boletín Oficial del Estado*, 8 July 1998.

38. Ibid., Article 7, page 283.
39. 'Plan Director de la Cooperación Española 2001-2004', *Diálogo Mediterráneo*, Vol.19 (Dec. 2000), pp.45–9.
40. See *Agencia Española de Cooperación Internacional. Memoria 1996* (Madrid: Ministerio de Asuntos Exteriores, 1997), p.113.
41. See *Memoria AECI 1999* (Madrid: Ministerio de Asuntos Exteriores, 2000), p.177.
42. 'Informe de política exterior y derechos humanos del gobierno español 2001: suben los intereses económicos y bajan los derechos humanos', www.a-i.es/esp/iape01.shtm, accessed 30 Sept. 2001.

European Democracy Promotion in North Africa: Limits and Prospects

RICHARD GILLESPIE and
LAURENCE WHITEHEAD

Less than a decade after the European Union started to extend its democracy promotion efforts to its southern neighbours, there are few if any signs of many tangible results. Without ostentatiously repudiating the European pro-democracy agenda, North African governments have contrived either to nullify its impact or to reorient it towards projects compatible with their own objectives. Of course, the fruits were never expected to appear in the short term, even by the most optimistic of democracy promoters. None the less, it is reasonable to enquire whether by this time the EU effort is starting to fuel processes likely to enhance the prospects of democracy in the long term. The contributions published in this collection raise serious doubts as to whether this really is the case. Given these doubts, this concluding assessment attempts to reassess the strategy upon which EU democracy promotion policies in North Africa have been based.

Such a discouraging first term report has not led the contributors to these pages to conclude on a note of fatalism. Nobody has argued that the EU should abandon this line of policy or replace it with a more modest enterprise, such as focusing merely upon 'good governance'.[1] The emergent consensus informing this collection has revolved around a number of commonly held propositions:

- authoritarian regimes are relatively well entrenched in North Africa, or at least they have demonstrated considerable powers of endurance;
- there are also many other factors other than EU policy that help account for the lack of fundamental political change in North Africa (political economy factors, emigration, non-European international support, fear of Islamist alternatives, and cultural factors, to list but some);
- given its limited leverage, the EU can act only as a facilitator of political change in the current circumstances of North Africa, and can only play

even a support role if domestic developments within the region provide the requisite openings;
- for all its shortcomings, the Barcelona Process is precisely that: a *process* that leaves open some possibility of rectification, and thus it is a worthwhile exercise to consider means of pursuing its objectives more effectively.

So far, the Euro-Mediterranean Partnership (EMP), as the multilateral framework for EU democracy promotion in North Africa, has constrained European efforts in this field more than it has generated new opportunities. It was probably inevitable that an ambitious 15+12 heterogeneous grouping such as this would place a premium upon keeping the partnership intact during its early years, particularly since it coincided with a brief phase of international optimism surrounding the Middle East conflict and provided a meeting place for Arabs and Israelis. This excluded any real prospect of there being much early focus on such divisive issues as democracy and human rights. In fact, the democracy agenda was something that was 'tagged on' to the partnership design after it was conceived, largely to satisfy demands made by the European Parliament. Spain and France, which are among the EU member states best placed to influence the EMP's evolution, displayed a distinct ambivalence towards its democracy agenda. Such attitudes may help to explain why, although the 1997 elections in Algeria were strictly 'undemocratic' as compared to those of 1990–91, nevertheless the EU presented them as progress. Despite (and perhaps even because of) such ambivalence in Europe, some Mediterranean partners – notably Egypt, Algeria and Syria – have demonstrated their concern about references to democracy and human rights, along with economic concerns, by engaging the EU in extremely protracted negotiations in relation to the association agreements envisaged in the Barcelona Declaration. At the outset, the political content of Barcelona would have been an obstacle to the launch of the process had it not been regarded as essentially declaratory. Since then, it has proved difficult to lend substance to the declarations because of the reliance of EMP activity on regime assent among the EU's partner states.

Yet, in the few years that have passed since the Barcelona Conference of 1995, the commitment to democracy promotion and human rights advocacy in general has been strengthened within the EU itself, both in terms of the content of its legal basis and in the practical work of one of its key institutions, the European Commission.[2] The European Union has itself come to acknowledge the need to reinforce this aspect of its relations with the Mediterranean partners,[3] and thus it may be assumed that constructive criticism of existing policy may have a role to play in future rethinking. On the southern shores of the Mediterranean, meanwhile, at least some countries (Morocco, Tunisia) have been prepared to engage in debate with EU partners on democracy and human rights issues through the Euro-Mediterranean Committee. Thus there is an enabling aspect to the Barcelona Process, even if it is one that thus far has been overshadowed by the constraints.

Under the Barcelona Process, when the EU attempts to formulate a democracy promotion stance towards the Maghreb, it treats the region as a whole and has to contend with certain realities (the colonial legacy, the role or Islam, the oil and gas linkages, the pressures of migration, the nature of linkages between Maghrebi diasporas in Europe and their home countries) which distinguish the Maghreb from other large regions (say the Mashreq, dominated by the presence of Israel, or sub-Saharan Africa, where colonialism left a different legacy). In contrast to southern and eastern Europe, for example, there is no Catholic church to transmit core European influences to a democratizing periphery, nor has the Socialist International established effective counterpart parties in North Africa. Whereas labour migration and the granting of political asylum to democratic elites built up goodwill towards the EU in the case of other democratizing regions, the experience of migrating from North Africa to Europe may generate more negative reactions. Such characteristics apply across the Maghreb as a whole, giving the entire region – and by extension the whole of North Africa – a somewhat common and distinctive orientation towards the EU, notwithstanding the great differences in regime type that separate Morocco from Algeria, Algeria from Tunisia, and Tunisia from Libya.

The fact remains that, for all the contrasts they exhibit, none of the regimes in North Africa are showing a commitment to democratization as understood within Europe. The one country whose authorities have come to make positive statements on democracy and human rights is Morocco, and it has also gone furthest down the road of expanding political pluralism. Yet, even there *alternance* has amounted thus far to the co-opting of only partially representative opposition parties, while power has remained lodged largely in the monarchy, an institution that enjoys a rare degree of legitimacy by the standard of the region. For all the changes of recent years, Mohamed VI has made clear that he does not intend to follow any European models of democratization and favours a 'strong, democratic *executive* monarchy' (our emphasis).[4] Regime mistrust of far-reaching democratic reforms has been reinforced by the persisting crisis and violence in Algeria, and the post-11 September 2001 'war against terrorism' is likely to generate plentiful further opportunities to resist reform without attracting external censure.[5] The main hope for some movement may be if a major Arab regime collapses as a result of its unresponsiveness to social demands at a time of renewed mobilization in Muslim countries. The post-11 September landscape is one in which radical Islamists will seek, with some prospect of success, to associate predominantly illegitimate North African regimes with a hostile or duplicitous Europe, now identified as an anti-Islamic threat as well as a source of support for policies of social exclusion. In some countries – notably Tunisia – economic progress is viewed as an ultimately surer safeguard against the Islamist challenge than the use of repression, so heavily used there since the late 1980s. But since most may be unable to deliver much short-term economic progress, there is a distinct possibility that some governments will seek to liberalize, within limits, in an attempt to defuse mounting popular pressure against participation in the international coalition. Clearly, the future policy of the United States government towards the Palestinian–Israeli conflict will be a crucial factor here.

For the EU, the aftermath to 11 September has made it urgent to reconsider Europe's relationships with Arab countries. The initial tendency, as in any project of partnership or coalition building, could be towards an accommodation with the powers that be, and to turn a blind eye to the repression of Islamist movements. But a possible longer-term scenario is that, once the alignments have crystallized, much greater thought will be given to ways of isolating core terrorist networks from peripheries within Islamist movements. Events since September 2001 do have some potential to give substance to 'clash of civilizations' scenarios, but also – for this very reason – they add currency to arguments based on the 'democratic peace' thesis. In any case, while international developments may heighten or lower the immediate importance of democracy promotion to the EU, it would be very difficult for the Union to backtrack completely on this issue. This is because of its value as part of the process of legitimation and identity-building in Europe at a time of growing integration, EU enlargement and efforts to develop as a global actor. In the long run the EU's credibility might increase, for example, if it succeeded in promoting democracy in other Muslim majority states or nations, such as Turkey, Northern Cyprus, Bosnia, Kosovo or Albania. More generally we need to distinguish between the formal and direct instruments of EU democracy promotion (which are poorly funded and constrained by bureaucratic rigidity and political timidity) and the *indirect* democracy promoting potential of a flourishing and politically liberal union of European states, which could eventually nurture the political freedoms of the Maghrebi diasporas housed within the EU. Some within Europe may therefore see it as a long-term moral imperative for the EU to persist with democracy promotion. They might also recall that European countries and the Community bear some historical responsibility for the consolidation of authoritarian regimes in North Africa, and may thus be duty-bound to make amends. Europeans did nothing to promote democracy as the region's regimes became consolidated after independence (in most cases from democratic France), and in more recent years the EU may be seen, in practice, as having bolstered elite coalitions rather than promoting political pluralism (see Dillman's contribution to this collection).

The analyses collected here lend considerable support to the view that the EU has for long proceeded too timidly with North Africa on the democracy front. Viewed purely through the prism of economic interests, and taking a collective EU view, it might be contended that ultimately Europe can afford to upset regimes in the region, notwithstanding the inconvenience of so doing. The EU's financial and commercial presence is distinctly modest, although crucially some individual member states have important energy interests in Algeria and Libya. For the EU in general, it is strategic thinking about security, more than economic advantage, that provides the motivation for pursuing good relations with North African governments: the latter are valued as part of European efforts to revive the Middle East peace process, to meet the challenge of increasing northward migration and now to isolate and counter Islamist terrorist networks on a global scale. Southern governments – seeing emigration as a means of defusing social pressures and as a source of valuable financial remittances – can facilitate it by turning a blind eye to people-smuggling activities. What gives them pause is their desire to retain some control over their diasporas for a mixture of political, cultural and financial reasons, and recognition that they cannot really afford to antagonize the EU in the long run.

The contributors to this collection favour a readjustment of the balance between top-down and bottom-up approaches to EU democracy promotion. The politically cautious EU has placed greater emphasis on the latter than on the former (although, as Haddadi points out, in reality this often amounts to a midway approach, in that support for civil society does not in practice extend to ordinary people). In principle, a bottom-up approach to democracy promotion would seem perfectly sound, since, once actual military intervention and occupation have been ruled out, democratization must be seen first and foremost as an endogenous process, involving social dynamics, and not confined to manoeuvres within a narrow political elite. However, in the context of North Africa, the limitations of a largely bottom-up approach to democracy promotion are evident, given the weakness of civil society organizations – at least of the kind that the EU would like to nurture. EU strategy is faulted in this collection for its simplistic, profoundly flawed assumptions about the relationship between economic and political liberalization; for its too limited a notion of civil society, effectively restricted to secular liberal society and excluding groups inspired by religious faith; and for the willingness to restrict civil society support to partners that are known to and approved of by Mediterranean partner governments. Such partners often turn out to be elitist associations close to government or associated with projects devised by transnational non-governmental organizations (NGOs), projects which may lack local ownership and perhaps sustainability. These problems are in addition to the institutional and procedural constraints on EU activities deriving from the Union's character as a 'clearing house for national interests rather than a unitary actor'.[6]

What then of top-down approaches? Chourou's survey of how post-independence Maghreb states avoided the road of democratization underscores the role of political leadership, and offers little prospect that current regimes will readily change tack on this issue. His thesis, that leaderships could have directed processes of democratization from above following national independence, is perhaps most persuasive in relation to Tunisia, a small country with a relatively cohesive independence movement. Elsewhere the weakness within most countries of popular organization, the emergence of a power vacuum when independence was abruptly conceded, French political disinterest (or distraction), the role of armed struggle in Algeria and the persistence of strong irredentist tendencies in Morocco all arguably made a democratic outcome more difficult.

Nevertheless, Chourou's account raises a crucial, and difficult to ignore, counterfactual issue. Could this region have democratized earlier? Were there clearly identifiable 'lost opportunities' (for instance if Morocco's main opposition leader Ben Barka had not been murdered in Paris in 1965 by the Moroccan government, with official French complicity)[7] that would need to be re-investigated by any democratic regime seeking to understand what went wrong during independence? This has a bearing on the question of what would need to be put right now in order to entrench democracy in the future. Such latent historical time bombs are liable to go off unexpectedly, and can destabilize processes of transition, unless defused by trustworthy procedures of 'truth and justice' investigation. If the analysis of North African politics is to move beyond the impasse of 'Islam versus democracy' conjured up by Samuel Huntington, then a more nuanced understanding of the complexities and cross-currents of the region's political history will be required. But such reconstructions may not prove costless to the EU. For as Chourou indicates, they are likely to highlight the interdependencies, or even collusions, linking some Maghrebi elites to certain European power structures, linkages that normally lie hidden beneath the cover of national independence and its foundational mythologies.

One of the current difficulties in the path of a top-down approach is that EU policy towards the Mediterranean is primarily driven by security motives and this, plus the partnership approach of the EMP, tends to lead to accommodation of authoritarian regimes rather than efforts to undermine them. In April 2001, the assisted flight from justice of a senior Algerian general accused in France of torturing his own co-nationals dramatized the extent to which such accommodations may go in some European countries.[8] So instead, the EU pursues long-range policies aimed at bottom-up democratization without conflict, forever trying to minimize political risks. Thus far, European policy-makers have acted as if, whenever the spectre of radical Islam could be invoked, that justified back-pedalling on political reform. As Chourou observes, however, whereas Islamists may be a threat to democracy, the authoritarian regimes are a negation of it. Moreover, after the massive bloodshed in Algeria in the past decade, the EU might well be advised to consider whether the actual outcome, to which it has lent a degree of support through accepting the military coup of 1992, has really been any better in terms either of stability or of morality than the likely results of accepting the electoral victory of the Islamic Salvation Front.

Top-down democracy promotion would imply more EU insistence at governmental level that EMP activity must be made visible in North African societies and greater determination to prevent North African regimes from blocking or diverting bottom-up democracy promotion activity. However a shift of the balance towards the 'top-down' pole of the continuum would need to be measured and modest, and could only involve an economical use of pressure. Persistence rather than intensity of pressure could be the key to the greatest success. One problem for the EU here is that 'strong' instruments such as the suspension of agreements can only be used highly selectively and exceptionally, yet relatively few less disruptive means of pressure are available to it. While there is further scope for positive forms of conditionality, there is no case for adopting a punitive form of conditionality on a sustained basis. It would be too extreme a measure to suspend association agreements over a remediable democracy or human rights setback, and such action could create a precedent for some future Islamist regime in the region to do likewise if it came to power and clashed with European interests. Yet, alongside the clearly preferred positive forms of conditionality, the EU could act more vigorously when faced with blatant violations of the Barcelona principles such as the detention of widely respected human rights defenders and pro-democracy leaders. Not to do so risks damaging Europe's reputation in the eyes of reform-minded North Africans and could breed mistrust of EU democracy promotion activities in the region.

However, it is essential to recognize the restricted range of direct methods available to the EU in its wishes to promote democracy in North Africa. Whereas in southern and eastern Europe the European Commission could offer the inducement of eventual EU accession, when Morocco applied for EC membership in 1987 it was told that this was impossible on geographical grounds. It seems that 'Europe' could extend eastwards to the former Soviet Union and beyond, and south-east to the Turkish frontier with Iraq, but it cannot incorporate Casablanca or Tangier. Given this, then the locus of European policy-making towards the Maghreb is always liable to shift between the multilateralism of the Commission in Brussels and the bilateralism of Paris, Madrid and Rome. But of course the countries of the Maghreb only escaped from French (and to a lesser extent Italian and even Spanish) colonial rule within living memory. In the particular case of Algeria, independence was won through a bloody eight-year war of liberation. Given these colonial antecedents, on the one hand, and the prohibition on entry to the Union on the other, it is patently clear that neither the EU nor its individual member states have any prospect of bringing about democratization in North Africa by any but the most tactful and diplomatic ('softly, softly') of approaches. There can, for example, be no Maghreb counterpart to the intrusive policies that Europe (and NATO) pursued in order to secure democratic reforms or regime transitions in the Balkans. Probably the most that can be hoped for is state-to-state diplomacy, co-ordinated within a broad framework of region-wide co-operation and political dialogue, perhaps afforded by certain non-intrusive programmes of material incentives.

But while a basic 'softly, softly' approach to democracy promotion may be the only realistic option, there is also an evident need to pursue it more consciously and coherently, and to be prepared to act more forcibly when the situation demands it. To go further, and adopt a 'big bang' approach aimed at using pressure to secure democratization in the near future, could well lead, at best, to the establishment of 'empty shell democracies' and, at worst, to anti-European reactions, providing undemocratic elites with opportunities to exploit nationalism in order to shore up authoritarian regimes. So, although something like the Barcelona Process is virtually inescapable, from the EU's point of view, so too is the imprecision of the associated provisions, particularly those concerning politics and human rights. This imprecision is more or less guaranteed by the need to iron out differences in perceptions and priorities *within* the EU, combined with the need to secure verbal consent from diverse North African governments – governments that resent European political interference and understand the limits of EU action. But even within these constraining strategic parameters, this collection has identified areas where democracy promotion efforts could be reinforced: in particular, as Youngs argues, the EU could do more to ensure wider participation in the implementation of existing policies, improved linkage between macro and micro levels of activity, and more co-ordination between activities in the three different chapters of the EMP.

Having established a partnership with the North African powers that be, it would be unrealistic to expect the EU to try to distance itself from them. Of course, this leaves Mediterranean partners, despite the asymmetry of the EMP, with some opportunities to exert leverage themselves. Poor disbursement rates under MEDA I were partly a result of southern partners holding out for more flexible arrangements for use of the funds; and several partners showed initial reluctance to sign association agreements with the EU. 'Deals' therefore still need to be struck so that European packages combining both the palatable and the unpalatable will be carried through. That said, the EU obviously has the greater leverage. The crucial instruments of the EMP – association agreements – are bilateral rather than multilateral. They enable partners to be dealt with individually without necessarily damaging the overall partnership, by an EU that (for all its limitations) is more united than the Arab Mediterranean partners. For this reason the EU has the edge over its Mediterranean partners within the Euro-Mediterranean Committee of the Barcelona Process and at ministerial and senior officials meetings. For all the complaints made by Mediterranean partners about asymmetrical arrangements, this is likely to remain a feature of the EMP.

It must be acknowledged, though, that the EU does not possess a wide range of strategic options in relation to North Africa, where conditions for democracy promotion are hardly optimal. Many would argue, for example, that there are no genuine NGOs in a country like Tunisia, such is the omnipresence of the state. One criticism of the EU is that it has adapted too readily to the weakness of genuine civil society organizations in North Africa by investing largely in projects devised by state-related or externally-sponsored associations. Several studies published in these pages bring out the skewed distribution of democracy assistance funds by the EU. This is a failing that the EU shares with other actors, including individual EU member states, US aid agencies, party foundations and international NGOs. None the less, EU activity does seem to be preoccupied with supporting familiar bodies, ones that appear similar to those that uphold democracy in western countries. In parts of North Africa, the focusing of projects on the formal political sphere – parliament, parties – may well prove fruitless since these are not representative, nor are they even markedly under-representative, of society. Particularly in those countries where political opposition and criticism can be expressed only in the mosque, it would seem essential for the EU to be doing more to promote dialogue across religions and to use its influence to encourage Islamist political participation. Seen by many North Africans as the only sector concerned about social exclusion, the Islamists will not go away just because the EU ignores them. There is some evidence from Morocco and Algeria that certain Islamist tendencies may be prepared to compete 'loyally' in the sense of accepting a pluralist form of political system, respecting the political and cultural diversity of their societies. There is even more evidence, from throughout North Africa, suggesting that democratization is unlikely to come from existing political elites following existing rules of the game.[9] In any case, democracy promotion must contend with a number of possible scenarios for future political developments in any country. It is too simplistic an approach to try to identify the democrats and then seek to assist them, as the EU has tended to do thus far. Potential democratic forces may only emerge in strength after more authoritarian forces have clashed and fought each other to a standstill, creating opportunities for new forces to compete for political influence. This may be the case of Algeria where, after a decade of hostilities dominated by military clans and Islamist extremists, mass popular protest and the articulation of democratic demands (including Berber cultural rights) erupted in the course of 2001. Equally (and hopefully) it could take a more peaceful form, although still involving a power struggle of some kind. In this perspective, as Dillman maintains, democracy promotion should involve initiatives that will actually stimulate political competition and even political (as opposed to military) conflict in countries that have entrenched authoritarian systems.

A major conclusion of our studies is thus that in the long term EU democracy promotion might be more effective if the bottom-up activity involved expanding the arena of political activity and facilitating associational development at the grass-roots, if all three chapters of the EMP were developed with this strategic political objective in mind, and if greater resolve were demonstrated in the face of obstruction by North African officialdom. Inevitably, this would involve, among other things, showing more awareness of ethnic diversity within North Africa and more recognition of the diversity of Islamist movements. Such displays of awareness would have to be practical in form and not just intellectual. This would imply a broadening of the scope of EU-funded projects to include Islamist sectors and minority rights groups that are prepared to co-exist peacefully with other forces within a pluralist context. As Jünemann's study demonstrates, political activists inspired by Islam have largely been excluded from the EMP thus far. A more open attitude towards so-called 'moderate' Islamists might have to be accompanied by reinforced opposition to the true hard-liners – a balance that may be easier to develop against the backdrop of efforts to establish a global coalition against terrorism, so long as this can avoid alienating Muslims in general. Yet even moderate Islamists represent viewpoints that clash with European democratic opinion, particularly with regard to gender separation. The important thing here is to encourage dialogue and partnership-building activities under the third chapter of the EMP – which is badly in need of development given its socialization potential – and not to exclude sectors whose views are simply a challenge to liberal democratic orthodoxy. The parameters of partnership would then be defined by attitudes towards political violence, rather than social values. What Europeans need to accept, however, is that any such extension of pluralism will require that they engage with unfamiliar, and to some perhaps unappealing, social and political forces, which will challenge the position of established elites.

On the longer run view, it seems that the EU may need to distinguish between two phases in its democracy promotion policies. There is (i) the current phase, before democratization has begun, when it is not known when, or even whether, it will begin, and when only low key or 'softly, softly' measures are possible. But there is also (ii) once local developments have put democratization seriously on the agenda, when events may begin to 'crowd in' hastily and unpredictably, probably inducing a sudden upsurge in demands for the EU to move into high gear, and to deliver on its longstanding but until then largely rhetorical commitments. EU activities undertaken in phase (i) are unlikely to produce many highly visible or direct results. They may even to some extent be understood as 'buying an insurance policy' against a future contingency that may not even arise in our lifetime. However, like an insurance policy, it makes a great deal of difference whether or not a clear position has been defined and agreed to in advance. Once regime change begins, it may be too late to start negotiating between member states and within the different levels of the EU bureaucracy over how to react, and how to encourage a more democratic outcome. In this case the EU could be insuring against an event it would like to bring about (contrary to most insurance decisions). So the EU has an interest in signalling the steps it needs to take to encourage democratization (however unlikely this may be) as well as to put itself on the side of the democrats once the action begins. Given all the imponderables, it is not possible to achieve great precision here. But in principle it should be possible to establish a strong and binding framework of commitments that can be honoured, and filled out, once the hoped for moment arrives.

If – or when – (ii) arrives, experience from elsewhere indicates that a long period of authoritarian stability can easily turn into brittleness and thus pave the way for an abrupt regime collapse (for example, in Tunisia power now seems so concentrated in the hands of the president that a succession crisis could easily prove difficult to manage). Once a regime change gets underway, there might well be a great upsurge of pent-up grievances directed both against authoritarian elites, and against their western allies. The EU needs to recognize that if democratization *does* begin somewhere in North Africa, it will almost certainly be resisted, both from within and from neighbouring countries. It is far more likely to gain momentum in just *one* country at a time than to arise in *all* at once. As a result, the instabilities that could well accompany democratization in the region could easily take *all three* of the following forms simultaneously: (a) Islamic protests against pro-western rulers; (b) popular protests against authoritarian controls; and (c) nationalist protests against governments seeking to shore up their internal weaknesses by seeking support from outside.

In short, if/when phase (ii) arises, and the EU has abruptly to contend with a serious attempt to transform (and potentially to democratize) a North African authoritarian regime, events are more than likely to proceed very fast, with much confusion and considerable scope for misjudgement and inappropriate responses. This is where – at least in principle – the Barcelona architecture might be developed to provide a framework capable of containing such dangers, and helping the European states to prepare the ground for a considered, co-operative and constructive response. But there is little evidence, as yet, that such preparations have been made.

One area where long-term planning is already needed, and where a more flexible approach could pay large dividends in Europe, is with respect to North–South human mobility. If EU actors wish to engage with a wider range of North African actors, travel restrictions as well as the design and development of aid programmes will need to be revisited. At present, there is no involvement of non-state actors from the Mediterranean partner countries in the planning and evaluation of programmes. On the other hand, neither permanent settlement of North Africans in the EU nor very short-term contractual arrangements simply concerned with using migrants for specific labour purposes would necessarily be constructive from a democratic perspective. Migration is an important opportunity for socialization, whose benefits will only be realized if the EU can help reduce the North–South economic divide across the Mediterranean and thus provide incentives for return migration. One cannot expect democratization in North Africa if an increasing volume of the region's youth continues to vote with its feet. Here, there are some potentially much more costly options that the EU might have to consider alongside relatively low-cost proposals for enhancing democracy promotion. Thus far, the EU has tended to see the project of building a Euro-Mediterranean free trade area as a panacea,[10] despite the palpable lack of enthusiasm shown by private investors in recent years. In another international regional context, Mexican President Vicente Fox has warned against this illusion, maintaining that one cannot have real democracy amidst huge inequality.[11]

North Africa remains a challenge for the EU. Its importance to Europe has grown through the successive processes of EC southern enlargement and European East–West reunification, the latter prompting the EU to devote more attention to its external relations, especially with regard to neighbouring regions. The events of 11 September 2001 have further focused European attention on North Africa along with other parts of the Muslim world. They have made it even more crucial for EU democracy promotion activity to extend to those parts of North African societies not reached by the Barcelona Process so far. A more sophisticated approach to such activity does seem to be emerging, following a number of EU innovations such as country strategies and greater thematic prioritization, although initially the former have been vague and the latter lacking in well-defined criteria.[12]

Whether the widely-held Muslim grievances exposed by the 11 September events will generate a more dynamic approach to EU democracy promotion towards North Africa may be doubted. There will certainly be voices in Europe both for and against suggestions that the EU should distance itself from authoritarian regimes in the region and engage more with North African civil society – a shift that could only be a matter of degree, in any case, if the EMP is to survive. Thus far nobody has advocated applying the notion of 'sub-regionalization' to the political agenda of the EMP, enabling subsets of the 15+12 to co-operate on democracy promotion projects.[13] This would probably only be feasible if political liberalization began to sweep a number of Arab states. Meanwhile, there is much the EU can do internally to make democracy a more attractive proposition to neighbouring countries. The obstacles to greater dynamism in democracy promotion are partly to be found within the EU, as the case studies of French and Spanish policy towards North Africa demonstrate. This collection has identified some areas where policy might be refocused sooner rather than later. But it has also acknowledged the importance of long-range activities based on dialogue and partnership building, whose value may not be reflected in immediate results, yet which may enable the EU to act with greater vigour when future democratic developments take place within North Africa.

NOTES

Our thanks go to Richard Youngs for comments on an initial draft.

1. For advocacy of such a move, see T. Niblock, 'Good Governance: Towards a New Framework to Guide the European Union's Involvement with Middle Eastern States', paper presented at the Conference on 'Good Governance and "Emerging Democracies"', University of Reading, January 2000; and D.K. Xenakis and D.N. Chryssochoou, 'Between Good Governance and Democratization: Assessing the Euro-Mediterranean Condition', Jean Monnet Working Papers in Comparative and International Politics, No.38, Department of Political Studies, University of Catania, October 2001.
2. European Commission, Communication from the Commission to the Council and the European Parliament, 'The European Union's Role in Promoting Human Rights and Democratization in Third Countries', COM (2001) 252 final, Brussels, 8 May 2001.
3. European Commission, Communication from the Commission to the Council and the European Parliament, 'Reinvigorating the Barcelona Process', Brussels, COM (2000) 497 final, Brussels, 6 Sept. 2000.
4. Interview in *Le Figaro*, 4 Sept. 2001.
5. This conclusion, unlike the other contributions, was written after the events of 11 September 2001.
6. Jörg Monar, 'Institutional Constraints of the European Union's Mediterranean Policy', *Mediterranean Politics*, Vol.3, No.2 (1998), p.39.
7. See 'La Verité sur la "disparition" au Maroc de Mehdi Ben Barka', *Le Monde*, 2 July 2001; and 'L'affaire Ben Barka face a l'omerta des Etats', *Le Monde*, 27 Oct. 2001.
8. In April 2001 former Algerian defence minister General Khaled Nezzar had to leave Paris in a hurry, departing on a plane sent specially from Algiers, to avoid appearing before a French judge considering charges of torture laid against him by three Algerians. *Le Monde*, 24 Aug. 2001, gave further details on the apparent Franco–Algerian complicities associated with this case.

9. See for example, in relation to Morocco, Rémy Leveau, 'Islam officiel et renouveau islamique au Maroc', in C. Souriau (ed.), *Le Maghreb Musulman en 1979* (Paris: CNRS, 1980), p.216.
10. Only up to a point, as several of our contributions reflect, has this tendency been countered by Commission and some member state initiatives of a social nature.
11. *El País*, 23 April 2001.
12. T. Schumacher, 'The Mediterranean as a New Foreign Policy Challenge? Sweden and the Barcelona Process', *Mediterranean Politics*, Vol.6, No.3 (2001), pp.92–3.
13. Sub-regionalization as a more general principle was included in the Common Mediterranean Strategy adopted by the European Council on 19 June 2000. For the text, see *Official Journal of the European Communities*, L 183/5, 22 July 2000.

Abstracts

The Challenge of Democracy in North Africa
BECHIR CHOUROU

Notwithstanding national peculiarities, a similar pattern of development can be discerned in Algeria, Tunisia and Morocco since independence. The early period was one in which political elites had an opportunity to initiate democratization yet quickly set aside the democratic arguments used during the independence struggle. Subsequent periods of economic crisis prompted reform efforts in the 1980s, which failed to prevent even deeper crises the following decade, bringing the threat of national disintegration, as seen in Algeria. Islamist movements have emerged as non-democratic alternatives to the existing authoritarian regimes, yet there are still some prospects of democratization. The EU has done little to promote democracy, for fear of the instability that a change of regime would bring. None the less, it retains some potential to influence the political process. An effective democracy promotion strategy would need to involve less tolerance of major examples of authoritarian behaviour by regimes and determined efforts to involve non-regime actors in projects undertaken in the context of the Euro-Mediterranean Partnership.

The European Union and Democracy Promotion in the Mediterranean: A New or Disingenuous Strategy?
RICHARD YOUNGS

The European Union's incorporation of a commitment to promote democracy in the southern Mediterranean reflects a notable evolution in strategic thinking. However, alongside this new approach more traditional doubts have continued to exist over the relationship between security and commercial interests, on the one hand, and political liberalization in the Arab world, on the other hand. Genuine uncertainty over strategic imperatives has conditioned a cautious approach to democracy promotion in the Mediterranean. EU strategy has eschewed coercive policy instruments in favour of an aim to generate socialization dynamics around a positive adherence to democratic norms. While this strategy has much to recommend it, the EU has in practice failed fully to abide by its own philosophy. The relationship between economic and political reform has been conceived in unduly simplistic terms, democracy assistance projects have been relatively limited in scope, and support for initiatives capable of engendering a convergence of political values has been hesitant. While standard critiques of EU policy fail to take on board key developments in European strategy, the Euro-Mediterranean Partnership has fallen significantly short of fulfilling its full potential.

International Markets and Partial Economic Reforms in North Africa: What Impact on Democratization?
BRADFORD DILLMAN

Contrary to assumptions that economic liberalization is likely to spill over to political reform, authoritarian regimes in North Africa have been able to use economic reform processes actually to strengthen their position. Market reforms encouraged by international organizations have imposed constraints on North African political elites but have also provided them with a means of bolstering their coalitions of support. Incumbent regimes have been able to dictate the winners and losers in the first stages of economic liberalization. Supporting concerns over the tendency for economic modernization to stagnate at a stage of partial reform, this has ensured North African governments the loyalty of winners, who have a strong incentive to oppose further, including political, change. Far from undermining the region's autocrats, the EU's incremental approach to democracy promotion has in practice provided resources that have been tapped by authoritarian regimes to shore up patronage networks.

From the Bottom to the Top: Civil Society and Transnational Non-Governmental Organizations in the Euro-Mediterranean Partnership
ANNETTE JÜNEMANN

Civil society co-operation is central to the European Union's conceptual approach to promoting democracy and human rights in North Africa. In practice, the EU has supported the Euro-Mediterranean Partnership's civil society dimension only very cautiously. The overwhelming share of assistance has been given to those civil society organizations in the Mediterranean region that are not highly politicized or critical of incumbent regimes. Rather, the EU has aimed to enhance forms of civil society capacity less directly confrontational to Mediterranean partner governments. The support given to the private sector has been mistakenly conceived as a means of strengthening independent civil society capacity, whereas in practice much of the business sector in North Africa is tied to the state through patronage networks. The EU has failed to recognize that its concept of civil society must address the issue of Islamist organizations if it is to be fully representative and inclusive. Civil society support has also been hampered by administrative problems, although in this area improvements have recently been made. One of the highest profile networks within the partnership, the Euro-Mediterranean Human Rights Network, demonstrates both the potential of genuinely transnational groupings, and the difficulty of reconciling different perspectives into a coherent focus on democracy and human rights.

Dancing in the Dark: The European Union and the Algerian Drama
HUGH ROBERTS

The European Union's position on Algeria with regard to the promotion of democratic principles and respect for human rights has been a pretension rather than an unrealistic ambition. Insofar as it has amounted to a policy, its objectives have not been to promote democratic principles in Algeria, but something else. The particular character of Europe's role in the Algerian drama has not been primarily responsible for the appalling way this has developed, but it has certainly contributed to this and has throughout been part of the problem, not part of the solution. That this has been so is a consequence of France's role in determining European policy, which continues to compromise the possibilities of democratic development in Algeria insofar as these are linked to European actions.

France, Democratization and North Africa
JEAN-FRANÇOIS DAGUZAN

France has modified its traditional realism, incorporating concerns with democracy and human rights into its foreign policy. This focus on democracy has still been extremely cautious in North Africa. However, pressure from public opinion, non-governmental organisations and the media have, as human rights abuses were progressively revealed in Morocco and Tunisia, forced significant changes in French policy. Relations with Algeria have been more complex, and infected with a uniquely delicate historical legacy. Divisions have emerged within the French political elite over the question of democratization in Algeria. The most notable development in French policy has been the willingness to support a certain degree of Europeanization of policy in North Africa. New democracy assistance projects have been supported, but to only a modest extent and mostly in an indirect fashion through NGOs and other non-official bodies.

Two Cheers for Whom? The European Union and Democratization in Morocco
SAID HADDADI

Relations between Europe and Morocco have been characterized by a series of agreements in which democracy and human rights issues have become increasingly evident. Morocco is undergoing a 'transition' in which real political power remains with the monarch and—despite *alternance* in 1998—has not been transferred from government to opposition. EU-funded democracy promotion programmes have not brought a notable strengthening of bottom-up democratization activity. They have benefited international non-governmental organizations (NGOs), elitist Moroccan NGOs and government projects, while neglecting an important part of Moroccan civil society, including that formed by non-violent Islamist associations. Democracy promotion might be more effectively targeted at a large number of small associations, where its socializing impact would be greater.

Spain and North Africa: Towards a 'Dynamic Stability'
BERNABÉ LÓPEZ GARCÍA and MIGUEL HERNANDO DE LARRAMENDI

Spanish policy towards North Africa is focused primarily on the Maghreb and characterized by a primary concern with economic and commercial interests. Promotion of civil society development in this region is very much a secondary concern and extreme caution is shown by the Spanish government over questions of political change and human rights, for fear of upsetting relationships with governments in the Maghreb. In principle, Spain favours 'dynamic stability' in North Africa, marked by a gradual evolution away from authoritarian structures, but the preoccupation with the pursuit of national economic interests has increased under the

People's Party, especially since it won an absolute majority in the 2000 elections. Reliance on a strategy of co-operation to strengthen interdependence, however, has not proven a firm guarantee against crises in bilateral relations, as recent disputes with Morocco have demonstrated.

List of Contributors

Richard Gillespie is Professor of Politics, Europe in the World Centre, University of Liverpool.

Richard Youngs is Senior Research Fellow at the Norwegian Institute for International Relations (NUPI) and the University of Portsmouth.

Bechir Chourou is a Professor of International Relations at the University of Tunis I.

Bradford Dillman is Assistant Professor of International Relations at Koç University, Istanbul.

Annette Jünemann is Associate Professor in the Faculty of Social Sciences at the University of the German Armed Forces, in Munich.

Hugh Roberts is Senior Research Fellow at the Development Studies Institute, London School of Economics and Political Science, University of London.

Jean-François Daguzan is *Maître de recherche* at the Fondation pour la Recherche Stratégique, Paris.

Said Haddadi is a PhD candidate in the School of Languages and European Studies at Aston University, Birmingham, UK.

Bernabé López García lectures in the History of Contemporary Islam at the Universidad Autónoma de Madrid.

Miguel Hernando de Larramendi lectures in the History of the Contemporary Arab World at the Universidad de Castilla-La Mancha.

Laurence Whitehead is Official Fellow in Politics at Nuffield College, Oxford and series editor of OUP's Oxford Studies in Democratization.

Index

Abassi Madani 115
Abdesselam, Belaid 112–14, 119, 126, 130n26
ACP states 40, 47, 55
Afak 163
aid
  conditionality 47–9, 109–11
  democracy promotion 185–6
  democracy-related 11–12
  MEDA *see MEDA*
Aït Ahmed, Hocine 115
Al Adl 157–8
Al Islah 157–8
Al-Aqsa 101
Algeria 13, 29, 49, 74, 76, 80, 81, 93, 149, 163, 170, 183
  army 30–1, 37, 63, 109, 114, 128, 133n85
  civil strife 43, 63, 92, 140, 152, 178–81, 194, 198
  debt repayments 72, 73
  democracy assistance 55, 185, 186
  democratization 139–44, 193, 194, 201
  elections (1991) 27–8, 31, 40
  elections (1997) 119–20, 126
  EU association agreement 47–8
  EU loans 109–12
  EU policy 106–7, 109–16, 125–9
  French policy 24, 107, 126, 126–9, 139–44, 146
  human rights 48, 139–44
  Islamist rebellion 112–14, 115, 117, 124, 140–1, 178–9
  MEDA programmes 123–4
  net transfers 72
  oil and gas 25, 74–5, 196
  partial economic reforms 70, 71, 78
  political reform 83, 84
  political rights and civil liberties 17, 67, 82
  post-independence 19, 22–3, 24
  Presidential elections (1995) 108–9
  Spanish policy 172, 178–81, 188
  uprising (1988) 26, 140
  war of independence 68
Algerian League for the Defence of Human Rights (LADDH) 116
Amnesty International 88, 155, 156, 187
Amsterdam Treaty 44
ANP 22
Arab Institute of Human Rights (AIHR) 163
Arab League 119
Arab–Israeli conflict 50
Arafat, Yasir 43
Armed Islamic Group 114, 141, 142, 147n22
Armée de la libération nationale (ALN) 22
Asmidal 74
Association Marocaine des Droits de l'Homme 157
authoritarian regimes 9, 11, 39, 91
  civil society 87–9
  economic liberalization 63–4
  Morocco 20
  North Africa 17–18, 35–6, 192, 196, 198, 201, 203, 205
  persistence 31
  retention of power 30–1
Averroes Committee 174
Aznar, José María 171, 172, 174, 175, 181

Balkhadem, Abdelaziz 172
Balladur, Edouard 141, 143, 144
banks, state-owned 70, 71, 81–2
Banque de l'Habitat 81
Barcelona Declaration 12, 33–4, 39n8, 40–1, 46–7, 52, 66–7, 68, 87, 88, 98, 106, 143, 150, 153–4, 161, 183, 193–4, 199, 200, 204
Barre, Raymond 110
Basri, Driss 150, 156, 159, 167
Ben Ali, Zine el Abidine 26, 28, 31, 63, 79, 81, 138–9
Ben Barka family 150, 197
Ben Bella, Ahmed 19, 22, 25, 115
Ben Brik, Taoufik 138
Ben Hadj, Ali 115
Ben Youssef, Salah 20
Benjedid, Chadli 28, 140
Betchine, Mohamed 123
BNP-Paribas 75, 76
bond issues 76
Boudiaf, Mohammed 111, 119, 126, 141
Boukrouh, Noureddine 115
Boumédiène, Houari 22, 23, 25, 140
Bourguiba, Habib 19, 20–2, 25, 26, 31, 138

Bouteflika, Abdelaziz 30, 124, 133n 85, 172, 180
BP 75
British Gas 75
business, civil society and 91–2

Canary Islands 177
Catalonia 177, 186–7
cellular phone licences 75
central banks 81–2
Cepsa 75
Cheysson, Claude 111
child labour 164
Chirac, Jacques 135–6, 138, 143
Chourou, Bechir 17, 197, 198
citizens, attitude to politics 31–2
Civil Forum 95–6, 101, 146, 186
civil liberties, North Africa 17
civil society 2, 4, 12, 15n12, 50, 66, 149, 153–4, 201
co-operation 87–9
contrasting views 89–93
  dichotomous and integrative views 90–1
  Egypt 63
  funding programmes 161–2, 163
  Maghreb 186–7
  Morocco 160, 186–7
  new groups 166
  organizations 145
  transnational co-operation 65, 98–101
  transnational networks 10–11
  clientilism 79, 80
Cold War 8, 25, 40
commercial considerations, Mediterranean policy 44–6
commercial credits, North Africa 73
Common Foreign and Security Policy (CFSP) 6, 44, 47, 106, 183
Common Strategy on the Mediterranean region 67
Confédération Générale des Entreprises du Maroc 79
Conseil Consultatif des Droits de l'Homme 155, 156, 164
constitutional reforms, Morocco 155–6
Cook, Robin 121, 128
corruption 45
  Morocco 159
Crédit Immobilier et Hôtelier 81

Daguzan, Jean-François 56, 135
Danielle Mitterrand Foundation 137, 145
De Gaulle, Charles 135, 136, 139
debt
  Algeria 113–14, 125
  conversion to investment 73
  relief 52, 72–3
Declaration on Human Rights 152, 160
Delors, Jacques 112
democracy
  discourse on 46–7
  nature of 28–9
  prospects 37–8
democracy assistance, Mediterranean 55–9
democracy promotion 1, 153–4
  Algeria 106–7, 109–16, 125–9
  EU strategy 2, 4–7, 46–51, 66–8, 82–4, 87–9, 192–4, 197–205
  Euro-Mediterranean Partnership 2, 4, 11–14, 30–1, 40–1
  explanations of policies 8–11
  Maghreb 194
  Morocco 150–1, 160–4
  North Africa 2, 35
  Spanish role 184–8
  strategy 46–51
Democratic National Rally (MND) 120
democratization 149
  EU policy 96–7
  French policy 135–6, 144–5
  gradual 88, 95
  limited 10
  Morocco 137–8, 149–52, 162–3, 165–7
  no private sector pressure for 45–6, 71
  North Africa 29–35, 64–8, 82–4
  possibility, post-independence 19, 23, 35
  socialization 47–50, 59–60
  Tunisia 138–9
Dezcallar, Jorge 178
Dillman, Bradford 54, 63, 196, 201
Djaballah, Abdallah 115, 119
Dumas, Roland 141

Eastern Europe, post-communist transition 69
economic interests, democracy promotion and 10
economic liberalization 12, 40–1, 48, 149
  authoritarian regimes 63–4
  link with political reform 51–4, 66–8, 82–4, 125–9
economic reforms
  Algeria 110, 111, 126, 128
  partial 63–4, 69–71, 82–4
  risks of partial reform 77–82
  winners and losers 69–71, 77–82, 83
EEC, enlargement 151
Egypt 4, 42, 47, 48, 49, 67, 82, 93, 163, 193
  authoritarian rule 63
  banking 82
  bond issues 76
  democracy assistance 57–8
  Industrial Modernization Programme 80

oil and gas 75
partial economic reform 70, 71, 72, 73, 78, 79
political reform 83, 84
privatization 76
Social Development Fund 53
telecommunications 76
tourism 74
Egyptian General Petroleum Corporation 75
Egyptian Organization of Human Rights 57
El-Malki, Abdallah 188
elections
fraudulent 47
free 83
elites
partial economic reforms 63–4, 69–71, 83
persistence 31
preferences 65
rent-seeking 67
resource flows 73
employers' associations 79–80
Enad 74
Endesa 75
ENI 74, 75
Estrella, Rafael 181
ETA 177
Ettahaddi 115
EU
Algeria (1991-94) 109–16
Algeria policy 106–7, 125–9, 142–4, 178–9, 180
civil society co-operation 94–7
democracy promotion strategy 2, 4–7, 46–51, 66–8, 82–4, 87–9, 150–1, 192–4
industrial upgrading programmes 80
Mediterranean policy 32–5, 37, 39n8, 41–6, 60, 182–4
Morocco policy 151–4, 160–4, 173
north–south split 44
resource inflows to North Africa 71–7
rivalry with USA 68
Rome Platform 117–19
EU Rapid Reaction Force 7
European Parliament 109
Euro-Maghreb Partnership 153, 154
Euro-Mediterranean Association Agreement, Morocco 150, 151, 154
Euro-Mediterranean Free Trade Area, prospective 51–3, 58–9, 78
Euro-Mediterranean Human Rights Network 2, 89, 98–101, 102
Euro-Mediterranean Partnership 2, 4, 11–14, 33–4, 40–1, 42, 78, 106, 107–8, 143–4, 150, 183
civil society 87–8, 99
democratic change 11–14, 46–51, 59–60, 66–8, 83, 151, 193, 200, 202
economic reforms 51–2, 54
Euromed Youth Action Programme 95
European Commission 5, 53, 55–6, 58, 88, 93, 94, 97, 193, 199
Democracy and Human Rights Unit 6, 59
FTA preparation 59
European Court of Justice 95
European Initiative for Democracy and Human Rights (EIDHR) 5, 95
European Investment Bank 73, 112, 124
European Parliament 89, 94–5, 102n 6, 109, 110, 114, 118, 122, 143, 152, 153
European Political Co-operation 153
European Union *see EU*

Filali, Abdellatif 174
FIS 27–8, 31, 40, 109, 113, 114, 115, 116, 117–18, 131n46, 178, 198
fiscal problems, North Africa 78
FLN 22–3, 111, 115, 116, 119, 120
Fonds de Solidarité Nationale (FSN) 81
foreign direct investment 70, 74, 77
Mediterranean 54
North Africa 72
privatization receipts 75, 76
foreign policy, EU co-operation 6, 7
Fraga, Manuel 182
France 2, 4, 119
aid 55, 56, 58
Algeria policy 24, 107, 126, 126–9, 139–44
colonial policy 24, 199
democratization and human rights 135–6, 193
FDI 74
Mediterranean policy 68, 86, 88, 101
Morocco policy 24, 136–8
North African aid 48
North African colonies 18, 19, 196
oil and gas investment 75
Tunisia policy 138–9, 181
France Telecom 76
free trade area, prospective Mediterranean 51–3, 58–9, 78, 125, 183
Freedom House 17
French settlers, Algeria 24
Front de Libération Nationale 22–3
fundamentalism 32, 36–7

gas, investment 74–5
Gaz de France 75
Germany 73, 74, 181
GIA 114, 141, 142, 147n 22
Gillespie, Richard 1, 192
Giscard d'Estaing, Valérie 136, 139

Global Mediterranean Policy 151
globalization, impact on economic reform and political change 65
good governance 10, 12, 45–6, 67, 149, 160
  assistance 58–9
GPRA 22
Greece 119, 151
Group for Democratic Development 57
GSM licences 76, 81
Gulf War, 2nd 40, 64, 73, 183

Haddadi, Said 149, 196
Hanoune, Louisa 116
Hassan II king of Morocco 20, 25, 26, 28, 63, 81, 136, 137–8, 150, 151, 154–6, 159, 174, 175, 176, 177
Hassan II Fund for Economic and Social Development 81
Helms-Burton Act 68
Henkel 74
Hernández Mollar, Jorge 128
Hernando de Larramendi, Miguel 170
Hosni, Nejib 138
human rights 64, 67, 87, 149, 199
  Algeria 121, 127–8, 180
  French policy 135–6, 144–5
  government-controlled groups 56, 57
  Morocco 48, 137–8, 152–3, 155, 156, 161–2, 174
  NGO activities 48, 88, 90, 99
  North Africa 3–4, 39n 8
  promotion 5, 41, 163–4
  Tunisia 138–9, 181–2
Human Rights League 145
hydrocarbon sector
  Algeria 113
  private investment 74–5

immigration
  common EU policy 44
  Morocco 163–4, 172
  pressures, EU 42, 204
imperialism, EMP regarded as 34
industrial upgrading programmes 80
industrialization, Algeria 22–3
interest groups, aggregation and articulation 29–30
International Federation for Human Rights 145
International Finance Corporation 75
International Monetary Fund (IMF) 12, 25–6, 70, 73, 111, 112, 115
international relations, democracy promotion and 8–9
intifada, Al-Aqsa 101
investors, views on Mediterranean policy 44–6
Iran 68
Iraq 40, 68
Ireland 75
Islam 83
  Algerian rebellion 112–14, 115, 117, 124, 140–1, 178–9
  anti-Western discourse 52
  attitudes to democracy and human rights 3–4
  civil society and 92–3
  EU involvement 50–1
  fundamentalism 25, 27–8
  political 9, 27–8, 37–8, 42, 67–8, 71, 84n 2, 93, 140, 157–8, 201, 202
  as security threat 64, 195, 196, 198
Islamic Liberation Front *see FIS*
Israel 50, 58, 101, 182
  Lebanon campaign 68
Istiqlal 20, 177, 187
Italy 68, 73, 74, 183, 199

Japan 114
joint ventures, FDI 74
Jordan 42, 48, 57, 67, 163
Jospin, Lionel 146
Josselin, Charles 139
judicial co-operation, France–Morocco 145
Jünemann, Annette 87, 202
Juppé, Alain 141, 142, 143

Kabbaj, Mohammed 81
Kabylia, violence 125
Kafi, Ali 112, 119
Keramane, Abd al-Wahab 81
Kouchner–Bernard 136
Koutla 156
Ksila, Khemais 138
Kuwait 40

Lamari, Major General Mohammed 115
Lamrani, Mohamed Karim 155
League against Racism and Anti-Semitism 145
Lebanon 49, 57, 59, 67, 68, 163
Léotard, François 141
Libya 4, 47, 152, 170, 182, 187, 194, 196
Ligue Marocaine pour la Défence des Droits de l'Homme 157
Locke, John 90
Lomé Agreement 47
London Club 73
López García, Bernabé 170
Lorca, Alejandro 188

Madani, Abbasi 178

Maghreb 55, 56
French policy 136–44
Spanish policy 170–3
makhzen 159
Malek, Redha 114, 115
MAN AG 74
Marín, Commissioner 143
Maroc Télécom 76, 81
Marzouki, Moncef 138
massacres, Algeria 121–2, 125, 140, 142
Matutes, Abel 173, 174, 175, 179, 180, 181
Mauritania 152, 172, 182, 186, 189
Mauroy, Pierre 110
MEDA Democracy Programme 55–6, 94–5, 151, 154, 161–2, 164, 165, 166
MEDA funds 47, 48, 52–3, 94–5, 123–4, 162, 181
MEDA I aid 73, 154, 161, 183, 209
MEDA II aid 73, 83
Medecins sans Frontières 135
Méditel 75
Mediterranean, EU policy 32–3
Mediterranean Forum 44, 143
Mediterranean non-EU countries (MNCs) 33–4
Messari, Mohamed Larbi 177
Middle East, peace process 42–3
Miguel, Ramón de 179, 182
Miskar gas field 75
Mitterrand, François 135, 136–7, 141, 142
Mobile phones, investment 76
MobileNil 76
Mohamed V king of Morocco 19, 20
Mohamed VI king of Morocco 4, 58, 138, 155, 158, 159, 175, 194
Montesquieu, Charles-Louis 90
Moratinos, Miguel Angel 178, 188
Morocco 4, 40, 48, 70, 72, 73, 74, 76, 79, 170
application to join EEC 151–2
banking 81–2
Barcelona Agreement 33, 34, 40
debt repayments 72
democracy assistance 55, 57, 58, 59, 60, 185–6
democratization 137–8, 149–51, 194–5, 201
economic crisis 25–6
economic reforms 63, 68
elections 1993 155–6
elections 1997 156–7
Euro-Mediterranean Association Agreement 150, 151
French policy 24, 136–8
Hassan II Fund for Economic and Social Development 81
human rights 48, 137–8, 152–3, 155, 156, 161–2, 174, 194–5
industrial upgrading programmes 80
monarchy 30, 37, 48, 150, 158–9, 167
opposition 158
political power 158–60
political reforms 83, 84, 154–60
political rights and civil liberties 17, 39n8, 63, 67, 82, 137–8
post-independence 19, 20, 23, 24
relations with EU 151–4
riots 26
Spanish policy 171–7, 188–9
telecommunications 75–6
tourism 74
Movement for Democracy in Algeria (MDA) 115, 116, 119
Movement of the Islamic Nahda (MNI) 115, 116, 119, 120
MSP 119, 120
Mubarak, Hosni 63
multinationals 10, 44–5
joint ventures 74

Nahnah, Mahfoud 115
National Indicative Programme 162
National Telecommunications Regulation Agency, Morocco 75
nationalism 9, 18, 19, 35
Néo-destour 20
NGOs 13, 96, 149, 200
Algeria 124
environmental 90–1
French 145, 146
human rights 48, 90, 95, 135
influence on decision-making 10–11
Mediterranean 50, 51, 56
Morocco 150, 160, 163
secular 93
Spanish 184, 185, 186
transnational 89, 90, 98–101, 197
non-governmental organizations *see NGOs*
North Africa (1980s) 24–6
authoritarian regimes 17–18
democracy promotion 2
demographic growth 25
EU policy 32–5
political change 3–4
post-independence 18–24, 35
resource inflows 71–7

Occupied Territories 43, 58
official development assistance (ODA) 54
conditional upon democratization 5–6
North Africa 48–9
oil, prices 152

oil companies, state-owned 74–5
oil and gas
  exports 76
  private investment 74–5
oil price increase (1973) 23
opposition parties, North Africa 32
Organisation Marocaine des Droits de l'Homme 155, 157, 163
Organization of African Unity 119
Oualalou, Fatallah 188
Oufkir family 137
Ould Lakhel, Mohamed Slem 182

Palestine Liberation Organization 43
Palestinian Authority 67
Palestinian Territories *see Occupied Territories*
Palestinian–Israeli conflict 195
Palestinians 101
Paris Club 73
Parti socialiste destourien 21
Party of Algerian Renewal 115
Party of Progress and Socialism (PPS) 188
Pasqua, Charles 141
Patten, Chris 39n8
peace process, Middle East 42–3, 50
Penal Reform International 164
Peres, Shimon 182
Perrault, Gilles 137, 155
Petronas 75
phosphates 152
  exports 76
Piqué, Josep 172, 177
Polisario Front 177
political change
  instability and 42
  international factors 1
  long-term 43
political liberalization 12, 41–2, 45–6, 48, 49, 83
  link with economic liberalization 51–4, 66–8, 125–9
political parties 56
  Algeria 115
  France 135, 136–7, 139, 146
  Morocco 156–8, 158–9, 187–8
  Spain 187–8
political prisoners, Morocco 137, 150, 152, 155
political reforms, Morocco 154–60
political rights, North Africa 17
politics, citizen attitudes 31–2
Pompidou, Georges 136
portfolio investment 70, 72, 74
Portugal 151
Portugal Telecom 75
power structures, unchanging 31
press, Morocco 164
primordial structures, civil society and 92–3
prisoners, rights 163, 164
private business, civil society and 91–2
private sector, weakness, North Africa 65–6, 71, 79–80
privatization 70, 91, 92, 128
receipts 75, 76, 81
public enterprises, joint ventures 74

Qadhafi, Muammar 182

Rally for Culture and Democracy (RCD) 115
recession 25
religion, civil society and 92–3
René Sedoux Foundation for the Mediterranean World 145
Renovated Mediterranean Policy 40, 152, 153
  rent-seeking
  elites 67
partial economic reforms 69–70
  rent-taking 77, 78
Repsol-YPF 187
resource transfers, net long-term 72–7
resources, government elites 80–1
Roberts, Hugh 106
Rome Platform 116–19, 126, 142
Royal Dutch Shell 75
rule of law 67, 149, 160

Saaf, Abdallah 188
Saavedra, Jerónimo 177
Sadi, Saïd 115
Saharan Arab Democratic Republic (RASD) 177
Saharawi 177
sanctions, democracy promotion 11
Schengen Agreement 44
secularism 92–3
security 64
  comprehensive approach 42
  democracy promotion and 8–9, 43, 198
September 11 2001, New York attack 195, 204
Serfaty, Abraham 137, 150
settlers, Algeria 24
Sifi, Mokdad 115
Soares, Mario 180
social funds 81
Socialist Forces Front (FFS) 115, 119
Socialist Union of Popular Forces (USFP) 187
Société de Banque Française et Internationale 76

society, primordial structures 92–3
Solana, Javier 173
Sonatrach 74–5, 113
Soulier, André 121–2, 127
Soviet Union
demise 25
post-communist transition 69
Spain 2, 4, 58, 74, 151, 199
Algerian policy 172, 178–81, 188
commercial credits to North Africa 73, 75
democracy promotion role 184–8, 193
Maghreb policy 170–3, 182–4
Mediterranean policy 68, 88, 96, 101
Morocco policy 171–7, 188–9
Tunisian policy 172–3, 181–2
within EU framework 182–4
Spanish Agency for International Co-operation (AECI) 175, 184–6, 187
state, relationship with civil society 90–1
state monopolies, exports 76
structural adjustment programmes 25–6, 52–3, 82, 112, 113, 119, 125, 128
Suárez, Adolfo 170
Suez Crisis (1956) 68
Sweden 75
Syria 40, 48, 59, 152, 193

TelecomEgypt 76
telecommunications, investment 75–6
Telefónica 75
Temmar, Hamid 81
Terrab, Mostapha 75–6
TotalFinalElf 75
tourism, investment 74
trade sanctions, US 68
trades unions 56, 90–1
transparency, lack of in commercial proceedings 45
Treaty of Friendship, Good Neighbourliness and Co-operation, Spain, Morocco 172, 175
Treaty of Oudja 170
Tunisia 4, 26, 37, 47, 48, 72, 74, 76, 79, 80, 81, 93, 149, 154, 163, 187, 189, 194
authoritarian rule 31, 63
Barcelona Agreement 33, 34, 40
democracy assistance 57, 185, 186
economic crisis 25–6
economic reforms 53, 58–9, 71, 78
Fonds de Solidarité Nationale (FSN) 81
French policy 138–9, 146
interest groups 29–30
oil and gas 75
political reform 83, 84
political rights and civil liberties 17, 39n8, 67, 82
post-independence 19, 20–2, 23, 24
Spanish policy 172–3, 181–2
telecommunications 76
tourism 74
Turkey 93

Union of the Arab Maghreb (UMA) 170
United Kingdom 119
United Nations 119
United States
democracy promotion 5, 8, 55, 66, 84
EU geopolitical rivalry 68
Palestinian-Israeli conflict 195

Védrine, Hubert 139, 146
Villar, Francisco 171, 178
Vivendi 76

war against terrorism 194
Washington consensus 66
Western Sahara 136, 150, 152, 170, 175–6, 186
Whitehead, Laurence 192
Wifak 156
women's rights 93, 160, 162, 163
worker remittances 76–7
Workers' Party (PT) 116, 119
World Bank 10, 12, 46, 55, 73, 80
World Organization against Torture 145

Yahia, Abdennour Ali 116
Yassine, Abdessalam 150, 158
Youngs, Richard 1, 40
Youssoufi, Abderrahmane 157, 164, 174

Zeroual, Liamine 43, 108, 109, 114–19, 123, 126, 141, 143, 178
zone of solidarity, North Africa 144

Titles of Related Interest

Opposition and Democracy in South Africa

Roger Southall, *Rhodes University* (Ed)

This collection of original essays, drawn from a variety of political perspectives, is the first consolidated attempt to explore opposition in post-apartheid South Africa. After discussions of the nature of political opposition and its appropriate forms and styles in a fragile democracy, analyses runs through the alleged narrowing space for opposition parties under ANC hegemony, the electoral prospects for the newly formed Democratic Alliance and the nature of this new formation (a merger of the liberal Democratic Party and the formerly ruling National Party), the use and misuse of 'race' as a category of opposition, the scope for internal opposition within the ANC, and finally the potential for the emergence of a labour-led opposition which could challenge the ruling party, which has increasingly espoused neo-liberal economic strategies, from the left.

256 pages 2001
0 7146 5149 4 cloth
0 7146 8173 3 paper
Democratization Studies Series
A special issue of the journal Democratization

Democracy Assistance

International Co-operation for Democratization

Peter Burnell, *University of Warwick* (Ed)

This book is the first to make a detailed study of recent developments across the full range of official and autonomous providers of democracy assistance. They include the United Nations, the European Union and multilateral development banks, as well as Germany's party foundations, or *Stiftungen*, and notable public and privately-run agencies in the United States. Democracy aid's performance in parts of Africa, Asia, Latin America, Russia and elsewhere is critically examined. Special attention is paid both to post-conflict situations and to semi-authoritarian regimes where democratisation has stalled. International efforts to support democratic decentralisation and civil society in particular are assessed. Although there are many strands to democracy assistance, the book argues that we cannot yet be confident that the total effort adds up to the sum of its parts. Indeed, there are a number of important political questions about what democracy assistance hopes to achieve, why and how effectively, and its implications for the evolution of world politics rather than just for the political relationships inside sovereign states. These outstanding questions should be addressed urgently by analysts as well as practitioners.

240 pages 2000
0 7146 5106 0 cloth
0 7146 8144 X paper
Democratization Studies Series
A special issue of the journal Democratization

FRANK CASS PUBLISHERS
Crown House, 47 Chase Side, Southgate, London N14 5BP
Tel: +44 (0)20 8920 2100 Fax: +44 (0)20 8447 8548 E-mail: info@frankcass.com
NORTH AMERICA
5824 NE Hassalo Street, Portland, OR 97213 3644, USA
Tel: 800 944 6190 Fax: 503 280 8832 E-mail: cass@isbs.com
Website: www.frankcass.com